D0773537

USELESS JOYCE

TIM CONLEY

Useless Joyce

Textual Functions, Cultural Appropriations

UNIVERSITY OF TORONTO PRESS
Toronto Buffalo London

Toronto Buffalo London
www.utppublishing.com
Printed in Canada

ISBN 978-1-4875-0250-8 (cloth)

Printed on acid-free, 100% post-consumer recycled paper with vegetable-based inks.

Library and Archives Canada Cataloguing in Publication

Conley, Tim, 1972–, author
Useless Joyce : textual functions, cultural appropriations / Tim Conley.

Includes bibliographical references and index.
ISBN 978-1-4875-0250-8 (cloth)

1. Joyce, James, 1882–1941 – Criticism and interpretation. 2. Joyce, James, 1882–1941. Ulysses. 3. Joyce, James, 1882–1941. Finnegans wake. 4. Art and literature. I. Title.

PR6019.O9Z5275 2017 823′.912 C2017-903064-7

University of Toronto Press acknowledges the financial assistance to its publishing program of the Canada Council for the Arts and the Ontario Arts Council, an agency of the Government of Ontario.

Canada Council for the Arts
Conseil des Arts du Canada

Funded by the Government of Canada
Financé par le gouvernement du Canada

Contents

Acknowledgments

In *Exiles*, Bertha Rowan reproves her husband Richard: "I am simply a tool for you" (588). Joyce is, as I hope this book demonstrates, very aware of what uses he makes of people, words, and ideas, even if his gratitude seems less than overwhelming. "Fair use" is a funny phrase, a formula by which scholars can defend their adoptions of others' work, and thus as much a legal fiction as paternity. I hope that I have made "fair use" of all named below.

Thanks first to various Joyceans from hither and yon, some of whom have thoughtfully discussed with me or carefully read some parts of this project, and some of whom have facilitated it in one way or another: Luca Crispi, Ronan Crowley, Anne Fogarty, Finn Fordham, Michael Groden, Terence Killeen, Sean Latham, John McCourt, Laura Pelaschiar, Fritz Senn, and Sam Slote. It is a privilege to count oneself in the company of these scholars. I am also appreciative of the support of my departmental colleagues at Brock University, a dynamic group with whom it is a pleasure to work. My students in *Ulysses* seminars and those in the *Finnegans Wake* reading groups I have organized (a verb that I doubt is apt) over the past several years have enriched my own ideas about those books and what we do with them. My research assistant Amber Halkes, a veteran of both of those environments, helped lay the foundations for the appendix of this book. Customary but always deserved and sincere thanks too to Stephen Cain.

Some chapters, or portions of them, have previously appeared, sometimes in slightly different forms, in scholarly journals and essay collections. "Misquoting Joyce" (chapter 2) was included in the volume *Joycean Unions: Post-Millennial Essays from East to West*, edited by Brandon Kershner and Tekla Mecsnóber (Amsterdam: Rodopi, 2013).

Chapter 3 is a blend and revision of pieces that appeared in *Hypermedia Joyce Studies* and the *James Joyce Quarterly*. Under a different title, the discussion of Lavergne's footnotes in the fourth chapter appeared in a special issue of *Scientia Traductionis* edited by Erika Mihálycsa and Jolanta Wawrzycka. Earlier versions of chapters 6 and 7 appeared in the *JJQ*. My thanks to all of the respective editors of these publications. Different and shorter versions of chapters 5 and 7 were presented as talks at the Joyce Symposium in Dublin and at the Joyce Summer School in Trieste, and I am grateful for the interest shown and the subsequent discussions produced by those audiences.

A grant from the Humanities Research Institute (HRI) at Brock University helped jolt this project into a comprehensible shape. A couple of months spent as James M. Flaherty Visiting Professor at Trinity College Dublin, thanks to a generous fellowship from the Ireland Canada University Foundation (ICUF), with the assistance of the Government of Canada, gave me time to see it through to its completion. I am grateful to James Kelly and Amanda Hopkins at the ICUF, to Chris Morash at the School of English at TCD, and for the hospitality and patient assistance of Sarah Barry at the Long Room Hub.

My editors at the University of Toronto Press, Richard Ratzlaff and Barb Porter, are as patient as they are professional. I also extend my thanks to the two anonymous readers for the press, whose perceptive suggestions and corrections improved this book.

The ongoing patience and support of Clelia and Simone has proved more than useful, but in ways and at such lengths as it is useless to try to count. My thanks and love to both.

Note on Abbreviations

The following citational abbreviations are used for works by Joyce:

D	*Dubliners*
FW	*Finnegans Wake* (New York: Penguin, 1976)
FW-O	*Finnegans Wake* (Oxford UP; ed. Henkes, Bindervoet, and Fordham)
FW-R	*Finnegans Wake: The Restored Edition* (Penguin; ed. Rose and O'Hanlon)
FW-RH	*Finnegans Wake: The Restored Edition* (Houyhnhnm; ed. Rose and O'Hanlon)
P	*A Portrait of the Artist as a Young Man*
SH	*Stephen Hero*
U	*Ulysses* (ed. Gabler)

The selection of Gabler's edition of *Ulysses* (or indeed of any editions of Joyce's works cited here) as primary reference should be understood as keeping with current scholarly convention, rather than as a critical endorsement of it over any other edition. Likewise the default text of *Finnegans Wake* here is distinguished from the most recent editions, which are themselves the subject of scrutiny in chapter 4.

USELESS JOYCE

To discover the various use of things is the work of history.
Karl Marx, *Capital*

Hands that can grasp, eyes
that can dilate, hair that can rise
if it must, these things are important not because a
high-sounding interpretation can be put upon them but because they are
useful.
Marianne Moore, "Poetry"

Clank it. Clank it. Miles of it unreeled. What becomes of it after? O, wrap
up meat, parcels: various uses, thousand and one things.
James Joyce, *Ulysses*

Introduction

Let us, the real Us, all ignite in our prepurgatory grade as aposcals and be instrumental to utensilise (*FW* 446.36–447.01)

At loose ends and unsure what to do with himself, Stephen Dedalus visits the dean of studies in the final chapter of *A Portrait of the Artist as a Young Man*. He finds the dean stooped before the fireplace, and Stephen asks, "Can I help you?" This question might surprise the reader a little, especially one who has read and been taught, again and again, that Stephen is a luciferian figure whose unfettered freedom and sovereignty are extolled with the decree *non serviam*. "Helpful" is probably not an adjective that most readers would attach to Stephen. It might also seem that it should be the dean who asks this question of the student who (to all appearances) comes to consult him, much in the way that the rector of Clongowes solicitously receives Stephen in his study in a parallel scene years before, in the first chapter of the novel. Declining the offer, the dean proposes a distinction between "the liberal arts" and "the useful arts" and lights the fire himself, an operation which Joyce depicts in slow technical detail:

> – Not too much coal, said the dean, working briskly at his task, that is one of the secrets.
>
> He produced four candle-butts from the side-pockets of his soutane and placed them deftly among the coals and twisted papers. Stephen watched him in silence. Kneeling thus on the flagstone to kindle the fire and busied with the disposition of his wisps of paper and candle-butts he seemed more than ever a humble server making ready the place of sacrifice in an

> empty temple, a levite of the Lord. Like a levite's robe of plain linen the faded worn soutane draped the kneeling figure of one whom the canonicals or the bell-bordered ephod would irk and trouble. His very body had waxed old in lowly service of the Lord – in tending the fire upon the altar, in bearing tidings secretly, in waiting upon worldlings, in striking swiftly when bidden – and yet had remained ungraced by aught of saintly or of prelatic beauty. (*P* 155)

This carefully inspired and nourished fire becomes not just an ostensible subject for the conversation that follows but a persistent metaphor. Even in this brief passage the eventual transition from the practical to the aesthetic can be seen as Stephen's thoughts move from the operative act (how to light a fire) to a lyrical, fanciful contemplation of the figure before him (the unusual Levite comparison is repeated as Stephen convinces himself of the image and embroiders it),[1] and his dawning realization of an incompatibility between "lowly service" and beauty. It is abundantly clear which of these "arts" might be Stephen's calling, and which one emphatically isn't.

Stephen might well be judged a rather useless young man. In fact, he sometimes seems to wear his incompetence like a badge of honour. He needlessly and perhaps shamelessly admits, "I am sure that I could not light a fire" in just the same way that he has minutes before told a flower girl that he has no money and later tells Mr Deasy in *Ulysses* that he is chronically impecunious. My students are inevitably amazed that Stephen is unable to figure out why "they put tables upside down at night, I mean chairs upside down, on the tables in cafés" (*U* 16.1709–10), a sure sign of his inexperience with serving. *I will not serve* may also mean (may proudly conceal) *I am unable to be of service*.

When the dean refers to "one of the secrets," the sense that this is a kind of initiation scene can be connected with the novel's epigraph from Ovid, which tantalizingly invokes "unknown arts." Does *A Portrait* reveal any "secret" or "unknown" arts? Perhaps the most – and only – practical thing the reader of the novel can claim to have learned is how to start a fire.[2] This utilitarian reading of the novel, however narrow or perverse or even other than "literary" it may seem, is nonetheless *a reading*: attentive, discerning, undeniably critical in its fashion.

This book investigates what it means to speak of the "use" of a text or work of art, with James Joyce's oeuvre as a focal case study. It proposes that James Joyce's work explores and interrogates this distinction between "the liberal arts" and "the useful arts" – a distinction that echoes the one that Aristotle, in his *Nicomachean Ethics*, posits between *poiesis* and *praxis*[3] – even as it continuously fosters what Louis Aragon called "that charming boy: the Sense of the useless" (49). Yet even as this book offers close and comparative readings of these works, on all points it is just as keen on examining the situating of the works and the contexts in which we read them – situations and contexts which, I suggest, have narrowed over time as readers (and here I am thinking particularly of those readers who would describe themselves as "educated" or "literary") have become neglectful of or even opposed to "the useful arts" of reading, in favour of "the liberal arts" of reading. The former is acquainted with literacy, a kind of necessary and minimal socialization, with which one can understand written instructions, select a meal from a restaurant menu, and the like, whereas the latter, often purported to be *the* critical form of reading by those who practise and teach it, is nonetheless invariably (if sometimes with embarrassment) defended in utilitarian terms: such reading constitutes a skill, which enriches one's life, sense of self, appreciation of the other, and so on. If these "uses" of texts are more abstract than, say, the customary "use" of a recipe for chocolate hazelnut cheesecake, that is because they are doubtless more refined, richer in ambiguity and irony and other seminar favourites; not really "use" at all.

One ripe example of this class struggle of reading aims and methods is the scene in *Ulysses*, in the "Wandering Rocks" episode, where Stephen is browsing at the bookcart:

> What is this? Eighth and ninth book of Moses. Secret of all secrets. Seal of King David. Thumbed pages: read and read. Who has passed here before me? How to soften chapped hands. Recipe for white wine vinegar. How to win a woman's love. For me this. (*U* 10.844–7)

Not the sort of books that Stephen was flaunting his knowledge of in the previous chapter, in which he imagined the life and mind of Shakespeare,[4] *The Irish Beekeeper* and *Pocket Guide to Killarney* are priced within his means, and, whereas in the library he spoke of authorship, now instead he wonders about other readers: "Who passed here before me?" He even makes the identification – and it is not, as the scene that follows demonstrates, altogether ironic – that seems the very hallmark of the most naive reader: "For me this." (Imagine if *Ulysses* had been titled *Homer for Dummies*.) However, the sudden appearance of Stephen's sister Dilly causes him to conceal what he is reading – "Shut the book quick. Don't let see" (10.856)[5] – and he answers her question of what he is doing by turning it back on her, and immediately focuses on the book that *she* is holding:

> He took the coverless book from her hand. Chardenal's French primer.
>
> – What did you buy that for? he asked. To learn French?
>
> She nodded, reddening and closing tight her lips.
>
> Show no surprise. Quite natural.
>
> – Here, said Stephen. It's all right. (10.867–72)

Stephen's question is, depending on how charitably one elects to read it, redundant, shockingly stupid, even more shockingly open-minded, or simply patronizing. It is a shame that Dilly does not ask her brother the same question about the volume he has just been perusing, and offer her considered opinion about whether it is "any good" (10.864).

Joyce is thus a most "useful" writer to examine in a discussion of what it means to assert that a text is "useful" or that a reader "uses" a text. He is, after all, the writer who made an epic hero of an advertising man prone to such notions as writing advice columns in newspapers and implementing civic designs to improve his city and the world. Leopold Bloom's pronounced interests in self-improvement and continuing education, whether they are taken as the objects of gentle satire or as documented qualities of the new, "modern" man (or, as this book understands them to be, both), have had noticeably little effect not just on resilient conceptions of Joyce as lofty elitist and his writings the frigid domain of scholars, but also, perhaps more insidiously, on the way that scholars have read the novel. There is irony in the fact that so much non-scholarly and uncertain contemplation of the novel in which the pragmatic Bloom appears frequently configures the novel as itself a means for such self-improving ends as Bloom favours: *Ulysses* is a "great" book whose reading, like a New Year's resolution to hit the gym more regularly, to figure out how to build that better garden shed, or to learn Japanese, seems perpetually postponed and just as perpetually re-recommended by authorities. The literary or cultural critic assumes the role of bodybuilding coach, handyman's helper, lifestyle guru.

It is easy to forget, for all of the diverting possibilities it keeps in play, how suffused the novel is with a sense of futility: the "paralysis" of *Dubliners* has been translated into a kind of shiftlessness. "A Little Cloud" climaxes with Little Chandler's furious recognition of how hopelessly remote are his dreams of Byronic success: "It was useless. He couldn't read. He couldn't do anything. The wailing of the child pierced the drum of his ear. It was useless, useless!" (*D* 79–80). The characters of *Ulysses*, none of them entirely pleased with their situation in life, seem more preoccupied than actually occupied. Though he is no gloom-giver, Leopold Bloom's frequent and sometimes telling use of "no use" and "useless" taps out a theme throughout the sixteenth of June:

> No use disturbing her. She turned over sleepily that time. (4.73–4)

> Cute old codger. No use canvassing him for an ad. Still he knows his own business best. (4.111)

> I noticed he had a good rich smell off his breath dancing. No use humming then. Allude to it. (4.529–30)

> Drop in on Keyes. No use sticking to him like a leech. Wear out my welcome. (8.1165–6)

> No use thinking of it any more. (5.211)

> Useless words. Things go on same, day after day (8.477)

> – But it's no use, says he. Force, hatred, history, all that. That's not life for men and women, insult and hatred. (12.1481–2)

> Useless. Washed away. (13.1259)

All of these expressions of a "useless" feeling are bound up with utterly distracting points of anxiety: judging the right moment and way to wake Molly or to approach someone as a canvasser, how to deflect the dangerous attractions of Boylan or the hatemongering in Barney Kiernan's pub, and generally trying to get on equitably with other people. (What Bloom is trying not to think about in the fifth quotation above is his father's suicide, and he later recalls "fractions of phrases" from the letter his father left him, among them "it is no use Leopold to be" [17.1882–3].) The theme of resignation ultimately becomes rhapsodic in "Ithaca" – "the futility of triumph or protest or vindication: the inanity of extolled virtue: the lethargy of nescient matter: the apathy of the stars" (17.2224–6) – before Molly's "yes" after "yes" after "yes" affirms nothing in particular, or at any rate nothing readers and scholars can agree on. Bloom is heroic in such a narrative because he *wants* to be useful, enjoys helping others, and regularly envisions changes to his world that would not profit him alone.

Finnegans Wake might seem quite a different case, for it so often seems and has been characterized as Joyce's most "useless" book. Its own reference to "his usylessly unreadable Blue Book of Eccles" (*FW* 179.26–7) conflates *Ulysses*, whose original cover was blue and whose main character lives in Eccles Street, with a directory or a parliamentary report (two documents both called, in the late nineteenth century, a "Blue Book") and, thanks to its inescapably centripetal force of association, with the *Wake* itself. As a book about "Everybody," written in an international melange of languages, the *Wake* is putatively aimed at a wider audience than any other book. Accessibility is a weighty and tricky question for both the kinds of books that Stephen imagines writing and those he surveys on the bookcart, and the *Wake* manages to be the most *and* the least accessible text around. In as much as the title *Finnegans Wake* may be read as a programmatic injunction (and by implication a promise of transformation if that injunction is heeded), it has more in common with *How to Be Your Own Best Friend* (1973) and even more sensational come-ons than it does with descriptive, thematic, and altogether more sedate titles like *Ulysses*, *Dubliners*, or *Exiles*. Moreover, the song from which the title comes has, we might say, a narrative function, in that it tells an amusing story about a drunken labourer's premature send-off, but a listener might also take warning from it (a warning that is only partly the effect of satire): that's not how to build a wall, right enough, nor any way to organize a decent funeral. Just as "Eumaeus" provides delight with its extraordinarily sustained performance of muddled writing, *Finnegans Wake* is, as it repeatedly, seemingly helplessly, admits, no proper way to tell a story. It is a monumentally ambitious negative example, the worst how-to book in the world.

And if these works do not themselves provide plenty of rich territory for a critical discussion of what terms like "use" and "useless" mean for cultural activities, there is Joyce's own cultural status, contested and contradictory as it remains (and in my view, usefully so). His name, image, and words have proved not just "useful" but downright exploitable for all sorts of Irish tourism schemes and products. Were it possible, it would be interesting, as an atypically quantitative measure of cultural capital, to have a comprehensive count of all the Joyce-themed coffee mugs, t-shirts, pens, puppets, and other such novelties on the market: surely few other authors could claim comparable numbers. First editions of Joyce are the darlings of antiquarian book fairs and auction houses, sought after by ardent collectors. Joyce not only knew about the fetishization of his texts but actively, playfully encouraged it. One could argue that *Finnegans Wake* is a kind of autofestschrift, a volume that reifies itself and the processes by which it is written, even as it tickles the bibliophile's anxiety by casting doubt on its authenticity, provenance, and value: "a notoriety, a foist edition" (*FW* 291.27). A distinguishing feature of Joyce's evolution as a writer is the way the winding paper trail behind each subsequent book becomes both longer and more conscientiously preserved. The extensive and widespread documentation of the processes of writing *Ulysses* and *Finnegans Wake* points to Joyce's awareness of what value – that is to say, what *use* – such notes and records might have for future readers.

Moreover, there are Joyce's methods as a writer to consider: his "use" of other sources, not perhaps unlike other artists and especially modernists in kind, but surely extreme in degree. In what might be called the fire-lighting sermon scene from *A Portrait*, Stephen remarks to the dean on his use of Aristotle and Aquinas, "I need them only for my own use and guidance until I have done something for myself by their light. If the lamp smokes or smells I shall try to trim it. If it does not give light enough I shall sell it and buy another" (*P* 157). Just as Stephen does not light his own fires[6] nor fashion his own lamps, but employs and disposes of what materials he may find for as long as they suit him, Joyce the writer appropriates, samples, and rewrites texts in a manner and scale – the magnitude and variety of which ongoing and continually astonished scholarship is still measuring – that, as my list of verbs may suggest, hopelessly complicates what it means to "use" another text in the process of writing one's own. Burtonian in number and unpredictable in format, Joyce's disposable sources include not just the usual suspects of Homer, Shakespeare, *Thom's Directory*, and all of the many others explicitly named or alluded to in his works, but a whole substrate of material traceable in the genetic record but not necessarily acknowledged in the published works, including encyclopedia entries, newspaper and magazine articles (on everything from golf to ladies' fashions), the private and published journals of others (by everybody from his own brother to Queen Victoria), and books on a dizzying, even ludicrous array of subjects, including Irish history, Egyptian burial rites, nursery rhymes, architecture, proceedings of criminal trials, magic, rivers of the world, advertising, and many more. Encyclopedias, directories, railway guides, and almanacs became habitual fuel for Joyce's last two decades of writing. When in a letter of 6 November 1921 Joyce asks Frank Budgen to send him a curious variety of publications, including a handbook on fortune-telling by cards, catalogues from department stores and booksellers, and a stamp collecting manual (*Selected Letters* 177), we see the parameters of what reading he finds "useful" widening so as to seem nearly indiscriminate.

Any suggestion of yoking "use" alongside "value," such as the one I have pointedly made above, immediately summons the spectre of Marx (a writer for whom Joyce did not have much use). Borrowing from Marx's definition of "the work of history" as the discovery of "the various use of things" (43), we might propose that "use" is in this respect akin to, if not the equivalent of, the subject of history, and "interpretation" is, by distinction, "the work of history," the narrativizing of the event. However, such a reformulation of the problem does not actually resolve it but rather starkly reveals its depths, since the writing of history cannot (especially in even the loosest Marxist terms) be separated from the subjectivity of history, the state of being within that ongoing, ever-constructed history. Our individual experience of history may be best demonstrated by the way we employ objects for purposes other than that for which they were designed and how they are commonly used: illustrative examples from *Ulysses* include a hat as a hiding place, a hairpin as a reading aid, and a biscuit tin as a projectile. Wittgenstein would undoubtedly ask whether these uses constitute interpretations – a question to which I will shortly return – but in any event the specific applications of an object are acts of individuation, and Marx's decisive adjective "various" means that histories must perforce be varied, and, we can add, those histories will in turn themselves have various uses.[7]

Just as uses are varied, so too, by association, have things become varied, in the sense that there are different classes of things distinguished by use. The recent field of inquiry known – not in an especially helpful way – as "thing theory" attends carefully to the way that the determination of purpose and the degree or extent to which an object is thus "useful" can result in a cognitive and rhetorical shift: an object that does not serve its expected purpose devolves into a mere "thing."[8] Anyone who has ever cursed at an uncooperative machine will recognize the compulsive force of this shift. Another way of putting this is that a thing is that for which we have no use, or can imagine none.

The language is revealing: one *uses* a spoon, but not a book. There is a large class of objects whose designed function requires no skill on the part of its operator that has to be verbally disassociated from the generic "use." One can use a jackhammer, a computer, a trowel, a key, a corkscrew, and a credit card. Yet one does not speak of using a car or helicopter, but of driving and flying one, respectively. The particular reasons for these differences are the stuff of social history, and well worth investigating as such, though for my purposes here it is enough to point out that reading is a highly specialized use, and thus books (and especially "literature") belong to the more concentrated class of objects that sometimes manage not to be thought of as objects at all.[9]

And yet they are objects, even if they are digital (reading devices are fragile and need power, and the much-vaunted information "cloud" in fact constitutes something of an unacknowledged real estate problem, since the necessary hardware for this illusion of intangibility has to take up space somewhere). For its heft, *Ulysses* might well make a better doorstop than *Heart of Darkness*, and, clutched to one's chest at just the right moment, it is more likely to stop a bullet than *All Quiet on the Western Front*. The misprint, the stuck page, the paper cut to a reader's finger all emphasize, with whatever degrees of inconvenience, irritation, or pain, the "thingness" of the book, just as Joyce repeatedly points to the very physical traits of text: the error in a telegram, the scent of a flower added to a letter, the dimensions of a newspaper (convenient for concealing the writing of a love letter).

In averring that "books are not just objects among others" (53), Georges Poulet compromises his proposed "phenomenology of reading." Such phenomenology needs, as I propose to do here, to be carefully tempered with materialist awareness. Just as there are inexorably economic reasons behind the aversion within the humanities to utilitarian or purpose-driven ideas and language (the corporatization of the university and the mercantilization of all intellectual exchange and knowledge production), books have the "economy" with which they are written and the economy within which they are produced, distributed, and – a word that may well seem even less satisfactory in this context than "used" – consumed. They also reflect economies, both real and potential.[10] Leopold Bloom is a compassionate observer of the poor use of people and resources in the Dublin around him. Joyce juxtaposes Bloom's ideas for improving the lives of his fellow citizens (such as those in the detailed index in "Ithaca" [*U* 17.1709–43]) with the menial, disagreeable "jobs"[11] and impoverished, dehumanizing situations in which he finds these same people. The use of humans as walking advertisements (it is pointedly the questioning letter "Y" who goes AWOL) and sexual objects may be the most biting examples, since they underscore a kind of oppressive hermeneutics: the subjugation in the reader's gaze. In this context the complexity of Joyce's writing is a kind of frustration of the routine of imposition and gratification that passive and presumptuous interpretation can amount to. Likewise Joyce repeatedly foregrounds the complexity of economic interrelations, without suggesting easy answers:

> A pointsman's back straightened itself upright suddenly against a tramway standard by Mr Bloom's window. Couldn't they invent something automatic so that the wheel itself much handier? Well but that fellow would lose his job then? Well but then another fellow would get a job making the new invention? (*U* 6.175–9)

Can and do "literary" books offer any kinds of answers to such questions? Despite the recognition of "cultural capital" as a palpable phenomenon and socio-political force of no small importance, questions of how interpretation relates to consumption and whether this capital is valued by exchange or use – in short, the very meaning of such terms and processes in this context – remain disconcertingly open. This is in part symptomatic of how hermeneutics and textual theory, abstract and materialist thought, have all too often kept their distance from one another, when they have not simply stood in mutual distrust and opposition.

Jean-Luc Nancy contends that manuals and treatises differ from other kinds of texts in that "they are means to ends located outside of themselves, in the world of theoretical or practical action" (5). Whether the "ends" of a work of literature are contained within the work, or even whether one can discern or speak of such works as having "ends" at all is a problem that again points to a reluctance in literary studies and among humanities scholars to imagine purposes and modes of interpretation connected to this "world of theoretical or practical action" (again, sometimes with plausible reasons for doing so). Yet just as to refuse to read *Moby-Dick* as a thorough manual on tracking, killing, and profitably carving up a whale would be a very deliberate misreading of that book, so should the possibilities inherent (but often unexplored) in reading other literary works as we do manuals, guidebooks, treatises, and other forms of writing designated "technical" or "functional" not be dismissed out of hand.[12] If, as Rodolphe Gasché has it, the "specificity proper to literature is commonly considered to consist in a use of language that is not exclusively logical" (2), then perhaps it is not surprising that the use of literature in turn need not be logical either.

Purposeful Reading

This book is the inverse of a "user's manual." Such manuals – not simply by custom but by their nature – do not seriously investigate their primary supposition and they tend to blur demarcations between description and prescription. I say "seriously" because of course prefaces and introductions to such books often contain highly rhetorical outlines of, say, the overriding importance of training one's dog to play dead on command, or the easiest method for tightening those abs. These gestures (not altogether unlike those to be found in academic books) ultimately seek to justify the existence of the guide itself more than they interrogate the rationale for the subject – they tend not to include in-depth discussions of the ethics of "training" dogs or "keeping" animals, for example, and seldom probe the economic and social implications of regulated body images and shapes. A guide does not ask (except perhaps rhetorically) "why do this?" but rather says "let me show you how to do this," often with the brand-minded emphasis on "me" as much as on "how."

When Molly Bloom complains of *Ruby: The Pride of the Ring* that "[t]here's nothing smutty in it" (*U* 4.355), she judges the book to be of no use for the expected or desired purpose for which it had been obtained and read. Her review is decisive and unapologetically partial – how many other books might she – or anyone else – dismiss by this singular criterion? (One thinks of Homer ...)

The agreeable, Kant's median aesthetic category between that which is good and that which is beautiful, is adaptable for argued distinctions between art and pornography. (Adaptable, I hasten to qualify, for Kant's word *Interesse* does not bespeak desire; though it is also essential to remember that ultimately desire does not itself determine purpose, though Kant does see purposiveness as subjective, as I am suggesting use is.) If it seems not quite the same thing to judge a work of art as a work of art, a disappointment, or a failure, or something along those lines, and to judge a work of pornography in the same terms, it is because "art" is understood to elude expectation and purpose in ways that "pornography" by definition does not. Molly's instruction to her husband to "get another" (4.358) is entirely comparable with Stephen's statement about the lamp: "if it does not give light enough I shall sell it and buy another." That which we find agreeable, that which gratifies us, is constitutively approximate to that which we find useful. And if one book doesn't do the necessary trick, one can always find another that will. Liberal arts and useful arts, yes, but also use value and exchange value.

Consider, in contrast with Molly's failed smut search, the telephone directory (remember them? – a text designed for use now rarely used, a book fallen out of the canon). One might read the book, however fancifully, as a novel with an extraordinary number and range of characters both distinguished from one another and interconnected by a portentous series of numbers; or, in a more sober critical mode, one might study the book as a sociological document, perhaps observing how business listings differ from residential listings, or how (especially in older editions) the patriarch's name signifies an entire household.[13] These are undoubtedly acts of interpretation, though they fly in the face of the (apparent) purpose of the text. Joyce's use of *Thom's Directory* for 1904 is literally at cross-purposes with the text, and consequently it is doubtful whether anyone now reads or "uses" it any other way.[14]

Simply to allege, then, that a given text is designed for use rather than interpretation is, rather than a neat solution to the problem, to birth a litter of new problems.[15] For one thing, this reifies intention in a way that most literary critics and theorists would otherwise balk at, but more subtly pernicious is the implied judgment in this binary, a judgment that favours one operation or design over the other. Terry Eagleton seeks to privilege "literary texts" when he characterizes them, however alluringly, as "those whose functions we cannot predict, in the sense that we cannot predetermine what 'uses' or readings of them may be made in this or that situation" (*The Event of Literature* 75). Why this same claim, which flatters those of us who study literature as having backed the winning horse in the hermeneutic races, cannot be made for "non-literary" texts – whatever exactly they might be – remains unaddressed: after all, Molly Bloom might find more smut in the telephone directory than in *Ruby: the Pride of the Ring*, if only because she might enjoy the nice names she would find there. "Literary" *a priori* implies a use (just as Eagleton elsewhere avers that "literature" is inherently ideological). Moreover, moral judgment, however unacknowledged as such, regularly colours efforts to distinguish "interpretation" from "use." A simple nod to the entangled question of whether the Third Reich's adoption of Nietzsche (or for that matter, Wagner) is an instance of "use" or "interpretation" makes the point. Valorizations of art tend to discredit aberrant appropriations in ways not unlike how demonizations of art strive to make direct connections between, say, violent video games and criminal behaviour.

Such problems stem from anxieties about hierarchies of subjectivity, or, more plainly, the "right" or "correct" way of understanding a text. Richard Rorty and Umberto Eco both seek to cleave a distinction between *interpretation* and *use*:

> To critically interpret a text means to read it in order to discover, along with our reactions to it, something about its nature. To use a text means to start from it in order to get to something else, even accepting the risk of misinterpreting it from the semantic point of view. If I tear out the pages of my Bible to wrap my pipe tobacco in them, I am using this Bible, but it would be daring to call me a textualist – even though I am, if not [in Rorty's terms] a strong pragmatist, certainly a very pragmatic person. If I get sexual enjoyment from a pornographic book, I am not using it, because in order to elaborate my sexual fantasies I had to semantically interpret its sentences. On the contrary, if – let us suppose – I look into the *Elements* of Euclid to infer that their author was a scotophiliac, obsessed with abstract images, then I am using it because I renounce interpreting its definitions and theorems semantically. (Eco 57)[16]

The passage from Eco quoted above comes from his book *The Limits of Interpretation* (1990), which attempts to put a leash on the previously free-range semiosis posited (or at least countenanced) by his earlier book, *The Open Work* (1989). "Interpretation" thus becomes defined by *evaluative* comparison with other interpretations, and "use" materializes as a category for all of those acts with texts that do not possess or demonstrate any of those constituent values. This definition, then, is less a phenomenological matter than, for example, recognizing a given object as a sombrero because it looks and fits like a sombrero, and because a friend knowledgeable about such things remarks, "Hey, that's a nice sombrero." Sam Slote notes that "a faith in facticity" is integral to what he calls "epistemological" errors ("An Imperfect *Wake*" 139); I would add to this formula a corollary faith in propriety, for readers who presume to identify such errors crave not just the state of being right, but to perform the act of being right. When Frank Kermode – in a kind of Platonist's reverie – wonders "[w]hat kind of mistake would you be making if you tried to sleep in Rauschenberg's famous Bed, which is a bed? You cannot mistake reality for reality" (Kermode 53), he is mistaking epistemology for ontology.

Eco's example of Euclid is rather odd because, as a Joyce scholar himself, he does not seem to think here of the splendid example of the second chapter of the second book of *Finnegans Wake*, in which Joyce reproduces a diagram from the *Elements*, demonstrating how to draw an equilateral triangle. The *Wake* can be read as a mathematics textbook, if an extraordinarily garbled one, and a reader can claim to learn this geometric lesson from this chapter. Scotophilia and sexual fantasies are also palpable "elements" of the chapter and the diagram, for in order to learn mathematics (counting in series, going forth to multiply), a student may first want to know its origins: what was the first number, where did this series of mathematics students of which he or she is a part come from. The reader of the *Wake* can read those geometric shapes as a simple drawing of what a child sees when it looks up its mother's skirt: the matrix in which all stories begin. Joyce allows semantic and semiotic (and/or, for that matter epistemological and ontological), readings to coexist simultaneously, but does not allow one to be given greater valence over the other.

Limits of interpretation indeed. Eco is plumping for design (assumptions of form, tending to be prescriptive) over subjectivity (possibilities of use, tending to be indeterminate). If we flip the terms of reference in his examples, questions emerge about how the writing on a tobacco packet can be read as scripture or whether a pornographic work might teach some principles of geometry. However unorthodox such interpretations are, they remain within the realm of the imaginable, once they are suggested.[17] And are they any more or less rebellious or unpragmatic than someone who, like Homer Simpson, when faced with a section of an official form that says, "Do not write in this space," writes "OK"? The boundaries that shape and limit uses of texts are nowhere better illustrated than in such bureaucratic documents and institutional forms ("for office use only"). Lisa Gitelman helpfully outlines how these documents alter the terms of textual interaction associated with "literature":

> whatever reading is entailed by genres like bills of lading and stock transfers, it is not reading that has very much to do with the sort of readerly subjectivity that came to such special prominence in the course of the eighteenth and nineteenth centuries, the subjectivities of literature in general and the novel in particular. Nor can genres like these strictly be said to have inspired identification among communities of readers in the way that newspapers have done because of the ritualized character of their consumption. Job-printed forms didn't have readers, then; they had users instead. Users have subjectivities, too, without question, but they are not exactly readerly ones. (30–1)

Put another way, readers are conditioned to respond to and engage with different kinds of texts with different senses of their roles in that process. Drivers do not, as a rule, debate too long about the meaning of a stop sign, but it must be added that not every driver understands what constitutes a "stop" in quite the same way, or even to what degree the information expressed by the sign applies to him or her. A driver who does not proceed after having stopped because the sign continues to say "stop" – never stops saying "stop," never says anything other than "stop" – might be characterized as too literal, too suggestible.

This readerly abjection is perhaps most sharply observed in such book titles as *The Complete Idiot's Guide to Beekeeping* (2010) and *Critical Thinking Skills for Dummies* (2015) – the modern equivalents of the books that Stephen finds on the bookcart – or rather in the popularity and the astonishing range of variations of the *Idiot's Guide* and *For Dummies* series. One need not invoke Althusser's concept of the answered call as subjection to ideology in order to understand that wilfully reading one of these books is an act of submission to authority (yes, I wish to learn to play the harmonica, meditate, and/or repair a truck, but I have to be addressed as a *complete idiot* when it comes to being instructed in these endeavours). Why does it seem that the attribution of greater subjectivity to a text seems to result in a diminishment of the subjectivity of the reader?

Recent proponents of a "new formalism" have flirted with "functional" readings but so far have not actually asked them to dance. For example, Caroline Levine adopts the term "affordance" from design theory to discuss "potential uses or actions latent in materials and designs" (6). This notion, she claims,

> allows us to grasp both the specificity and the generality of forms – both the particular constraints and possibilities that different forms afford, and the fact that these patterns and arrangements carry their affordances with them as they move across time and space. What is a walled enclosure or a rhyming couplet *capable* of doing? Each shape or pattern, social or literary, lay claim to a limited range of potentialities. Enclosures afford containment and security, inclusion as well as exclusion. Rhyme affords repetition, anticipation, and memorization. (6)

Emotional response does not appear to be an affordance in this scheme. Might it then be classified as a side effect, or some sort of dangerous supplement? (Recall how very different is Shelley's claim in his *Defence of Poetry* – a favourite text of Joyce's, and one that also meditates on the starting of fires – that "utility" is a way of expressing "the means of producing" the reader's pleasure: "whatever strengthens and purifies the affections, enlarges the imagination, and adds spirit to sense, is useful" [514].) For that matter, does all interpretation and response hew to the affordances, or vice versa? Is use "latent in materials and designs" or in the eye of the user?

Effectual Reading

"All art is quite useless" (Wilde, *Picture* 4). Wilde's notorious aphorism is remarkable precisely because of its frequent use out of context both by those who salute it as an artistic credo and by those who fret about the social effects and responsibilities of art. In fact, this slippage between polarized understandings of the aphorism underscores its implicit point about "all art" as a rhetorical and conceptual figure that disallows context. Rather than simply the rejection of a social function for art, the careful sequence of propositions and provocations that acts as preface to *The Picture of Dorian Gray* identifies art as a matter of affect in action, as a relation between "use" and "admiration": "We can forgive a man making a useful thing as long as he does not admire it. The only excuse for making a useless thing is that one admires it intensely" (4).

If we can look past the *too*-dandified caricature of Wilde that might make us forget his socialist thinking, it can be argued that Wilde anticipates – one might even go so far as to say prefigures – Horkheimer and Adorno, for whom "[c]ulture is a paradoxical commodity. So completely is it subject to the law of exchange that it is no longer exchanged; it is so blindly consumed in use that it can no longer be used" (131). In this context it is crucial to observe that, in Wilde's novel, Dorian Gray *uses* the enchanted picture of himself: he hides it away, not unlike a stash of pornography, for his own private and shameful viewing. (Octavio Paz writes that a poem's "value and usefulness cannot be measured; a man rich in poetry may be a beggar. Nor can poems be hoarded: they must be spent" [154]. Dorian is a would-be miser of time and pleasure.) Wilde, an ironic pragmatist, literalizes the idea of art as a means to immortality, a formula whose own longevity indicates how unobjectionable it has been to even the most fervently anti-utilitarian humanists and artists.[18] As biographers and annotators habitually remind us, Joyce himself adopted (and adapted) it: "I've put in so many enigmas and puzzles that it will keep the professors busy for centuries arguing over what I meant, and that's the only way of insuring one's immortality" (Ellmann 521). Everyone who uses this line is being used by Joyce.[19]

When Marjorie Garber claims that "poems and novels do not have answers that are immutably true; they do not themselves constitute a realm of knowledge production" (*Use and Abuse* 28), she (perhaps inadvertently) posits a misleading equation between knowledge and immutability. What one knows is unavoidably circumstantial and contingent, and this is precisely what poems and novels avow. There is knowledge in the hidden portrait of Dorian Gray and in the missing letter of *Finnegans Wake*, but more important is how they engender knowledge that is multiple, subjective, and often contradictory in the minds of people. Rita Felski observes that it is a predicated understanding of literature as ideology that determines "that literary works can be objects of knowledge but never sources of knowledge" (7).

To sidestep the inhibitions implicit in privileging the question of intention or "design" (whether it be *intentio auctoris, intentio operis*, or *intentio lectoris*), we can instead – and to no insignificant liberation – ask about what a text does, what its effects are. Yet as deft a strategy or countermove this seems, it invokes another, equally troubling problem, of what distinction may be made between an effect and a function. Put another way, if a certain poem in my view *does X* (and X can be as superficial or as sophisticated as you like: the poem makes me sad, or the poem parodies the hegemonic suppositions of normative linguistics), to what extent is my view shaped by utilitarian assumptions about what language, texts, or poems can do, in general or in particular? Do I observe that the poem *does* X because I perceive X to be *useful* to me? If I cannot perceive any usefulness in X – that is, if I cannot see how or why the poem should sadden me, if I cannot conceive of a purpose for which I might observe such an effect – can I even perceive X?

Such questions have deep and disquieting phenomenological, ideological dimensions, and by the same token they may seem absurd – if or when they seem useless. In reading the rationale given in "Ithaca" for Bloom's shaving at nighttime, a reader might judge this as a practical notion and take up the practice, but there are many more reasons why a reader might not (not everybody shaves, for one). This example points to why the monkey-read, monkey-do conception of literature is flawed: use is contingent in ways that meaning is not. The example is simple and pragmatic, but the point applies to representations of other behaviours and even moral principles that readers are encouraged to emulate. The hermeneutics of *Finnegans Wake* depend upon what connections or allusions readers may find "useful," what interpretive suggestions give coherence of context, however provisional, local, or momentary, to a text defiant of any other kinds. Whether that transitory meaning has any "use" outside of the text is another question again, but it is the use (of words, of images, of sounds, of associations) that allows for meaning, a reversal of the customary understanding of interpretation preceding and governing use.

Adapting Vico's cyclical stages of history, readings of the *Wake* – and, I would suggest, readings of any text, though I will retain the *Wake* as an illuminating because extreme case study – can be classified as theocratic, aristocratic, and democratic. Their differentiation lies in how the reading manifests itself, how it responds to the degree and kind of authority that the author locates in or bestows upon the text. In a sense, what I am proposing is a "new science" of the phenomenology of reading, albeit realized in broad strokes. This taxonomy of the "uses" of texts, like Vico's cycles, points both to the social and political immediacy and specificity of these manifestations of reading *and* to how they are inseparably part of a continuum of readings.

Theocratic readings, first of all, find an urgency in a work of writing that may overpower all other ideas and considerations. Noel Riley Fitch recounts how in 1954 a young man sent dozens of letters and telegrams to his family and friends as well as to Sylvia Beach, warning them to evacuate Paris. He explained that "he had 'solved the riddle' of *Finnegans Wake*: When would World War III break out?" (394). Joyce's book was a coded prophecy, a "new science" for an atomic age, and this alert reader acted upon this interpretation. Any chuckling we may be tempted to do at this instance might rightly be somewhat nervous, for the force behind this interpretation is enviably zealous, even righteous, in a way that other readings are not, and yet lunacy is not exclusive to such a reading. The reader electrified by the word-for-word truth of scripture and the reader who throws down a mystery novel to call the police and report the murder are both theocratic readers, for they see the text before them as an invasion into the world at large, a new reality that expands or irrevocably alters their own. Censorship is invariably a product of theocratic reading: it is very much an inspired act. In connecting poetry with the sacred, Georges Bataille points to the essence of theocratic reading: "[S]acrifice returns an element of use value to the world of sensibility" (148).

The aristocratic reading, in effect the default mode of academia, reifies rather than deifies the authority of the text, and treats the text as an invitation to share that authority. The aristocratic reading transforms a reader into an author, and its typical fruits are the lecture, the essay, the monograph (though also, less directly, other forms such as the biography, the novel, and so on). Blogs and book reviews and even private diary entries about one's impressions of a given book all belong to this category. Where theocratic readings instigate changes to the reader's relationship with the world in which he or she lives, aristocratic readings primarily seek to change the reader's relationship with the text (not as separate or distinct from the world, but as another way of being in it).

Finally, democratic readings prompt changes to relationships between readers. Such readings are multiple, non-monologic, contradictory, aggregative. Embodied by conversation, the open exchange of ideas and interpretations, democratic readings do not typically yield publications precisely because they are by definition at odds with the investment of stabilized authority into a particular person, as the publishing industry has come to expect. The most obvious example in this context is the phenomenon of the *Finnegans Wake* reading group. Such groups are, in my experience, strikingly egalitarian spaces that can feel at once utopian, frustrating, and not unlike a group therapy session. (Not all such reading groups are equally or even functionally democratic, of course, and within any group dynamic there is the possibility of aristocratic or even theocratic tendencies.) A really good *Wake* reading group empowers readers together. Democratic readings primarily seek to change the reader's relationship with other readers.

Despite what valences, attractive qualities, or problems that political systems designated as "theocratic" or "aristocratic" or "democratic" might hold, none of these three *modes* of readings is inherently superior to the others (the interpretive insights of an online chat group, taken together as a democratic mode of reading, are not by definition any more or less profound than those of a sermon, nor any more or less prone to folly). In fact, because these Viconian terms suggest a graduated and shifting spectrum of readings, the distinction between one and the next can in some cases be rather hazy. A scholarly monograph could conceivably venture into theocratic pronouncements (though he demurs that he is no academic, John P. Anderson's obsessive study of *Finnegans Wake* and Kabbalah – at the time of this writing in its tenth volume! – is an example to behold, an enterprise which explicitly says that the *Wake* "fits no known category other than wisdom literature" [12], and so reads it accordingly). A university seminar discussion is often a site of struggle between aristocratic and democratic tendencies, while the decision to tattoo another's poetry onto one's body is a more or less theocratic gesture, depending on whether and how that tattoo is shown to others.

Cyclicality is also important to this appropriation of Vico, for just as interpretation is ongoing, always in revision, and constantly supplemented and qualified, so too are the terms of "use" for whatever "things" come to hand. Bloom, observing the newspapers in production in "Aeolus," thinks forward to the afterlife of the stuff, the reuse and recycling of information and matter: "the obedient reels feeding in huge webs of paper. Clank it. Clank it. Miles of it unreeled. What becomes of it after? O, wrap up meat, parcels: various uses, thousand and one things" (7.135–8). Joyce encourages an understanding of both production and use as co-dependent but not synonymous, one ever and continuously imagining the other, and vice versa.[20]

As I have already suggested, "literature" is not customarily thought of as material that can be either purposed or repurposed, but is instead reified by many writers and readers as some more mysterious or metaphysical phenomenon that cannot be harnessed to base "use." The tautological thinking of "art for art's sake" was never confined to nor laid to rest in late nineteenth-century aestheticism, but finds comfortable refuge in postmodernism. In conversation with Osvaldo Ferrari, Jorge Luis Borges explains how to answer a question of use with useless questions: "Last week I was asked in several places – two people asked me the same question – what's the use of poetry? And I answered them with: What's the use of death? What's the use of the taste of coffee? What's the use of me? What's the use of us?" (Borges and Ferrari 111–12). But if the notion that literature is "useless" is likewise too much to bear, one can always celebrate the freedom of literature from mastery. Garber, for example, writes: "[a]t times when meanings are manifold, disparate, and always changing, the rich possibility of interpretation – the happy resistance of the text to ever be fully known and mastered – is one of the most exhilarating products of human culture" (*Use and Abuse* 30). The rhetorical swelling of this assertion almost obscures the fact that *possibility* is itself being presented here as a *product*.

Bloom sounds like the advertising man that he is with the jinglish "various uses, thousand and one things,"[21] but he does not sound so very different from Garber's promise of ever further acts of interpretation. Beyond the fact that we do use books – to keep records and extend memory, to furnish a room, to divert and entertain, to teach us, and to make yet more books – lurks the possibility that uses not yet thought of may await their moment, just as death or the taste of coffee or even Borges may yet prove useful. Marx's formula can be tweaked to imagine an alternative history composed of the various times and ways in which certain things have been reckoned useless. In a sense *Finnegans Wake* is just this sort of history, a rubbishy archive of disjecta, an overgrown midden heap of verbigeration, words nobody knew they needed. If literary history is to map the "various uses" that comprise its subject, the boundaries of "plurabilities" must not be peremptorily fixed and the "useless" ought to be recognized as an undiscovered country. There is always a lesson to be had from the carefully discriminating and shockingly practical Molly Bloom, who thinks of her husband as not "much use" but "still better than nothing" (*U* 18.999).

About This Book

This book's central axiom is an extrapolation of the powerful refrain from William Carlos Williams's *Paterson*, a poem considerably influenced by Joyce. To Williams's assertion, "no idea but in things" can be added *no interpretation but in use*. How readers interpret this book will materialize in their uses of it – whether that's as fodder for a dissertation or as kindling for a fire. By extension, an inability to find any use for it represents a kind of interpretation, albeit a disappointing and uninteresting one. In any event, there are more uses of a text than are dreamt of in an author's philosophy.

The first of this book's two parts is devoted to specifically textual questions of use, distinguished as "Textual Functions." It examines the activities that might be most readily understood as "uses" of a text in the context of textual production, as it may be broadly conceived. These activities include quoting and citing ("using" a text by transplanting it), editing (shaping a "useable" version of a text), annotating and translating (transforming text for use by readers otherwise unable to "use" it), each of which constitutes a chapter's slippery subject.

"Guidance Systems," the first chapter, examines how populous is the crowd of guidebooks jostling to stand next to Joyce's books on the shelves, and asks about the nature of and assumptions behind this relentless endeavour to introduce and explain this author to a hypothetical, benighted audience. This book's second chapter is called "Misquoting Joyce" – the first word may be a gerund or an adjective – because Joyce challenges what it means to use another's words, and whether accuracy has anything to do with the activity. As I have already suggested, the quoter of Joyce is also a means to Joyce's ends, a way in which a text can count on the further dissemination and longevity of his work. Editing, the processes by which a "useable" text is shaped, is the province of the third chapter, "Limited Editions, Edited Limitations." The textual travails of *Ulysses* have been repeatedly chronicled elsewhere, so this chapter compares two recent editions of *Finnegans Wake* not merely to appreciate the more than slightly intimidating job such work represents, but to consider what purposes such editions have for what readers. Translation and annotation, intertwined processes of magnifying (and thus inevitably distorting) a text, are the subjects of chapter 4, "Translation, Annotation, Hesitation," which takes as its focal study the case of Philippe Lavergne's singlehanded translation of the *Wake*. Like editing, translation and annotation prescribe and to no small degree circumscribe subsequent uses of a given text.

"Cultural Appropriations," the second part of the book, turns from textual production to textual consumption. Declan Kiberd has acclaimed *Ulysses* as a "modern example of wisdom literature" (31), a "sort of 'self-help' manual" (245), and the second part of this book not only happily accepts this suggestion but adopts it as a kind of reading practice.[22] If we understand Joyce as a self-help author, what advice and instruction await in the pages of not just *Ulysses*, but *Dubliners*, *A Portrait of the Artist*, and *Finnegans Wake*? These chapters may be approached as kinds of *jeux d'esprit* in cultural studies, and collectively as an ironic (but not dismissive), self-reflexive assessment of a critical disposition of time past, when fiction and poetry were held to offer readers directives (usually moral) for living. By asking what *uses* these books may have and stooping to consider uses which may well seem improbable or irreverent – and, equally important, without set or predetermined conceptions of what uses literature as an institution might be supposed to have (a careful provision meant to prevent teetering into such chasms as Leavisite moralism) – we find ourselves reading these books in ways that enable unexpected and sometimes stimulating interpretations and connections.

In probing such hermeneutic questions, the titles of this section's chapters themselves make precisely the kinds of extravagant promises made in the titles of guidebooks like *How to Win Friends and Influence People*, *A Guide to Rational Living*, and *Teach Yourself Tantric Sex* – and my own inventions may even seem more modest by comparison with real titles such as these, while the subjects at issue in them are both typical and popular in self-help books. The first of these chapters, "Make a Stump Speech of It," whose title comes from some mock-encouragement in the "Circe" episode, reads Joyce's work as a (kind of) guide to public speaking, a subject whose fascination for the author can be seen in the various ways he returns, again and again, to dramatizing. The next, "Win a Dream Date with James Joyce," consults various guides to dating against the courtship rites and wrongs represented in Joyce's works, and in turn weighs what special attractions someone with a knowledge of Joyce might be able to flaunt. Diet is the subject of the seventh chapter, "The Stephen Dedalus Diet," re-examining our understanding of *Ulysses* as a book of gastronomic extravagances with questions about what exactly Stephen Dedalus eats, how Joyce composes his text, and what narrative and political significance lies in eating choices.

It can be chastening to ask whether literary criticism might or can be one of the "useful arts." How applied are its methods and insights, does it have functions apart from textual ones? Bloom's reading of *Matcham's Masterstroke* in the jakes, itself a kind of use (a diversion from the operation under way and "his own rising smell" [4.513]), ends with what might well be an interpretation: "He tore away half the prize story sharply and wiped himself with it" (4.537). Whether this constitutes a theocratic, aristocratic, or democratic reading I leave to others to judge, but if this can be seen as a gesture of literary criticism, a masterstroke of its own, then our own acts of criticism may be uses of texts not yet recognized as such. One function begets another.

PART ONE

Textual Functions

Mark my use of you, cog! Take notice how I yemploy, crib! (*FW* 464.03–04)

1
Guidance Systems

Under what guidance, following what signs? (*U* 17.1991)

The comedian Steven Wright tells of asking a bookstore employee where he would find the "self-help" section. "If I told you," she replied, "that would defeat the purpose." We might compare this joke with the story of Robert Schumann performing a new composition for his students. When he was finished, one listener admitted the difficulty of the piece and asked the maestro whether he might explain it. By way of assent, Schumann promptly sat and played it again.

That the notion of "difficulty," taken up by many writers and critics,[1] almost always arises in direct relation to works of modernism reveals at least as much about the (ongoing) reception of modernism as it does about *The Waste Land*, say, or *Tender Buttons*, and perhaps even more about how, at this moment in history, we conceive of reading and of aesethetic reception more generally. The discourse of difficulty inevitably ties itself in knots, for, stirred by the suggestion that readers may not on their own have sufficient resources (whether that means a specific literacy, cultural awareness, or access to pertinent extratextual information) and will need assistance, the writer who addresses this problem can only confirm it: he or she cannot say "you do not need any help" without thus having offered some. Both Schumann and Wright's bookstore employee *have* rendered a kind of assistance, even if this particular kind might not inspire much thanks.

There is, then, a difficulty with difficulty: there are swathes of literature, most strikingly works of high modernism and Joyce's works most of all, utterly surrounded by "help." The offers of "help" are so numerous that simply seeking it has become far less a problem than discerning which offers to accept. Feeding the plaintive phrase "help me I have to read *Ulysses*" into Google produces nearly four million results.[2] The past decade has seen a noticeable proliferation of new Joyce guides, books written by scholars but aimed at a general public. In 2009 alone, half a dozen appeared: Declan Kiberd's Ulysses *and Us: The Art of Everyday Life in Joyce's Masterpiece*, Edmund Lloyd Epstein's *A Guide Through* Finnegans Wake, Philip Kitcher's *Joyce's Kaleidoscope: An Invitation to* Finnegans Wake, W. Terrance Gordon's glossy *Everyman's Joyce*, Peter Mahon's *Joyce: A Guide for the Perplexed*, and Lee Spinks's *James Joyce: A Critical Guide*. That these books are optimistically, ostensibly aimed at a wide, unacademic readership (and in some instances not so optimistically aimed rather away from Joyce scholars) shows how much the publishing world has invested in the enterprise of framing and reframing Joyce for the "average" or "general" reader. Kiberd's argument that the titular "masterpiece" *Ulysses* has been unjustly kept from "real people" (11) by what he calls "specialist bohemians" (30) strategically ignores the identifiable genre of which his book is just one recent example.

And to this bibliography might be added the growing number of websites on Joyce, the graphic novels and comic book biographies, the publication of (at least some of) the Buffalo *Finnegans Wake* notebooks,[3] and the appearance of the third and fourth editions of Roland McHugh's *Annotations to* Finnegans Wake (in 2006 and 2016, respectively). All of this deserves more attention than the cynical (but not inaccurate) comment that the "Joyce industry" is thriving; here we see many serious efforts to expand the readership of and fan curiosity about books still often written off as hermetic obscurities, wastes of time, useless things. (As one Amazon.com reviewer of *Finnegans Wake* summarily judges, "I award [the author] no stars and may God have mercy on his soul.")

It is one thing to affirm, as Frank Delaney does in *James Joyce's Odyssey: A Guide to the Dublin of* Ulysses, that the body of Joyce scholarship has, "by its size and daunting diligence, come between Joyce and the non-academic reader, the enthusiast" (9), and quite another to assert that one's own guide is somehow not part of this intervention: "This is a plain man's guide to a novel, perhaps *the* novel, of the plain man" (11). I'll return to the rhetorical strategy at work here later; for now it is sufficient to remark that this novel of the plain man is evidently not so plain that its plainness does not need pointing out.

Voicing the Trend of Modern Opinion

Modernism, often thought to be utterly opposed to the self-improvement creed of Victorianism, is in fact a kind of remodelling of this impulse. While modernism has its undeniably elitist qualities, embodied by sometimes cartoonish Eliotic critical disaffections, there is another aspect comprising and simultaneously confronting a full-blown industrialization of "self-help." Modernism's transformative mandate – inherited and modified from that of Romanticism, and perhaps best emblematized by Rilke's solemn pronouncement, "du mußt dein Leben ändern" – had a conspicuously pedantic streak. Witness the very titles of Pound's *How to Read* and Stein's *How to Write* (and the uncertain degrees of irony in these titles do not overwhelm this agenda). To "become modern," to "modernize oneself": these are the phrases used to denote a qualitative change in the constitution of the self, however obscure that change might be, and this change is in principle not defined by or exclusive of class or gender.[4]

Even the prurient view of modernism as the ravaging of taboos and the publication of naughty words represents an understanding of modernism as a form or means of instruction. How many eager young readers have consulted *Lady Chatterley's Lover* as an illicit kind of instruction manual? Whether or not D.H. Lawrence actually makes for edifying or riveting sexual education (or should that be studies in labour relations?) is beside the point: such use and reputation are a significant part of the book's reception and history. *Ulysses* offers a wider array of self-improvement avenues than whatever tips of a similar nature might be feverishly sought in its notorious last chapter, but the novel still retains, nearly a century after its first publication, a reputation as educatively naughty. Judge Woolsey's characterization of the novel as an "emetic" agent, rather than as a means of erotic arousal, replaces one unflattering function with another: what benefits would a reader seeking out *Ulysses* for just this purpose, on this judicial endorsement, discover? Might *Ulysses* serve as a kind of Wonderworker? "Recommend it to your lady and gentlemen friends, lasts a lifetime" (*U* 17.1832).

One could go so far as to suggest that one of modernism's defining disputes with modernity is its gradual separation of forms of reading, which I touched upon in the introduction. "Only a fool reads poetry for facts," declares the first sentence of a recent critical study of poetry and poetics, Daniel Tiffany's *Toy Medium: Materialism and Lyric* (11). It is not that modernity has sowed scepticism of textuality – that task, I have argued elsewhere, *modernism* undertakes – but rather has delineated specific kinds of text to which may be attributed specific kinds of authority, or in other words, certain texts for certain uses. Tiffany points to how modernism brought a kind of "scientific" discursive quality to poetics, though perhaps he understates the matter. The unself-conscious blend of scientific inquiry and poetry percolating in Lucretius is tellingly unmatched by anything produced in the last four hundred years. Joyce nods to the premodern hybridities of poetry and science, nature and use, by giving as the assigned essay theme for Lucretius in the children's lessons chapter of *Finnegans Wake* "The Uses and Abuses of Insects" (*FW* 306.31). Does an earwig have a use, and how does one abuse an earwig? "Insects" is also, throughout the *Wake*, suggestive of "incest," the prohibited intermingling of related subjects. *De rerum natura* is "incestuous" only to purists who do not like their discourses and methods mixed, but by the same token it is not "interdisciplinary" any more than a cow is proof that God loves hamburgers. Use is not synonymous with design, and the materiality of texts and reading underscored by modernism loosens the dictates of how these things are used.

Yet guides constrain, or at any rate narrow the conceivable uses and interpretations, and so seem at odds with the emancipatory agenda of modernism. The fact is that modernism has a fascinating, conflicted relationship with "guides" as such. For all of the ridiculing of jittery travellers dependent on their baedekers, there are many concentrated efforts to map, in fiction and poetry, the streets and routes of urban itinerants (think of *Ulysses*, Woolf's *Mrs Dalloway*, Aragon's *Paris Peasant*, Henry Miller's *Tropic of Cancer*, and so on), and works such as Hope Mirrlees's *Paris*, Eliot's *The Waste Land*, Basil Bunting's *Briggflatts*, and *Finnegans Wake* are stocked with (more and less helpful) footnotes.[5] For all of the avant-garde denunciations of museums and the past, there are poems "including history" (in Pound's formulation), steeped in classical allusions and ancient languages. For all of the scorn for nineteenth-century moral codes and watchwords, there are various, no less earnest exhortations to "make it new," to become "absolutely modern."

Misled by an Oracle

Guidance is itself an interesting, inextricable theme of both *A Portrait of the Artist as a Young Man* and *Ulysses*, though that theme is treated differently by each book. The former casts great suspicion on institutional authorities. These authorities are by turns abusive, coercive, intimidating, posturing, colonial, and ignorant – and Stephen ultimately arrives at the brink of becoming one of this intelligentsia. Disregarding the teachings of the church is flagged as a danger to his soul: "God spoke to you by so many voices, but you would not hear" (*P* 104). The recognition and blandishments afforded by various advisors, teachers, and paternal figures are alluring, for Stephen is torn repeatedly between being a good pupil and a rebel, between "futile isolation" (82) and belonging (heeding the call, the "vocation": "We are your kinsmen. And the air is thick with their company as they call to me, their kinsman" [213]). Yet when, at the end of the novel, Cranly "seized his arm and steered him round," although Stephen is "thrilled by his touch" (208), he nonetheless abandons his confidant (and will recall that guiding arm ambiguously when Mulligan presumes to guide him in "Telemachus" [1.159]).

For most of 16 June 1904, Stephen is following someone else's lead, and he is still plagued with worries about whether he is to be included or whether to exclude himself from this or that event or group or opportunity. His first decisive action in *Ulysses* – which happens so passively that first-time readers might miss it, and re-readers might argue about whether it happens at all – is his resignation from teaching:

> – I foresee, Mr Deasy said, that you will not remain here very long at this work. You were not born to be a teacher, I think. Perhaps I am wrong.
>
> – A learner rather, Stephen said.
>
> And here what will you learn more?
>
> Mr Deasy shook his head.
>
> – Who knows? he said. To learn one must be humble. But life is the great teacher. (2.401–7)

"I foresee": Mr Deasy's prophecy is uncharacteristically sage and correct, though he immediately thereafter tumbles again into hoary pedantic formulas. But who is speaking the unspoken line, "And here what will you learn more?" Stephen, evidently thinking to himself, has internalized a master's voice (just as we later see in "Aeolus" that Father Dolan's voice echoes readily if unbidden in Stephen's mind: "See it in your face. See it in your eye. Lazy idle little schemer" [7.618]). "Learner" suggests a distinction from "student," and its etymology reaches back to a sense of seeking the right track to follow. It is telling that in the following chapter, absentminded Stephen will walk farther than he intended, and lose track of himself. Unguided, he gets lost, and it may be more than simply ironic that "Proteus" is the very chapter where many first-time readers of the novel get lost and give up.

I have already pointed out that Bloom's heroism in *Ulysses* lies in his wish to be of use to others. Among other things, he is only too happy to (attempt to) improve Molly's vocabulary while serving her breakfast, offer assistance to Menton and Parnell with their respective hats, and lead the blind stripling across the road. He keeps a "sharp lookout" (16.1778) for the hazards of traffic around himself and others, warning Mrs Breen of the fixed trajectory of Cashel Boyle O'Connor Fitzmaurice Tisdall Farrell and Stephen Dedalus of the oncoming steamroller.

Without regard to time and place he explains scientific phenomena to those who care even less than they understand (erections resulting from hanging in "Cyclops" and the origins of thunder in "Oxen of the Sun"), and shares garbled notions of political economy with a young man too far from sober to respond in more than a few words. The thanks he receives for these and similar gestures are almost inevitably muted, and when they are not, it is because Bloom has been *unwittingly* helpful, such as the occasions of his providing the newspaper with a name to an unknown mourner at Paddy Dignam's funeral, and of his offering a gold tip on a horserace, which Bantam Lyons, to his regret, later changes his mind on. And of course the novel pivots on a moment of selfless assistance, Bloom's rescue of Stephen.

This heroism of the potentially useful often veers into the ridiculous: one can, in a sense, be *too useful*. What great role at the newspaper does Bloom most fancy? That of the advice columnist, of course: "Dear Mr Editor, what is a good cure for flatulence? I'd like that part. Learn a lot teaching others. The personal note." (*U* 7.95–7). Later in the day Bloom will get the chance to give such prescriptions (if only in his own mind):

> PISSER BURKE
> For bladder trouble?
> BLOOM
> Acid. nit. hydrochlor. dil., 20 minims
> Tinct. nux vom., 5 minims
> Extr. taraxel. liq., 30 minims.
> Aq. dis. ter in die.
>
> (U 15.1648–54)

This is the Bloom admired in "Circe" for his wisdom on an array of questions. He dispenses "[f]ree medical and legal advice, solution of doubles and other problems" (15.1630–1). His authority is unquestioned: "*Bloom explains to those near him his schemes for social regeneration.*

All agree with him" (15.1702–3). Lest anyone complain that "Circe" is too long, let it be noted how wryly compact is the use of indirect discourse here. What schemes, precisely? It doesn't particularly matter at this point, when the reader has come to know that Bloom is full of schemes for the improvement of this, that, and the other, but they are seldom clearly expressed and even more seldom given serious consideration by anybody else. And Bloom's knowledge assumes unforeseen and inexplicable depths in "Circe": not only does he have, ready upon demand, the exact measures for Pisser's prescription, he mysteriously knows that Bella Cohen has a son in Oxford, to her amazement. Such occult knowledge is a reminder that Homer's Circe is ultimately an important counsellor to Odysseus, providing him with useful directions. In Joyce's rearrangement of *The Odyssey*, "Circe" is the episode in which Bloom's fantasies of being useful expand to the point where he is himself roughly used, and thereafter he returns from fantasy to the practical world and gives assistance to Stephen.

Joyce is playing with conventions of the guide in the epic: the need for directions, mentoring, protection, supplied by the Cumaean Sibyl in *The Aeneid*, the spirit of Virgil in Dante, angels in Milton, and by a number of characters in Homer: Mentor (Athena) primarily, but also Nestor, Proteus, Tiresias, and Circe. One could say that the epic is by definition a series of consultations with advisors, punctuated by sequences of voyage and action. No goddess of wisdom can be located in *Ulysses*, though the novel is, as later chapters of this book will show, awash in advice. The Homeric "parallel" of the milkwoman in "Proteus" with Mentor is impossible to take straight, for she offers no guidance of any kind in the chapter (Stephen is unsure whether she is there "[t]o serve or to upbraid" [1.406], a binary that lays bare his maternal anxieties and general difficulties with women). By contrast, Buck Mulligan ("I must teach you" [1.79]) and Haines ("Pay up and be pleasant" [1.449]) are zealous counsellors. More follow in subsequent chapters: Mr Deasy, Myles Crawford, and so on, culminating in Bloom.

When Bloom nervously confuses the terms "admirers" and "advisers" in "Cyclops" (12.767), he signals the ambivalence the novel has for these various guides. Perhaps Joyce's use of the Roman name Ulysses rather than the Greek Odysseus for his title is a significant nod to Dante, who placed the hero (Ulisse) among the false counsellors in hell (see Canto 26). Pyrrhus, that disappointed bridge, was "misled by an oracle" (*U* 7.568–9) as the ponderous pundit Professor MacHugh reminds us: a classical inheritance of subsequent narrative is to be seen in how much of it is propelled by misconstrued advice. In a protracted distortion of the moral instruction heaped on Ophelia by her father and brother, and on young women in general by patricians and primers, *Finnegans Wake* recommends: "Trip over sacramental tea into the long lives of our saints and saucerdotes, with vignettes, cut short into instructual primers by those in authority for the bittermint of your soughts" (*FW* 444.21–4). "Long lives cut short" hardly sounds like careful study of saintly examples, and ordering one's life and thoughts in the manner that one sets out tea (bitter or mint) in cups and saucers is not much of a philosophy. The authorities of the classics and the church are most interesting to Joyce because they are so misleading.

Doubtful, too, is the practice of taking Joyce himself as a guide to his works. Included as often as a map to Dublin in editions to *Ulysses*, and sometimes treated as maps themselves, the so-called Gilbert and Linati schema can be too reverentially treated. With unforgiving judgment, Vladimir Nabokov recounts how "[o]ne bore, a man called Stuart Gilbert, misled by a tongue-in-cheek list compiled by Joyce himself, found in every chapter the domination of one particular organ ... but we shall ignore that dull nonsense too" (*Lectures on Literature* 288). Regardless of whether one agrees with Nabokov about Gilbert or the "tongue-in-cheek list" or the domination of organs, the matter of what one chooses to ignore, what information or suggestions or guidance one filters out, is at least as important as what such things a reader may accept for consideration. Daring explorers know that the most intriguing and alluring signs in the museum are not those that cue authorial voice-overs and constitute the stations of the guided tour, but rather the ones that say STAFF ONLY and NO ADMITTANCE.

On Your Gullible's Travels

Guidebooks to reading Joyce frequently liken the experience to a journey. This analogy obviously reflects the time commitment involved and suggests a kind of reward, if only bragging rights, at the journey's end, but the question of the role of the guide in the journey is addressed in different ways. For instance, Michael Murphy's 2004 guide to Joyce, published by Greenwich Exchange (which, according to the book's back cover "aims to appeal to both the specialist and the general reader"), acknowledges the "bewildering array" of scholarly introductions this way: "As with a guidebook to a favourite city, they should repay repeated reading, nudging one's shoulder at a particular view from a bridge, making suggestions about the best restaurants, pointing out a beautiful still-life in a corner of the museum" (xviii). Are guidebooks really matter for "repeated reading"? The guide has in this formulation subtly replaced the destination as the voyager's primary focus. It is not the "favourite city" that merits revisiting and close attention, but the guide with its invaluable nudges and suggestions.

Frank Delaney recasts the relationship between novel, reader, and guide when he writes that "*Ulysses* may, if you wish, become a guidebook, a literary Baedeker, by which a trip to Dublin becomes enlivened" (11). In this formulation, *Ulysses* is itself a guide, and thus by implication Delaney's *Guide* is a guide to a guide. How good, how clear and reliable a guide can *Ulysses* be if one needs a supplementary guide to it? At the back of this one can hear Chico Marx calling out, "tootsie fruitsie ice cream," the scam with which he fleeces Groucho in *A Day at the Races*. For every guidebook that Groucho buys in pursuit of a hot tip on the day's horse race, Chico tells him he needs to buy yet another to decode the one before it. When Peter Mahon, in his *Joyce: A Guide for the Perplexed*, calls Joyce guides "a way into the labyrinth" (xi), his choice of preposition may be more apt than intended. Guides lead us "into" the labyrinth but not "through" it, either because they desert us or because they themselves get lost.

Writing on the valences of knowledge and ignorance in reading Joyce, Fritz Senn remarks:

> If Odysseus had set out from Troy with a copy of *The Mediterranean on Five Drachmas a Day* he would have saved himself enormous trouble, but the *Odyssey* would have become a much more tedious epic or, more likely, none at all. Commentators also like to think that a final, clinching gloss supersedes all the previous trials and errors when the best glosses, actually, can hardly be anything else. (*Joyce's Dislocutions* 74)

Senn makes a strong point about the limits of annotation,[6] a subject taken up again in chapter 3, but I would prefer to examine *The Mediterranean on Five Drachmas a Day* before passing judgment on its possible influence in (or on) Homer's poem. Of the "World's Twelve Worst Books" helpfully listed in "Circe," at least three are clearly self-help guides: "*Care of the Baby* (infantilic)," "*Expel that Pain* (medic)," and "*Pennywise's Way to Wealth* (parsimonic)" (15.1577–84). Exactly what makes them among the "worst books" is left to the reader's imagination (and this right before "Eumaeus"). How might the first of these books have helped Little Chandler, who instead had recourse to Byron? Byron's poetry is clearly a useless guide to childcare, and makes for a poor lullaby besides. Again, assistance is defined by situation.

How often those who would read Joyce are told that they should read something else, even before trying whatever work by Joyce they are interested in. There is no general difference between scholarly criticism and popular guidebooks in this emphasis on the ineluctable intertextuality of Joyce's writing, but this advice does trouble the journey motif. At worst, it might be the equivalent of answering questions about directions with "you can't get there from here." At best, it's the kind of directions that dissuade the traveller, however gently, from her stated purpose: "Well, to understand Dublin, you know, you have to have seen Rome and New York and Venice or else you won't have any basis for – what's that? You haven't seen Venice? Oh, you really must see Venice before you can appreciate Dublin."

"How should you read *Ulysses*?" asks Jefferson Hunter in the first sentence of *How to Read* Ulysses *and Why*. "It would be a good idea to begin, as most readers do, with Joyce's earlier works of fiction ... As time permits you might read at least the first half of Homer's *Odyssey*" (1). "As time permits" is a splendid example of guidespeak, always considerate of expense (of time, capital, or labour), never wishing to appear frivolous in this regard. And readers are assured: "most readers" take these steps, so there is no need to worry about any irregular or unorthodox methods: no deviating from well-beaten paths here.

In some ways the Grand Tour, that Enlightenment trajectory by which one acquired a well-rounded cultural education, itself a kind of neoclassical odyssey, is mimicked in miniature by the Bloomsday circuit of Dublin. These pilgrimages earn cultural capital: walking in Bloom's footsteps is understood to enhance our reading of Joyce's novel, or even dispel its necessity. In turn this "tour" has again transformed, now into an immersion into digital information, and vexed students turn first not to Gifford but to Google. Yet it is the gaps and variations within the routes through Joyce's Dublin that function both as a critique of predetermined, set trajectories of reading, travel, and self-determination, and as an invitation to readers to forge new paths of their own. This plural needs underscoring, for Joyce shows us – in his engendering of so many guides and so much commentary, and in the way that *Finnegans Wake* reconfigures reading as a continuous, collaborative process rather than as a solitary act[7] – that the "civic selfhelp" that Bloom invokes entails a sharing of resources and ideas; a journey taken together.

Self-help and Self-improvement

The exact origins of phrase "self-help," which appears, appropriately enough, in "Ithaca" (unhyphenated, of course [*U* 17.29]), are elusive, but its popularity stemmed from Samuel Smiles's book of that title, published the same year as *The Origin of Species*. A collection of exemplary anecdotes of success through perseverance, *Self-Help* "sold a quarter million copies by the end of the century and was translated into all the major European and Asian languages" (Rose 68). "The Smiles philosophy," writes Jonathan Rose in *The Intellectual Life of the British Working Classes*,

> was more than a crude success ethic. He was a radical who favored universal suffrage, had some sympathy with Chartism and the ten-hour workday, and strongly supported the Co-operative movement and adult education. He condemned class-bound standards of respectability and denounced pure economic individualism as empty and selfish.... He preferred to write about workingmen whose achievements were intellectual rather than commercial, though he ruefully noted that his business success stories sold much better. (68)

Rose acknowledges such precedents to Smiles as G.L. Craik's *The Pursuit of Knowledge under Difficulties* (1830–1), Thomas Dick's *On the Improvement of Society by the Diffusion of Knowledge* (1833), Timothy Claxton's *Hints to Mechanics, on Self-Education and Mutual Instruction* (1839), and William Robinson's *Self-Education* (1845).[8] There were, in previous centuries, published guides on health and medicinal matters, as well as some agricultural guides, but it was in the nineteenth century that the ethic "self-help" became a popular publishing genre, which in the twentieth century exploded into a whole market of its own.

The creation of the Everyman series of books in 1906 (Rose 48) was part of a growing effort at broadening education in the United Kingdom. In *Ulysses* Bloom is something of a standard-bearer of such efforts, presented with a complex mixture of affection and irony. As we have seen, his thoughts readily tend to "schemes" of instruction, and he regularly endorses similar enterprises, such as that of the temperance movement in the (delightfully named) Coffee Palace:

> To be sure it was a legitimate object and beyond yea or nay did a world of good, shelters such as the present one they were in run on teetotal lines for

> vagrants at night, concerts, dramatic evenings and useful lectures (admittance free) by qualified men for the lower orders. (16.793–6)

In a sense, this is a description of "Eumaeus" itself: free lectures and dramatic performances by men of the world (Bloom, Murphy, Skin-the-Goat) for the improvement of drying-out listeners.

But it is in the early twentieth century that "self-help" all too quickly transforms from communally-inspired initiatives to commercial ploys. The "self-made man," as we understand him today, is so emphatically an individual that his success and his lack of dependence on others are virtually synonymous. There is more than a hint of this idea in Deasy's "*I paid my way*" (2.251). This is quite different from the lessons of "mutual improvement," advocated by the inheritors of Smiles, which held "that no autodidact is entirely self-educated. He or she must rely on a network of friends and workmates for guidance, discussion, and reading material" (Rose 76).

Mass publishing of "self-help" manuals and magazine columns not only usurped the role of these networks but refocussed the means and goals of "self-help" away from social improvement to individual insecurities. Eva Illouz has documented how "[i]n the 1920s, advice literature, like the movies, was an emerging cultural industry, and it would prove to be the most enduring platform for the diffusion of psychological ideas and the elaboration of emotional norms" (*Saving the Modern Soul* 52). At the same time, the business of explicating and annotating the new, difficult, modernist art and literature to a mass audience was taking off: the first guide to *Ulysses*, Paul Jordan Smith's *A Key to the* Ulysses *of James Joyce*, appeared in 1927. This business would also prove an "enduring platform" and would elaborate its own kind of norms.

Finnegans Wake, in no small way a digest of the assorted critical and popular responses to *Ulysses*, offers numerous parodies of the "crude success ethic." The myth of the "selfsufficiencer" (240.14), so potent in a colonial context, repeatedly tells of a man who rises from humble, even oppressive origins to incontestable triumph that is at once worldly and religious:

> There grew up beside you, amid our orisons of the speediest in Novena Lodge, Novara Avenue, in Patripodium-am-Bummel, oaf, outofwork, one remove from an unwashed savage, on his keeping and in yours, (I pose you know why possum hides is cause he haint the nogumtreeumption) that other, Immaculatus, from head to foot, sir, that pure one, Altrues of

> other times, he who was well known to celestine circles before he sped aloft, our handsome young spiritual physician that was to be, seducing every sense to selfwilling celebesty, the most winning counterfeuille on our incomeshare lotetree, a chum of the angelets (*FW* 191.09–19)

Seducer and celibate, companion of angels and counterfeiter of lottery tickets, this "handsome young spiritual physician" is all the more extraordinary for being "one remove from an unwashed savage," a man not just better than his circumstances but, owing to his gumption ("nogumtreeumption") and self-will, better than his relations and nominal peers. Most of these encomiums in the *Wake* are connected with Shaun, the local boy who has made good:

> Still in a way, not to flatter you, we fancy you that you are so strikingly brainy and well letterread in yourshelves as ever were the Shamous Shamonous, Limited, could use worse of yourself, ingenious Shaun, we still so fancied, if only you would take your time so and the trouble of so doing it. (*FW* 425.04–08)

His brother Shem, too, though ever the hopeless case, is a study in guided selfhood: "Of course our low hero was a self valeter by choice of need" (184.11), instructed by "Sharadan's *Art of Panning*" (184.24), a book that seems a blend of Thomas Sheridan's *Ars Punica* (a list of rules for punning published pseudonymously in 1719 and for some time attributed to Swift), a handbook for gold prospectors, and an essay on severe criticism. To be a "self valeter" is presumably to be one's own servant, though R.J. Schork, observing that in Latin *valet* "means 'he is strong,' 'he is healthy,'" suggests that Shem is "his own doctor or pharmacist" (238). Which is better, the "self valeter" or the "young spiritual physician"; the self-medicating dope or the cure-all authority; the fool who reads self-help books or the fool who writes them? The *Wake*, though it infamously contains its own running meta-commentary, leaves answers to these problems to the reader, the mark of its complete failure as a self-help guide. Yet, as Joyce informed Harriet Shaw Weaver in the spring of 1927, his crazy work in progress, the composition of which partakes of all sorts of discourses and methods and "arts and crafts," was meant "to teach everybody how to everything properly so as to be in the fashion" (*Letters* 252).

According to Gail Brenner, "The self-help industry is fundamentally flawed. It perpetuates the myth that we are limited, damaged, inadequate selves who need to be fixed" (9). This claim is the basis for Brenner's own recent self-help book, *The End of Self-Help: Discovering Peace and Happiness Right at the Heart of Your Messy, Scary, Brilliant Life* (2015). Brenner contends that the stable and stabilizing force of self-awareness makes for a path to happiness – or, rather, "a pathless path – pathless because it goes nowhere but to the realization of being here now, awake and alive" (6). The rhetorical circuit here (the aspersions cast on an "industry" that does not speak to real people and from which the author thereby removes herself, followed by broad, inspirational claims for her own work) is not only characteristic of many self-help books but of the popular Joyce guides discussed above – or even, in some ways, academic writing more generally, where writers sometimes all too mechanically discredit predecessors and even the entire field of study as prologue to advancing their own new and redemptive ideas. (The appendix to this book offers, for the reader's consideration, comparative publishing chronologies of popular guides to Joyce and self-help books.) Strange to say, self-loathing may be the key ingredient to self-help as a popular, marketed discourse, despite all of its motifs of encouragement and affirmation and "positive" thinking. Not only does the discourse clearly capitalize upon the needy despondency of its consumers, it is predicated upon an understanding, however sublimated, of its own ongoing endeavour as almost entirely illegitimate, fraudulent, or ineffective.

In *The* Finnegans Wake *Experience* – a title that has a certain new-age vibe to it – Roland McHugh professes "a natural distrust of gurus" to explain his avoidance, for his first three years of reading the *Wake*, of "any kind of critical account" (1). Yet it is this very distrust of guides that he claims licenses his own status as a reliable guide: "I hardly intend that my present readers should repeat my example [and it might be noted that it is too late for that, if we already reading his book], but I feel that the experience qualifies me to introduce [*Finnegans Wake*] to them in a particularly helpful manner" (1–2). This is the same move made by Delaney, quoted earlier: present as evidence of the complexity and difficulty of Joyce's works the enormous corpus of commentary that has grown up around those works, and then suggest that *your* guide is unique for its clarity, accessibility, relevance, concision, and whatever other demagogic values cannot, implicitly or explicitly, be attributed to the *Wake* (or any other volume deserving of a guide) on its own or to those other commentators.

Here we can revert to Nancy's definition of manuals and treatises, quoted in the introduction, as "means to ends located outside of themselves, in the world of theoretical or practical action" (5). The notion that other forms of writing, including all of those forms that are generally recognized under the rubric of "literature," do not have or are not intended to have "ends located outside of themselves, in the world of theoretical or practical action" is more than a little dispiriting. Do the forms of writing collectively categorized as "literature" utterly contain all possible effects (and affects) and inspired actions they may produce in readers? If manuals do not represent ends in themselves, or at any rate do so less than other kinds of texts, why is it that *Men Are From Mars, Women Are From Venus* has sold many more copies than *Finnegans Wake*?

What is interesting is that in so far as guides and manuals may point to "the world," they point *away from themselves*. Just as signs are semiotically different from symbols, because the former denote something other than themselves, we might be tempted to adjust Nancy's distinction in similar terms, with manuals gesturing to a realm of interpretation and action outside of themselves, and literary texts the equivalent of symbols, gesturing to themselves and to some meaning beside or beyond themselves. Yet this is merely a posture. Beneath their modesty is the messianic tendency of guides: through me, the way. In contradistinction to this show of transparency, authority, and a contradictory sense of "uselessness," modernism stresses materiality and opacity, dramatizes the erosion of reliability, and diminishes trust in the narrator as guide.

Mr Deasy's paranoia about "backstairs influence" (2.343–4) ought to yield more than the reader's scorn for his antisemitism. This pathetic, lonely man, sure of and free with his own opinions, wants to influence others but avoid any reciprocation. His example can be taken as a kind of caution against worrying so much about bad advice that one heeds none. Instead of appraising how "influential" Joyce – or, for that matter, any other writer – is, we might talk in terms of how open to influence he is. In Joyce's case, we would have to say that he unusually becomes more open to influence, rather than less, as his writing career continues, if we take into account the diversity and number of "sources" (to use an unsatisfactory word to cover a lot of ground) that he draws from, adapts, and uses in his later works. This point applies equally to reading as to writing (since, as I said in the introduction, one function begets another). A reader who comes to a text without influence, peremptorily shunning all introductions, guidebooks, and other commentary is the crucial ingredient in tediously recycled myths of a "pure" reading (the equivalent of what so many defunded institutions have come to call a "self-guided tour"). In an otherwise rich and thoughtful book about the different ways in which the awareness of a reader of *Ulysses* develops, Margot Norris refers to "virgin" readers, again hearkening to an illusory vision of innocence that makes Gerty MacDowell seem guileful.[9]

Outlining his aesthetic ideas to Lynch in *A Portrait*, Stephen says that "the artist prolongs and broods upon himself as the centre of an epical event and this form progresses until the centre of emotional gravity is equidistant from the artist himself and from others" (*P* 180). The "event" of *Ulysses* can be disputed, though as I have noted, a good case can be made for Bloom's finally proving himself useful to someone (as a kind of guide to Stephen), even if he is not perhaps as useful as he might have hoped, but the terms of Stephen's definition share the same degree of abstract metaphor and narcissism as numerous "self-help" guides. "Emotional gravity" is a ripe example: in distinguishing the epic's displacement of the self from the lyrical mode, Stephen uses science as a metaphor without acknowledging it *as* a metaphor, to give a semblance of disinterested objectivity to a (richly) subjective matter. A book like *Emotional Equations: Simple Formulas to Help Your Life Work Better* (2012) does likewise with the same phrase:

> Gravity is a universal force that affects the physical world, but you may not have considered how it also affects the human condition – and not just by keeping us on Earth. Gravity shapes our physical bodies; we often get shorter and closer to the ground as we age. Gravity can also shape our emotional selves. Emotional baggage, for instance, is a form of gravity; we acquire more of it as we grow older, and it weighs us down. The more *emotional gravity* we're fighting, the more force we require to move forward. And force moving against gravity causes a lot of friction. (8; emphasis added)

The author of *Emotional Equations*, Chip Conley – no relation! – invites readers to think of him as their "emotional concierge" (13), whatever that means.

Rita Felski outlines how literature serves as a kind of guide to selfhood:

> As selfhood becomes self-reflexive, literature comes to assume a crucial role in exploring what it means to be a person. The novel, especially, embraces a heightened psychological awareness, meditating on the

> murky depths of motive and desire, seeking to map the elusive currents and by-ways of consciousness, highlighting countless connections and conflicts between self-determination and socialization. Depicting characters engaged in introspection and soul-searching, it encourages its readers to engage in similar acts of self-scrutiny ... One learns how to be oneself by taking one's cue from others who are doing the same. (25–6)

This is no new claim, of course, but practically an article of faith among critics and professors of the humanities who have flourished it when the "usefulness" of their studies has been questioned. Joyce, however, overruns with self-reflexivity and at the same time continuously undermines the various "cues" and guidance that seem to come at the reader from all sides.

Finnegans Wake hazards a prayer for its reader: "guide them through the labyrinth of their samilikes and the alteregoases of their pseudoselves, hedge them bothways from all roamers whose names are ligious, from loss of bearings deliver them" (*FW* 576.32–5). In "bothways from all roamers" is a faint echo "all roads lead to Rome," yet it is "from" and not "to": thus readers are not coming to the same place but, with notable uncertainty, even about who they are ("pseudoselves"), heading in different, unknown directions. Individuation, self discovery, or "what it means to be a person" has no straight path, and any single guidance system can no more handle or anticipate all of the problems and demands of such a process than the most exhaustive compilation of annotations can get a reader home to Ithaca or Eccles Street any faster than it takes. Our selves and our guides have changeable uses of each other. As Giorgio Agamben, drawing upon Foucault, observes, the definition "self" is inextricable from a definition of "use": "[t]he subject of use must take care of itself insofar as it is in a relationship of use with another" (34). This relationship, more complex (especially ethically) than Felski's "taking one's cue," may stir unresolved curiosity about who is being guided by whom at any point. To his readers, who remain likewise unsure of how they properly "use" not just his texts but the many guides that seem to usurp their relationship with those texts, Joyce can be encouraging but his guiding "tips" (a loaded, recurring word in *Finnegans Wake*) and his promises never inspire much confidence: "they will prove for your better guidance along your path of right of way" (*FW* 432.28–9).

2
Misquoting Joyce

Misquotation is, in fact, the pride and privilege of the learned. A widely-read man never quotes accurately, for the rather obvious reason that he has read too widely.

– Hesketh Pearson, *Common Misquotations* (1934)

Mistakes are the portals of discovery.

– "Attributed" to James Joyce, at Wikiquote[1]

Jorge Luis Borges once suggested, in an eminently quotable way, that every reader of Shakespeare *is* Shakespeare ("A New Refutation of Time" 323). While the argument from which this quotation is drawn is really one against the sequentiality of experience and thus the consistency of identity, it is also about language and, less directly, the particular kind of textual "use" that is the focus of this chapter, quotation. The notion of becoming Shakespeare is, on the one hand, thrilling and uplifting: the promise of such shared eloquence is utopian. In the most recent edition of *Fowler's Modern English Usage*, R.W. Burchfield sighs: "In a perfect world, familiar lines or passages from the great classical works of English literature, or from famous speeches, would never be misquoted" (498): the perfect world is characterized and perhaps itself created by the practice of accurate quotation. On the other hand, though, this promise of an inner Shakespeare waiting to possess us is stunningly constraining: the finitude of expression, bearing down upon every user of words, makes plagiarism inevitable and individual expression perhaps impossible. What if in that roomful of monkeys inexplicably pounding away at those typewriters there is even one particularly pathetic primate who above everything does *not* want to reproduce the works of Shakespeare, perhaps wants to find his own voice and write his own opus – isn't he doomed by both proverb and probability? "This is the monkey's own giving out" (*Othello* 4.1.124): in this light, that is a somewhat sad way to introduce a quotation.

Does Borges's remark about Shakespeare apply to Joyce? In an earlier book, I suggested that we readers, scholars, and editors all misquote Joyce.[2] But, as I also tried to make clear, this is not our fault – at least, not entirely. We are vexed by a very high degree of textual instability in Joyce's works, by which badly stretch-marked phrase I collectively refer to the sometimes bellicose history of publication, translation, and litigation of those works, plus the fascinating, frustrating aesthetic of error that Joyce himself explored as the complexity of his texts grew exponentially. (Allow me to stress that I do mean "complexity" and not "difficulty": the former is quantifiable and subject to, for example, certain fairly intuitive theories and laws of communication and logic.) Neither this history nor Joyce is wholly to blame. In the spirit of Ralph Waldo Emerson's remark that correctness is not the most prized quality of the scholar, and in response to Borges, I'd like to argue that every reader of Joyce is him- or herself, unique in his or her errors.

This chapter draws out this crucial point by a sort of *reductio ad absurdum* trajectory. If we attempt to define misquotation, we may map out specific categories, recognizable "kinds" of misquotation. The *OED* serves as a cautionary tale, however, defining as it does, "misquote" (noun) as "an incorrect quotation" and, as a verb, "quote incorrectly." (The entry is complemented by no quotations demonstrating usage – a badly missed opportunity.) No less vexing is the definition provided by Wikipedia, that storehouse of received, recycled, and unreviewed wisdom. Consider how, for example, the syntax and vagueness of the following undermine the unknown quotable author's claims:

> Some people are thought to have said certain things, but there is no evidence of these words in any of their surviving writings: when this is the case, the words have merely to be attributed [*sic*] to them. Many quotations are routinely [?] incorrect or attributed to the wrong authors, and quotations from obscure writers are often attributed to far more famous writers by lax quoters. Good examples of this [*sic*] are Winston Churchill, to whom many political quotations of uncertain origin are attributed, and Oscar Wilde, who has said far more witty things than he possibly could [*sic*].[3]

I will have more to say about both Wikipedia later; for the moment I wish to highlight the presence of Wilde as well as the strangely near-Steinian tone of the first half of this quotation ("some people are thought to have said certain things" sounds like a fugitive phrase from *The Making of Americans*).

The eminently quotable (and, of course, equally misquotable) Oscar Wilde[4] makes an apposite distinction between the creative and critical faculties in "The Critic As Artist." Contrary to popular wisdom, asserts Wilde's polished mouthpiece Gilbert, the creative drive is mechanically repetitive, while criticism represents real innovation and difference (1021–2). (To accept this insight of Wilde's, one need not also agree with Gilbert's preceding claim that "all fine imaginative work is self-conscious and deliberate" [1020] – at least, not to the maximal degree that Wilde implies, whereby every effect of a work is determined by the artist's "self-conscious" intentions.) In a lecture delivered forty-five years later, Gertrude Stein announces her agreement: "The question of repetition is important. It is important because there is no such thing as repetition" (494). This statement not only illuminates Stein's own work, which represents perhaps the closest approximation to repetition in writing, but Joyce's, wherein one "yes" from Molly may be distinguished from another if we listen to her carefully.

Anyone can quote, but misquotation is a "portal of discovery" (*U* 9.232), the threshold of art, and an original "use" of others' work.

Ellipsities

What seems like the most straightforward approach at a definition of "quotation" is the insistence upon a repetition of a sequence of words in their original order, without either omissions or embellishments. (For now let us not be fussy with such niceties as page layout – why, I continue to wonder, do so many students so like to *centre* verse quotations? – or what might seem like fanatical details, like, say, typeface) *Ulysses* is notoriously loaded with such misquotations: indeed, according to this definition, it might be difficult to say just how many "correct" quotations are actually to be found in the novel.

On his way to lunch, Leopold Bloom spies a well-fed "squad of constables" – the use of the collective plural "squad," like a pod of whales or a pride of lions, is a taxonomic gesture, for these coppers are a different species, walking "[g]oosestep" while "out to graze ... Bound for their troughs" (*U* 8.406–13). Hungry Bloom muses about these animals:

"Policeman's lot is oft a happy one" (*U* 8.409). Of course, W.S. Gilbert's own lyric properly runs: "When constabulary duty's to be done, / A policeman's lot is not a happy one." *The Pirates of Penzance*, which hinges on misunderstandings and incorrect information, is a resonant source of misquotation for *Ulysses*, a book keen on the voyages of all kinds of seafarers, no matter how dubious. This particular song ("When A Felon's Not Engaged") employs choral echolalia: the sergeant leads and his fellow officers repeat the last few syllables of each line, a method of quotation conspicuously similar to the way partial phrases echo in Joyce's novel.

Yet why the misquotation? The problem here is less the matter of who and what is being quoted than it is a question of who is doing the quoting and to what purpose. Determining the former is sometimes thought to be the mandate of the critic of modernism, but the difference is between suavely sipping the wine to identify the exact vintage and evaluating the reasons why your host wants you to drink precisely this glass.[5] Is Bloom quoting Gilbert and Sullivan, or is this one of those slippery instances in which Bloom's consciousness is, as it were, quietly upstaged by the novel's own metaconsciousness, which enjoys knowledge not presumably known by the character in focus? (A well-known example involves another opera: the play of Lenehan's "Rose of Castille" riddle in or around Bloom's thoughts, even though Lenehan's telling of the riddle occurs when Bloom is not present [*U* 7.514, 7.588–91].)

Familiarity with this popular operetta would not be unusual for Bloom, though we are more accustomed to his appreciation of Italian opera. Moreover Bloom generally seems to think of men in uniform as music hall characters: he is titillated by a tune of the Tilley Sisters in "Calypso" – "O please, Mr Policeman, I'm lost in the wood" (4.179) – and, again thinking of *The Pirates of Penzance*, he casts his father-in-law as a modern "Majorgeneral" [15.779]). It is the thought of Corny Kelleher, followed by the phrase "Police tout" (5.14), that leads him into his musical rumbling, "tooraloom, tooraloom" (similar to "Tarantara, tarantara!," the hearty cry of the timid police of *Penzance*). This connection is confirmed at the end of "Circe" when Corny manages to assure the bobbies about Stephen and Bloom: "(*He lilts, wagging his head.*) With my tooraloom tooraloom tooraloom tooraloom. What, eh, do you follow me?" (15.4827–8). This satisfactory giving of a cryptic musical password is followed by Bloom's unctuous "Naturally. Quite right. Only your bounden duty" and the Second Watch's echoing, apologetic agreement: "It's our duty" (15.4849–51). (It is worth remembering here that the alternative title to *The Pirates of Penzance* is *The Slave of Duty*.) The police then "move off with a slow heavy tread" (15.4856), from which we may gather that indeed – taking one consideration with another – a policeman's lot is not a happy one.

Although the problem of who is quoting Gilbert and Sullivan may be answered by the argument that *both* Bloom and the meta-consciousness (or "arranger")[6] of the novel do so, the question of who omits the "not" from "A policeman's lot is not a happy one" (and replaces it with "oft") stubbornly remains. Is this Joyce's error or Bloom's, and with what irony should we read it, and why? Joyce repeatedly confronts us with such problems. The act of quoting is typically understood to be a show of authority, and Eloise Knowlton writes that "one quotes to control, to establish identity and dominance over others' words, over others" (38). This is one way of getting around the problem: by accusing Joyce of being a powermonger, a great and terrible "Wizard" (Knowlton 63) determined to control his readers. While there is definitely some justice in this approach – one need only reflect on Joyce's resolve to protect his own copyright by petition, lawsuit, and even matrimony – it is not the only one, and indeed it overlooks the open dialectic, the choice that Joyce offers his interpreters. Simply to call the sentence "Policeman's lot is oft a happy one" a quotation or a misquotation is not enough: the reader must independently and subjectively evaluate, here as at so many junctures, what authority to bestow to which character, speaker, author, interpretation. What *use* is being made of the words?

This mode of misquotation – omitting the "not" – is not indicative itself of error, since it is the name of a common and accepted practice in quotation: *ellipsis*, from the Greek for "defect." This classification is still depressingly imprecise: Burchfield notes that Quirk's *A Comprehensive Grammar of the English Language* "needed more than fifty pages to list, illustrate, and label" all of the acceptable grammatical forms of ellipsis (245); accordingly, we may imagine that even a ruthlessly concise index of erroneous and illegitimate uses of ellipsis could probably constitute a small library. Yet this word is useful, for we find Joyce pondering its meaning near the end of *A Portrait* and again in the "Nightletter" of *Finnegans Wake*, both scenes from a schoolroom and both combinations of mathematical and literary discourses. In the former, a professor who is rumoured to be "an atheist freemason" and who clearly enthralls Stephen Dedalus with his "spectrelike symbols of force and velocity" (*P* 160), uses quotation to enliven his lecture:

– So we must distinguish between elliptical and ellipsoidal. Perhaps some of you gentlemen may be familiar with the works of Mr W. S. Gilbert. In one of his songs he speaks of the billiard sharp who is condemned to play:

On a cloth untrue
With a twisted cue
And elliptical billiard balls.

– He means a ball having the form of the ellipsoid of the principal axes of which I spoke a moment ago. (*P* 161)

Here Gilbert and Sullivan are quoted not to substantiate a point or justify a claim but as an example of error, which the professor stoops to amend: "He means ..." Yet the fact that the professor is himself being quoted here (it may well be that Joyce lifted this pedagogical aside from his own experience as a student) prompts two questions: why the novel itself should quote Gilbert, and why the novel quotes (as it were) the professor quoting. The answers complement each other. The song is the Mikado's outlining of his supremely humane policy "to let the punishment fit the crime," though those misdemeanors may be truly no more than potentially irritating eccentricities. Its inclusion here in the final chapter of *A Portrait* serves as an ironic counterpoint to the "fitting torment" promised by the sermon on damnation in the third chapter (110), and offers further, subtle evidence that this older Stephen no longer cringes in fear of hellfire. That sermon, too, had employed quotation to rhetorical effect, but whereas the sermon itself is textually represented in full, the mathematics lecture is itself only sampled, "quoted." Dramatized for the reader is Stephen's new awareness of the ineluctable partiality of the quotable, of what words lose and gain in reproduction, of how quotation is necessarily elision.

Joyce revisits "ellipsis" in the *Wake*, where the children take a lesson in Euclidean geometry: "evertwo circumflicksrent serclhers never film in the ellipsities of their gyribouts those fickers which are returnally reprodictive of themselves" (*FW* 298.16–18). The overlapping circles and facing triangles that they examine (*FW* 293) represent both the turning reels of film, whose flickering images especially entertain Issy, and an upskirt view of their mother's genitals, the site of reproduction. Yet there are more elliptical possibilities, too. The two centres of the circles, taken as foci, can suggest an ellipse (which would be contained within the two circles) at whose perimeter point π may be found. An

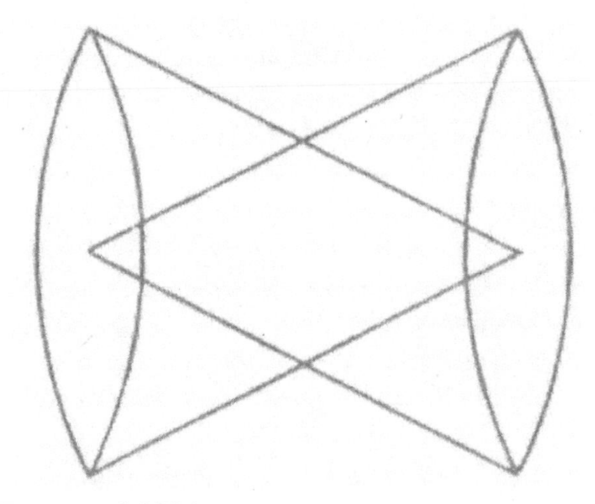

Figure 1. The gyres of *A Vision*.

egg, where life begins and which (or *who*) may one day fall from a wall, has the profile of an ellipse. Perhaps we are looking into the "ancient, glittering eyes" from the poem nodded to in the phrase that introduces the diagram ("in the lazily eye of his lapis" [*FW* 293.11]) or, as I most like to think, into a compressed sort of Yeatsian gyre (suggested by "gyribouts" and the earlier exclamation "Gyre O, gyre O, gyrotundo!" [*FW* 295.23–4]). An ellipse is just a conic section, a cross-section of a gyre, and a distorted circle, in the same way that a quotation is a distorted utterance, as deformed as any stream run through a tundish. In the same way that the students misread Euclid, Joyce misquotes Yeats.

Taken together, these meditations on "ellipsis" in *A Portrait* and the *Wake* point to the arithmetical roots of quotation itself: the word comes from *quotāre*, "to number." Both diagrams presented here suggest mathematical transformations, the specifically defined re-coordinations and substitutions of forms. An eclipse occurs when one body obscures another, when one form aligns with another within our line of sight (Bloom thinks about "parallax" in the same chapter in which he misquotes *Pirates*). A misquotation is a sort of eclipse, in which a form is repeated while it is simultaneously obscured.

"Policeman's lot is oft a happy one" is a misperception of the song lyric, not unlike the remixed Hendrix "excuse me while I kiss this guy"

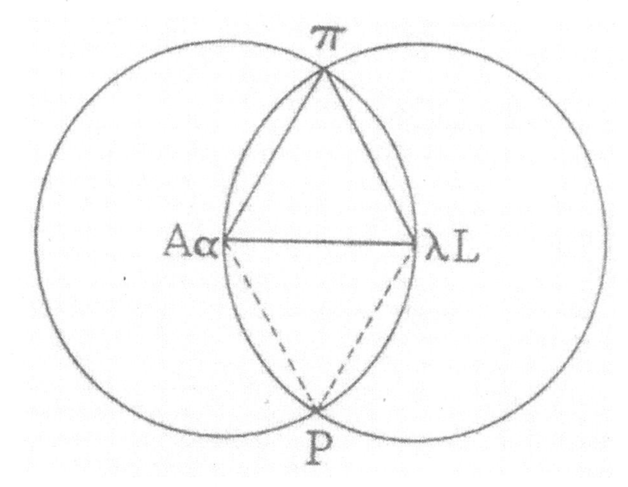

Figure 2. The circles of *Finnegans Wake*.

and other popularly misheard tunes, but determining how and why the quoter's senses are deranged or distorted is, as I have indicated above, ever Joyce's reader's problem.

Similar Sounds

The second kind of quotational offence I'd like to consider is usually known as quoting out of context. As Joyce shows, however, this kind of error is an even less absolute affair than literal misquotation. Probably the most obvious example of quoting out of context comes from Mr Deasy's financial advice: "But what does Shakespeare say? *Put but money in thy purse*" (*U* 2.239). Joyce's use of italics on this last phrase – or, as these italics represent a potential source of textual dispute, let us say instead the use of italics in so many published editions of the novel, from the Shakespeare and Company original to Gabler's and even Rose's editions – is especially sardonic: this is a somewhat unusual instance of authorially (or textually) inscribed irony. The italics are doing the work for which another author, happy to use conventional "perverted commas," would dangle scare quotes. Deasy's implied attribution of Iago's sentiments to Shakespeare irks Stephen, the pedant who murmurs the speaking character's name but not for Deasy's benefit.

Yet does not Stephen himself drip with quotations from Shakespeare, most wetly in his algebraic "proof" about who is speaking and being quoted in *Hamlet*? Context does not seem to matter very much in Stephen's allusive and associative argument, and although he may not "mince words" in the way that Deasy does (*U* 2.331) – in fact, Deasy's own phrase about mincing his words is another appropriation from *Othello*, a play apparently much on this paranoid and jealous man's mind[7] – he is not above some slicing and dicing. Our reading of "Scylla and Charybdis" ought to take into consideration both this irony and Stephen's own misquoting of Shakespeare's ghost: "*Hamlet, I am thy father's spirit*" (*U* 9.170). In the play, the ghost does not name his son. One could argue that Stephen is not quoting Shakespeare at all, but rather Leopold Bloom, whose uneven knowledge of Shakespeare is displayed in the previous chapter, a few minutes before he sees the squad of constables:

> *Hamlet, I am thy father's spirit*
> *Doomed for a certain time to walk the earth.* (8.67–8)

Bloom's ghost walks the earth instead of the night, for a time rather than a term, but, as he says, "That is how poets write, the similar sounds" (8.64). Close enough is the stuff of art. Bloom rewrites Shakespeare and Stephen quotes his spiritual father. Stephen's argument about Shakespeare thereby becomes more difficult to assess: at the very least we can see that Stephen will not be the servile reproducer of the wit and wisdom of such fathers as Simon Dedalus, Mr Deasy, Plato, or even Shakespeare, ghost father of a ghost son. The questions of paternity and authorship swirling in this discussion are significantly dramatized by the hurriedly changing contexts for these flashing quotations.[8]

Marjorie Garber has, with a little uncertainty, wondered whether "*every* quotation is a quotation out of context, inevitably both a duplication and a duplicity" ("Quotation Marks" 134). Readers (and especially quoters) of *Finnegans Wake* are familiar with such an extreme-seeming proposition: every phrase and quotation is rearranged at each time and place it reappears, a phenomenon comparable to those genetic mishaps that occur when the transporter is on the blink in *Star Trek*. The *Wake* is simply the most aggressive way in which Joyce's work offers the power to define "context," but this same tendency begins with the very open questions about narration and title in *Dubliners*. One of the most playful, slippery words in *Ulysses* is "metempsychosis," whose definition remains elusive and whose form itself disintegrates in the course of the day ("Met him pike hoses" [*U* 8.112], thinks Bloom, moments after his own *Hamlet* misquotation). Metempsychosis may explain why this novel is named *Ulysses*, and in a sense it exonerates Joyce of plagiarizing Homer (or Shakespeare, or anyone else). In *Religio Medici*, Sir Thomas Browne understands the reproduction of past ideas and thoughts

> as though there were a *Metempsuchosis*, and the soule of one man passed into another, opinions doe finde after certaine revolutions, men and mindes like those that first begat them. To see our selves againe we neede not looke for *Platoes* yeare; every man in onely himselfe; there have been many *Diogenes*, and as many *Timons*, though but few of that name; men are lived over againe, the world is now as it was in ages past, there was none then, but there hath been some one since that parallels him, and is as it were his revived selfe. (66–7)

If Shakespeare appears in 1904 Dublin (whether in the face of Martin Cunningham or in the words of Stephen Dedalus), we should thus expect him to be translated by his circumstances. Misquotation is a metamorphosis as much as it is a revival.

Bloom – or is it Joyce? – recognizes Shakespeare as a source of infinite jest: "Quotations every day in the year. To be or not to be. Wisdom while you wait" (*U* 11.905–6). While this insight might seem hackneyed, it hits upon as profound a truth as any of spoken earlier in the day in the library, and indeed puts in a nutshell the quotational method of argument employed by Stephen in "Scylla and Charybdis" and recommended by Walter Benjamin. Benjamin saw Shakespeare not just as a source of quotations, but as a model of a *user* of quotations. His diary entry of 17 June 1931 recalls a conversation with Brecht about Volumnia's speech in *Coriolanus*. "'It's a miracle,' Brecht says of Shakespeare, 'where he could have got this speech from; he must have spent enough time looking for it'" (483). The works of Shakespeare are simply building blocks, raw material for ambitious readers, writers, and monkeys to modify, vary, or change to suit the day at hand.

In composing these snappy advertising jingles for William Shakespeare – "Quotations every day of the year" – Bloom may even be more astute than he knows, since the word "quotation" has the same etymology as "quotidian." As Browne says, there have been many Timons, and so many Hamlets and Cleopatras too, "but few of that name." The everyday world is a reshuffling of quotations. (This is why

Benjamin's monumental *Arcades Project*, a tower of quotations, remains unfinished. His study of modernity as material, sensory experience disallows a single, momentary context, so the book remains a kind of jigsaw puzzle which readers assemble as they may.) Context is inescapable and ever a work in progress: the lifetime of the quoter is the context for each quotation as much as the critic's interpretation contextualizes the quotations he or she uses – allegedly to shape that interpretation.

As Quotad Before

My third and final definition of misquotation concerns authenticity. Spurious attributions and apocryphal quotations are the wild boars of the academic forests, hunted down with great zeal by those who go in for that sort of thing. In their 1989 boar slaughter entitled *They Never Said It: A Book of Fake Quotes, Misquotes, and Misleading Attributions*, Paul F. Boller, Jr, and John George report that Wellington's phrase "Up, boys, and at them" (sometimes given as "Up, guards, and at them") was denied by the Iron Duke himself, who claimed to have instead barked the far more prosaic "Stand up, Guards!" before the ultimate charge at Napoleon (Boller and George 130). By contrast, Wikipedia's vast "Wikiquote" index acknowledges "Up Guards and at them again" ("often misquoted as 'Up guards and at 'em'") with reservations: in October 2006, it was called an "attributed" rather than a "sourced" quotation (though not a "misattribution"), and ten years later, the entry reports that "Wellington himself, years later, declared that he did not know exactly what he had said on the occasion, and doubted that anyone did."[9]

Wikipedia, characterized by Jaron Lanier as a distressing form of online collectivism, tries to be a "meta" reference, all too often at the expense of accuracy and, as Lanier despairs, context.[10] *Finnegans Wake* is a similar enterprise that engenders similar anxieties. In fact, it might be more "meta" than Wikipedia in that the *Wake* cheerfully admits all doubtful, even erroneous attributions into its folds. There Wellington changes his name – at one point he is "Wikingson" (*FW* 241.18), son of Wiki! – as regularly as he alters (or forgets) his battle cry. These Wellington mutations range from "*Hoploits and atthems*" (272L4), where military bravado is associated with the vanity of exploits and anthems, to "Upanishadem!" (303.13), a Vedic variation found in a cluster of badly mixed-up "Irish" clichés. With his gift for understated illumination, Fritz Senn calls this practice of distortion "an instinctive metamorphosis."[11] This phrase is more instructive than any I might invent.

Finnegans Wake's fascination with illegitimacy and the forms of language that so consternated philosophers such as Plato and Heidegger includes a love of misquotation: indeed, the *Wake* misquotes itself over and over again. It merely exaggerates a tendency that Joyce shows considerable sympathy for in all of his work, the tendency to resist mechanical repetition. Consider, for example, beleaguered Farrington in "Counterparts," who inadvertently writes "*Bernard Bernard* instead of *Bernard Bodley*" (86) and seems to be doomed to a life of repetition, called "You impertinent ruffian! You impertinent ruffian!" (87) and entreated to with "I'll say a Hail Mary for you ... I'll say a Hail Mary for you" (94). Knowlton suggests that Joyce overtly challenges "modernity's quotational project," the idea that "one can *say the same thing twice*" (71). A slave to this modernity, Farrington's only freedom (if not hope) lies in the insignificant range of variation he can make from otherwise mindless "faithful copy," like his elaborate version of office events in Davy Byrne's. One could likewise read *A Portrait of the Artist as a Young Man* as Stephen's struggle with rote learning. An imperfect young copyist, he discovers that the supernumerary word "nearer" is heresy (*P* 66), and yet, even at his most abject and chastened, he resists parroting. While the other boys at chapel "repeated the act of contrition, phrase by phrase, with fervour," Stephen's tongue is "cleaving to his palate" so he is left to pray "with his heart" instead (*P* 114). Joyce's dramatizing of this "phrase by phrase" ritual, doubling each of twelve lines, might seem to little purpose – other than, perhaps, to convey to the reader Catholicism's great love of redundancy – until it is observed that it is a misquotation, that a significant phrase from the act has been omitted. Repetition may repeat error, but the error is general, just as the collective prayer and vow "to amend my life" treats those lives and their sins as anything but individual and creative.

The *Wake* refuses the servitude of authenticity; it is an entirely unfaithful copy of unauthorized sources. Its metamorphic instinct, its tendency towards error, is appreciable as a stark sort of freedom, the will to change. It quotes itself wrongly over and over again.

Borges's "A New Refutation of Time," wherein the quotation with which I began is found, ends with a double-irony.[12] The essay's dispirited concluding words are equally well-known to his readers: "The world, unfortunately, is real; I unfortunately, am Borges" (332). Just as there is no total escape from time, there is no complete escape from the self. (Maybe after briefly being Shakespeare one is jettisoned onto a grassy shoulder of the New Jersey Turnpike, like those who have briefly been John Malkovich in the film of that name.) Attempts to do so are, says Borges, "secret consolations," but his essay does not end with his own name, Borges, but with a quotation from another author, another time. He quotes Angelus Silesius:

> Freund, es ist auch genug. Im Fall du mehr willst lesen,
> So geh und werde selbst die Schrift und selbst das lesen.
>
> Friend, this is enough. Should you wish to read more,
> Go and yourself become the writing, yourself the essence. (332)

Among the other paradoxes cherished by Silesius is the heresy that God and Man are indivisibly one. *Finnegans Wake* goes further: The Duke of Wellington is and isn't Thor, Shem is and isn't Shaun, God is and isn't Man. Everybody is "themselse" (*FW* 3.07): themselves and everybody else, too. Thus, in the compressed gyre of the *Wake*, where opposites meet, to quote someone else is also to quote oneself, and unlike the reader of Shakespeare, who reverts to Shakespeare, we readers of Joyce find that Joyce – ahead of us, as usual – is already us.

Defining misquotation, like defining error, is quantifying variation. None of the "kinds" of conventionally recognized misquotation that I have outlined here provides an absolute rule or airtight definition. Rather, as Joyce demonstrates (and one can depend on Joyce to trouble definitions), because authority, context, and freedom are never wholly stabilized or conscribed, quotation is not a constant. When it comes to error and distortion, the best one can hope for is to establish a rule of probabilities, and even within that modest allowance lies the further realization that the orders of magnitude involved for even the simplest text – such as the uncomplicated examples of words from Gilbert and Sullivan, Shakespeare, and the Duke of Wellington that I have referred to here – are way too big for any kind of practical consideration. In plainest words, there is no discernible end of ways to screw up any one thing. This is good news for the individuated monkey, great news for literary critics. It means that we can never be Joyce, but it also means that Joyce prompts us, in our every attempt to read and quote him, to be ourselves.

3
Limited Editions, Edited Limitations

"Books are for reading; editions are for use." So pronounced (and repeated) Hans Walter Gabler at the 2012 Dublin James Joyce Symposium. This pat-sounding distinction produces more questions than it answers. Used for what, used by whom? Are "reading" and "use" antonyms? (What about written instructions: how to operate this fire extinguisher, stop when these lights are flashing, and so on?) Danis Rose and John O'Hanlon, the editors of a new *Finnegans Wake,* agree that there is a distinction, though their terms and tone are different from Gabler's, even if they are no less puzzling: "The ultimate function of a book, however, is to be read, not to be looked or picked at" (522). How does one read a book without looking at it? What does it mean, to "pick at" a book? And exactly what is meant by "ultimate" here?

It cannot be too often or too emphatically recalled that for students of Joyce, a plurality of editions is an asset, not an obstacle. Given the complexity of books like *Ulysses* and *Finnegans Wake* and their sometimes byzantine textual histories, it is valuable to have comparisons. Even as minor differences may be noticed between the various printings of the book available today, the need for a more substantial basis for such comparisons has become gradually more apparent. One could readily assemble a substantial anthology of commentary and debate on the editorial efforts and skirmishes over *Ulysses.* Among its chronicles would be the "Joyce Wars" waged over the Gabler edition of *Ulysses,* the legal folderol of Danis Rose's "Reader's Edition" (with its curious echoes of the Samuel Roth affair), myths of the Kidd edition (the ghost ship that has never yet sailed or been tugged into port), and, most recently, the text as "remastered" with perverted commas by Robert Gogan in 2012. *Finnegans Wake,* by contrast, has for decades been left untouched by editorial hand, apart from Anthony Burgess's bizarre abridgement and occasional conjectures and prophecies of an eventual "restoration."

This situation has now changed with the appearance of two new editions of the *Wake* in the past few years: one prepared by Rose and O'Hanlon (which I will refer to as the Penguin *Wake*) and another by Finn Fordham, Robbert-Jan Henkes, and Erik Bindervoet (the Oxford *Wake*). In this chapter, I'd like to compare these texts and their respective conceptions of their function, or even their "ultimate function." To help bring the problem of function (or "use") and readership into focus, let me recount a joke, an old and idiosyncratic favourite of mine.

A man goes to a baker and orders a German chocolate cake. "Come back this afternoon," the baker tells him. When the man returns and flips open the lid of the cake box, his face falls. "What's wrong?" asks the baker. "Oh, nothing," the man says, but the baker insists. "Well, it's perfect, really, but I forgot this morning to be more precise: I wanted a German chocolate cake *in the shape of the letter B*." The baker tells him to come back the next day, when he'll have just that item for him. The next afternoon, the man returns and flips open the lid of the cake box, and again is disappointed: "This is wonderful, really, but I should have been more precise: I wanted a German chocolate cake in the shape of a *lower-case* B, and this one is as you can see an upper-case B." The baker, who will not take his money, is adamant about satisfying his customer: "Come back tomorrow morning at the very instant that we open and I will have it ready." So early the next morning the man returns, flips open the lid of the cake box, and beams with joy: "Absolutely perfect!" The baker, also thrilled, asks, "Shall I wrap it up for you?" And the man says, "No thanks, I'll eat it here."

Why this joke is funny – if it is: in more than one sense it is a matter of acquired taste – has much to do, I think, with the problems that any editorial effort faces with so convoluted a text as *Finnegans Wake*, and with the particular questions I think we ought to pose to these new editions. Amid the eccentric-seeming demands of his customer, the baker loses sight of the specific purpose of his work – cake is to be eaten, and you can just eat it here, without its being wrapped up or transported – and we laugh, if we do, because we too have momentarily lost sight of this purpose. How we want to eat a cake is linked to its form, and how we read a text is linked to its presentation. If we want a new *Finnegans Wake*, it would be best if we knew what we wanted it *for* (how we'd like to eat it) even before we start the oven. How might it be read or "used," by whom, and what workable distinction might there be between its being "read" and being "used," if any?

My interest here, then, is in discussing the editorial mandates of these new *Wakes* – what we might call seeking to understand how the editions understand themselves – as well as plausible conceptions of future editions, with only a few remarks on methodology. This is not to suggest, though, that mandate and method are separable, but my comments on methodology will by and large be confined to their conceptual and theoretical implications. Jerome McGann's concept of "bibliographical codings" proves useful to us in reading not (or at any rate, not merely) the text of the *Wake* that this edition proffers, but the ways in which it shapes a reader as well as a literary and cultural history. McGann is also worth invoking here because Rose has pointedly done so in his stated "Rationale" for his ill-fated *Ulysses: A Reader's Edition* (1997), though in truth McGann's thinking is brought up on that occasion only to be effectively dismissed in favour of "the traditional approach" of editors such as W.W. Greg (Rose, "Introduction," *Ulysses: A Reader's Edition* xiii–xv).

Writes McGann in *The Textual Condition*:

> As the process of textual transmission expands, whether vertically (i.e., over time), or horizontally (in institutional space), the signifying processes of the work become increasingly collaborative and socialized.... authors (and authorial intentions) do not govern those textual dimensions of a work which become most clearly present to us in bibliographical forms. (58)

It might well be argued, too, that editors (and editorial intentions) do not absolutely or entirely govern these dimensions, and for this reason it seems best to try to attain a careful balance between consideration of stated or otherwise discernible editorial intentions and the editorial effects, if we may call them such, so as neither to privilege the former nor neglect the latter. And this seems a wise course even if, as I suspect, Rose and O'Hanlon would have us see every aspect of their edition as meticulously deliberate on their part as they assert that each word in the text is Joyce's, as verified by themselves. Examination of the aspirations and contradictions of the mandates and productions of the Penguin and Oxford editions yields useful considerations of the problems faced by current and prospective editors, publishers, scholars, and readers of the *Wake*.

"Circumstances" and Circumstantiality

In 2010, Houyhnhnm Press appeared with a limited edition *Finnegans Wake* – or, more accurately, two variations of a limited edition. The first, called the "standard," is a hardcover book of 493 pages (i.e., 135 pages shorter than the 628 pages of previous editions), enclosed in a cardboard slipcase and accompanied by a paper-cover booklet containing a note by Seamus Deane, a brief preface by the editors, a foreword by Gabler, an introduction by David Greetham, an afterword by the editors, and a list of acknowledgments. Only 800 copies of this book were printed and priced at 300 euros (or, as the exchange was then, $410 US). The second version is "the special version," bound in black calfskin, with hardbound booklet and a full cloth slipcase. And that's not all – these 150 books are signed (not exactly by the author), stamped, and numbered, all for just 900 euros (or $1200 US), postage not included.[1]

Obviously the limited print run points to a pretty small "reading public" and the expected outlay is rather out of tune with the swelling chorus of Joyce guides and introductions discussed in the first chapter – texts optimistically aimed at a wide readership, and in some instances not so optimistically aimed away from Joyce scholars – which exhort new readers to join the fun. Meaningful discussion of book costs has often proved tricky for literary history and criticism – where, that is, such discussion is attempted at all. (I remember seeing several years ago a review by a left-leaning Canadian politician of a new collection of Orwell's writings in a national newspaper. His praise for a writer he clearly judged essential was unchecked by even a mention of the collection's exorbitant price.) Although Joyce is one of the first of the still relatively few cases where twentieth-century literary studies stoop to ponder price tags, the attention has been primarily on *Ulysses*, first because of the narrative of its travails (antipathy of publishers, piracy, censorship), then its inexorably heady rise in collector value, and later because of the counternarrative of elitism presented by critics such as Lawrence Rainey, who posits the marketing of *Ulysses* as symptomatic of a modernism in which "aesthetic value became confused with speculation, collecting, investment, and dealing ... modernism and commodity culture were not implacable enemies but fraternal rivals" (76).

It is worth recalling a few of the details of that 1922 publication precisely because Houyhnhnm Press so clearly has Beach's advertising model in mind (prospectus, order form, etc.). The "private" first edition of *Ulysses* that was offered to subscribers by Shakespeare and Company had a print run of 1,000 copies and came at three different prices, depending on paper quality and the inclusion (in only 100 copies) of Joyce's signature. Rainey handily points out that the least expensive of these (150 francs) was half the cost of a month's rent for Ezra and Dorothy Pound, then newly arrived in Paris (63). Thus it might be pointed out in defence of the price of this *Wake* that Paris apartments now cost more than twice the "standard" volume – but here we must remember why these comparisons are misleading. The historical differences between 1922 and 2010 are not to be judged by prices but by economic systems, and the economics of publishing is now a very different affair.

Just as it has been useful for scholars to study the original list of subscribers for the 1922 *Ulysses* (the marketing of which appears to be directly reflected – though perhaps with some magnification – in the scheme used by Houyhnhnm Press, with its round figure of 1,000 copies), it would be interesting to know who bought the Houyhnhnm *Wake*, what percentage of buyers were scholars and university libraries, and how that figure corresponds with the editors' conception of their readership. Although Deane (in what amounts to an extended blurb) heralds it as "a critical edition," Rose and O'Hanlon do not seem to intend their edition for scholarly purposes as such but, rather like Rose's ill-fated "Reader's Edition" of *Ulysses*,[2] for a readership that the book has not heretofore attracted.

In 2012, the year the copyright on *Finnegans Wake* expired in the European Union, a new, far more affordable hardcover of this edition was brought out by Penguin (though no paperback has yet materialized). This new Penguin *Wake* is titled *The Restored Finnegans Wake*, so as not to cause catalogue confusion with the other edition that Penguin fortunately intends to keep in print. The rapid metamorphosis from Houyhnhnm to Penguin has left some horsefeathers on the fowl. For instance, the preface refers to "this short introductory volume" (ix), clearly referring to the booklet format in which the preface first appeared, and, in warily acknowledging that there might be some sort of aesthetic role for error in the text, Greetham's introduction says that "surely Vicki Mahaffey in justified" (509), a nicely ironic typo not corrected from the Houyhnhnm edition. No great editorial care is in evidence in this transition, but there is another absence of change between them that is far more troubling. The process of the editing remains concealed. Readers are repeatedly told of how much hard and honourable work has gone into the restoration, but the work itself is kept out of view and thus away from judgment.

While there is ample room to doubt the emendations, it is important that we should as readers come to new editions in good faith – without, that is, the kind of sentimental chauvinism that results from an attachment to a favourite reading copy, with its standardized and familiar pagination and lineation. Several of the changes in the Penguin *Wake* seem to me by turns plausible and intriguing. Take a most overt example: the end of II.2, where Rose and O'Hanlon have displaced the concluding "NIGHTLETTER" (308.16–25 in the original) to a page of its own (237). There is a published precedent for doing this, namely the 1937 Corvinus Press printing of *Storiella As She Is Syung*; but one wonders why Joyce didn't remark on what would seem like a glaring layout error in his hundreds of corrections to the published *Wake*. Maybe the Penguin editors have a very good story to explain this, but Rose and O'Hanlon's promise in the Houyhnhnm book remains just a promise in the Penguin: "the full analysis will be made available to scholars and the interested public in the form of an electronic hypertext as soon as circumstances permit" (ix).[3] Made available how? When (even roughly)? What "circumstances?"[4] Unanswered questions even now. "Our isotext" – the idiosyncratic term that Rose and O'Hanlon use for what may be a variation on Gabler's "continuous copy-text" – "might exceed the limit of reasonable readerly ease of comprehension" (515). That is an extraordinary suggestion to make to a reader of *Finnegans Wake*. Likewise extraordinary is Gabler's proposal that "while we await information from the data bank ... we may take it on general trust" (501) that the editor's emendations are reasonable. I shall also await my Fields Medal for an outstanding accomplishment in mathematics – though the revolutionary proof of my theorem is, alas, not available for scrutiny – and we'll see which arrives first.

The Houyhnhnm/Penguin text is, significantly, a *computer-generated edition* of the *Wake*, which edition is in turn being advertised by website. The innovations and advantages of digital editing are the wizard kept hidden behind the curtain, and besides needlessly making a great and terrible mystery of the processes of textual production, this disparity between production (computer-assisted) and dissemination (pricey books) is as inconsistent as delivering gas-guzzling SUVs with a solar-powered truck. Certainly it makes sense to web-publish the isotext, but if that is to prove a legally viable enterprise, then so would an electronic text of this reset *Wake*. But the nature of the use of computers in the editing process cannot be deduced without the release (and, preferably explanatory notes to) the "isotext." Here is how Rose defines this term in his 1997 "Reader's Edition" of *Ulysses*:

> an isotext is an error-free, "naked" transcription of the author's words as written down by him or a surrogate, positive faults and all, with their individual diachronic interrelationships defined. It is not a transcription, however edited, of any single text, but a blending together of the members of a series of texts. ("Introduction" xii)

The second sentence sounds somewhat like a description of Gabler's "continuous copy-text," but the first pointedly does not. In what is called "a very brief overview" of the editorial methodology of the new *Finnegans Wake*, posted on the publisher's website, Rose offers this noticeably different definition: "an electronic hypertext databank specifying, differentiating and layering all authorial/non-authorial (scribal), documented/undocumented, valid, suspect or corrupting textual operations." This sounds rather like that list that Santa Claus keeps of who's been naughty and who's been nice, not only because it has a certain abstract, authoritarian quality that befits and even fortifies the mythological, but because it seems to be two lists somehow codified as one (naughty and nice together, valid operations weighed with or against suspect or corrupting ones).

If, as McGann has observed (and Rose, at least in his *Ulysses* project, has registered agreement), the meaning of a text is effectively synonymous with the social history of that text, a critical edition without an apparatus or even a substantial narrative or history of its production is an edition that seeks to efface meanings other than those which it explicitly or implicitly endorses. There may well be more than a hint of the isolative in these isotextual practices, an attempt to assure (or "restore") a purity to the text that extends to the hermeneutic. The booklet of editorial commentary included with the Houyhnhnm volume is pointedly "separated out," the editors explain, "as a final gesture of deference to the monumentality of *Finnegans Wake*, a book that brooks no equal" (Rose and O'Hanlon, "Preface" [*FW–RH*] 8). Among the authors whose various paratexts comprise this gesture of deference (not to say outright idolatry: *thou shalt have no other texts before me*), there is no agreement as to whom they are addressing and why. Deane writes with astonishment of the "miracle" achieved by the editors, seemingly to a reader reasonably aware of what he rightly calls "the sheer agglomerative scale of Joyce's undertaking," with a sidelong acknowledgment of a particular class of readers, "Joyceans," who are "acclimatized" to the vagaries and controversies of the *Wake* (*FW–RH* 5–6; *FW–R* vii–viii). Greetham's contribution, which has the most footnotes, has a curatorial quality: the scholar opening an exhibition not in his field to an audience likewise interested but unfamiliar. Gabler, for his part, offers more a defence of the general principle of critical editions ("*texts can always be otherwise*," he emphasizes ["Foreword": *FW–RH* 15; *FW–R* 501]) and the benefits of multiple editions than a justification of the specific decisions made by these editors, which are as unavailable to him as to us. This "foreword" ought perhaps to be read as a caution against resurgent and unnecessary "Joyce wars," and as such represents a direct address to Joyce scholars.[5]

Deane lauds the editors for having achieved "the clear reading text":

> There has always been a large majority of readers for whom *Finnegans Wake* is, as part of its rationale, unreadable; indeed, unreadability has always been part of its attraction, the pseudo-suave explanation for never having read it. That view of, approach to and refusal of the work are all now outdated. The new edition brings *Finnegans Wake* to its audience again, but this time with the barriers of twentieth-century critical reception (if that is the word) cleared away. (*FW–RH* 5; *FW–R* vii)

Not only does it remain unclear just what "barriers" have been "cleared away" by this edition – a confusion rather similar to that felt by many readers and scholars at Rose's previous suggestion that hyphenating "snotgreen" and punctuating the monologue of "Penelope" were revolutionary feats which cleared the way for previously obstructed readers into *Ulysses* – it seems all too likely that new barriers are here in the offing, and we return to the anxious "elitism" against which critics, editors, teachers, and readers have had to struggle (and against which, it could well be argued, Joyce posed his book about, for, and in a sense by "everybody").[6] To imagine that the "twentieth-century critical reception" of the text, a most obvious part of its social history, can or ought to be removed, is to envision editing as a process of purgation rather than enrichment.

Just to Administer Correction

In their "note on the text" included in the Oxford *Wake*, Robbert-Jan Henkes and Erik Bindervoet oddly state that "no thorough attempt has been made to create a corrected text" (xlviii) but nod a little later in a footnote to the Houyhnhnm *Wake*.[7] Perhaps there is an implied difference between "emended" and "corrected," but at any rate the Penguin edition is a substantive revision and the Oxford one isn't. Nor does the Oxford *Wake* assume the quasi-messianic rhetoric of purpose that seems to come naturally to Rose and O'Hanlon. By comparison, the editorial apparatus of the Oxford *Wake* has less cheerleading and more in the way of technical assistance for the reader: roughly thirty pages of introduction by Finn Fordham, followed by a "chapter by chapter outline," a truncated but clear and instructive textual history by Henkes and Bindervoet, a six-page select bibliography, and a chronology of Joyce's life by Jeri Johnson. An appendix of fifteen pages in small type provides an invaluable list of "variants" to consult, with specific cross-references to the relevant *James Joyce Archive* volumes.[8] This handy appendix alone – composed of 2,235 "instances of what we think is an oversight, and unintentional error which, once restored, will be beneficial to the structure of the sentence" (*FW–O* xlviii) – makes the book a necessary item on a Joyce scholar's shelf. Another way of saying this is that the book is not just for reading, but for reference, and opinions may well divide on whether "reference" is definitively reading or distinguishable as a kind of "use."

Nearly fifty years ago, Jack P. Dalton expressed dismay with the only published *Wake* left to us: "I find the text less than perfect, and I have determined to carry out a textual critique, to result commonly in emendation" (133). It is not entirely clear what "commonly" might imply here, but in that word can be heard the snap of the proctologist's enthusiastically assumed rubber glove. Dalton guesses that he would make 7,000 emendations; Rose and O'Hanlon claim to have made "about 9,000" (ix); both figures are immediately followed by the assurance that they aren't so big when one takes into consideration the length and complexity of the whole shebang (the voice from behind saying, "this won't hurt much at all"), all of which does make for something of a paradox. Henkes and Bindervoet note that their own much smaller count is not an "exhaustive" conclusion, but a specific collection of findings made in the process of translating the *Wake* into Dutch. Both the Penguin and the Oxford editors place emphasis on improving syntax, but of course therein lies an extremely muddy quandary: which syntax of which language?[9] It is not exactly incontestable that *Finnegans Wake* is written in English, "at any sinse of the world" (*FW* 83.12).

If we try to peek into the revisionist mechanics of the thing, we can make out that Rose and O'Hanlon do follow Dalton's lead. For instance, take the paragraph beginning "Yad" and ending "Yee" in Book IV (*FW* 605.04–606.12), which includes this passage:

> at sextnoon collected gregorian water sevenfold and with ambrosian eucharistic joy of heart as many times receded, carrying that privileged altar *unacumque* bath (*FW* 605.30–2)

Rose and O'Hanlon's changes exactly correspond to those proposed by Dalton:

> at sextnoon collected Gregorian water sevenfold and with Ambrosian eucharistic joy of heart as many times receded carrying the lustral domination contained within his most portable privileged altar *unacumque* bath (*FW–RH*/*FW–R* 472–3)

And in this version, the paragraph ends with "Yed" rather than "Yee." Luckily, the Oxford edition's appendix is here to point out the textual sources for these changes (*JJA* 63:38ce, 63:63; 63:141, 63:301) and again underscore the value of having multiple editions to compare.

Let's take another example, the last phrase of the first page: "since devlinsfirst loved livvy" (3.24). In a "a very brief overview" of their "editorial methodology" found on the Houyhnhnm Press website (but not included in the Penguin edition), Rose and O'Hanlon observe that "some scholars" (whoever they might be when they're at home: none are named) "would insist on retaining ['devlinsfirst'] ... on the grounds that Joyce might be considered to have 'passively' accepted the joined-up words when he neglected to correct the error at the time he changed the case of the 'D'. We do not take that view."[10] Although the possibility that the compound might be one of those "happy faults" that Joyce sometimes allowed to enter his text is rather sniffily recognized as a "view," the scare-quotes handcuffing the word "passively" seem meant to discredit the very idea that Joyce was capable of doing anything "passively." Rose and O'Hanlon instead suggest, again in the "Rationale" offered online: "On the proof in question, for example, the word is spread over two lines – 'Dev-' at the end of one, and 'linsfirst' at the beginning of the next – making it less likely that Joyce (who was revising, not correcting, the proof) would have noticed the absence of a space." Though the editors gradgrindingly pronounce their text to be "shaped and logically determined by the *facts* of the manuscript record," the "devlins first" is a matter of *conjecture* based on the manuscript record. There is nothing wrong with conjecture, in so far as it is part – even if seen as a necessary evil – of the editorial process, and thus one might as well own up to it.[11] But this one might be a little more persuasive if the proof's splitting of the word (and thus the hyphen, punctuation that Joyce eschewed in all instances but the word "no-one") had occurred not after "Dev" but between "lins" and "first."

Be that as it may, Joyce's poor eyesight is often invoked by Rose and O'Hanlon in contradistinction to the purity and genius of his intentions, and *Finnegans Wake* is effectively characterized as a physically disabled text. As the healers set out to make the blind author see and the lame text walk, they perforce shift their focus from *what the author has done (or not done)* to *what the author would have done if he could have*. The latter provides the impetus for the "colourization" of black-and-white movies: the filmmakers would have used colour had the technology been available. Yet it is all too short a step from conjecture to fantasy in this privileging of some idealized and highly localized conception of intention over the larger material and psychological realities of production.[12]

Neither the Penguin nor the Oxford editors venture to annotate – and who can blame them – but both by necessity assume the responsibility of introducing Joyce's beguiling book to a new audience, and this task must involve no simple blend of contextualization, explanation, appreciation, and perhaps too justified frustration. (I will return to annotation in the next chapter.) Fordham's introduction, written with his characteristic clarity, enthusiasm, and verve, offers this nice melange of characterizations, taken from admirers, critics, and Joyce himself:

> the dream-like saga of guilt-stained, evolving humanity; an ark to contain all human myths and types; organic, living with its own life; a cold pudding of a book; a little Negro dance; music; a war on language; a hypermnesic machine; the most profoundly antifascist book produced between the two world wars; a wonderful game. (viii)

Fordham, like Rose and O'Hanlon, sees the *Wake* as a novel – as many but not all do – and introduces it as such, though without undue insistence on the point. He aptly calls the *Wake* "an exegete's dream" (*FW–O* xxxii), though more might have been made of the manner and continuousness of its various exegeses.[13] I can expand this quibble with reference again to "since devlinsfirst loved livvy." In that phrase we can hear *Much Ado About Nothing*:

Sing no more ditties, sing no moe
Of dumps so dull and heavy;
The fraud of men was ever so,
Since summer first was leavy. (2.3.64–7)

For the purposes of an introduction to the *Wake*, pointing out this allusion (and in turn how many fertile Wakean themes are hinted at with it: deceit, marital strife, the heaps of miseries and the laughters low, "hey nonny, nonny," etc.) is of less importance, I think, than pointing out that McHugh's *Annotations* neglects it. That the sleepless industry of Joyce scholarship, with all of its guides and notes and glosses of varying degrees of insight and depth, has so far overlooked a reference to Shakespeare on the very first page testifies to how much is still being discovered in the *Wake*. This, in my view, is the crucial note to strike in introducing readers to the book. Fordham, for his part, celebrates how the book has served as a powerful inspiration for artists and intellectuals, from Marshall McLuhan to Joseph Beuys, and suggests that the "potential" inspiration is more powerful still.

Rose and O'Hanlon's introduction adopts an entirely different approach. Their reader is soothed:

> Gentle reader, were you to ask *How should I read this book?* we would answer: passively, like any good book, neither too fast nor too slow. Do not pause because you cannot understand a word or words: you are not expected to understand it all. Imagine yourself a child, leaning over the banisters, listening to the grown-up banter going on below. ("Preface": *FW–RH* 8; *FW–R* x)

From this recommendation to read "passively" and take comfort in our not being "expected to understand it all," and remembering that "passively" is precisely the adverb that these editors scorn in considering how Joyce wrote, readers can fairly extrapolate a general theme and principle to the text, and the very limited role they are supposed to have in it. The "gentle reader," that premodernist chestnut that Joyce himself ridicules in the *Wake*,[14] may take the further hint that *the edition itself* is best read in this trusting, passive, uncomprehending way. Fordham imagines a participatory role for the reader, the specific effects and results of which he sagely does not presuppose, while Rose and O'Hanlon suggest that there are tacit if unspecified and not exactly encouraging "expectations" of the reader.

How "unusuable"

Limited editions of a text that so exuberantly defies limitations make for a disservice rather than merely a contradiction or misreading. If a wider audience for the *Wake* is what's truly wanted – and not merely greater remuneration for specialized intellectual work – a print-on-demand option makes more sense than a deluxe volume of limited number and high price. Moreover, the force of Joyce's blurring of the distinction between "producers" and "consumers" (*FW* 497.01–02) can be felt in attempts to find a second-hand copy of *Finnegans Wake* without marginal scribbles, and one wonders how many calfskin-bound volumes will be so liberally (and liberatingly) defaced. A more fluid and participatory model, one which would record within itself the history of and conversation about the text, is with each passing day more and more technologically possible. These possibilities depend on a clearer conception of who reads the *Wake* and how than Rose and O'Hanlon demonstrate.

Readers and scholars will have to decide, each for him- and herself, to what degree this or that edition is for reading or for use, which seems if not "definitive" (in Joyce studies? Perish the thought) *sufficiently* authoritative and accommodating, in a book not usually thought to be either. Future editors of the *Wake* will need to reflect seriously on both how Joyce's text represents conceptions of circulation and consumption different from those of *Ulysses*, among of course many other texts, and how readers have, over the nearly eighty years since it was first published as whole, engaged with that text, rather than taking us back to a nursery introduction and/or neglecting the particular needs and wishes of such readers. If readers should refrain from dismissing the initiatives and experiments of critical editions, so too should such editions refrain from underestimating readers, perhaps especially those perpetual readers of *Finnegans Wake*, who are not passive but the very opposite: relentlessly active, ever stumbling forward and sometimes back. We are demanding, and as idiosyncratic and precise in our demands as the baker's customer, because this idiosyncratically and precisely demanding book has made us so. We want to have our *Wake* and read it too.

4
Translation, Annotation, Hesitation

Typically, a footnote in a translation is understood to be a white flag waved as discreetly as possible, sighted where the translator explicitly admits some degree of defeat. Perhaps "typically" ought to be underlined here, for of course there are not simply exceptions but a range or spectrum of exceptions, since the theory and practice of translation ought to be understood as always plural and, as I would like to argue here, because translation is the trafficking of exceptions rather than a set of or obeisance to traffic rules, the footnote is not only the symptom of a given translation's failure – the flipside of Walter Benjamin's titular "task" (*Aufgabe*) is, as Paul de Man pointed out, "surrender" – but also its opposite, a refusal to surrender, a mock-surrender, and is in effect the emblem of the inherently flawed process of translation itself.[1] In short, if you want to assess a translation, study the footnotes.

Perhaps the strongest of temptations faced by a translator is the temptation to explain – to explain some quality or meaning of the "original" text, or to explain the aims, philosophy, or method of his or her translation, though these both ultimately come to the same thing. The relationship – or the conceptual distance – between translation and annotation can be as difficult to fix or measure as the more acknowledged one between reading and translation, and as usual *Finnegans Wake* makes the point. The *Wake* is a text that is not "read" in the usual sense that one uses the word, or at least it requires that the reader be willing to "translate" as much as "read"; and yet, on the other hand, to speak of "translating" this book invites incredulity. In addition to these commonplaces we can add two curious facts. First, this book that merrily annotates itself (not just in II.2, with notes in both margins and at the foot of the page, but within its roundabout composition, wherein it rewrites itself and even other texts written about it) is itself probably one of those most annotated by readers (as I noted in the previous chapter, looking through used copies in bookstores finds a strikingly uneven ratio of the scribbled-upon to the virginal). Second, *mirabile dictu*, *Finnegans Wake* does get translated, and sometimes those translators are so shameless as to annotate.

Philippe Lavergne took only slightly less time to Frenchify Joyce's text than Joyce did putting that text together: the first excerpt appeared (in the pages of *Tel Quel*) in 1967 and the completed book in 1982.[2] This feat, the first full translation of the *Wake*, accomplished by a single translator, should give anyone pause. Jacques Derrida in "Two Words for Joyce" nods to Lavergne – appropriately enough, as we shall see, in a footnote – by noting a specific effect lost in the French version, which version is "nonetheless very commendable," and he then diplomatically adds: "But let us never malign translations, especially this one ..." (159n10). There seems little danger of such maligning, since critical discussion of translations seems invariably to be a celebration of translation itself, of its very possibility, and this undoubtedly has much to do with the utopian impetus of translation, remarked upon by Ortega y Gasset, Lawrence Venuti, Emily Apter, and others. We do not *malign*, but this business of studying translations and comparing texts is ever a matter of continually *realigning*, for utopia is not and cannot be a fixed destination, and travellers must always be redrawing each others' maps, taking new bearings, and deciding where next to turn. Translation, like utopia, is always a work in progress.

I come to Lavergne's *Wake*, then, neither to bury nor to praise.[3] Where criticisms and questions appear in this discussion, they are part of the broader purpose: to observe how *qualified* even so ambitious a translation as this one is, and to consider, with this extraordinary example as a focus, how intimate and yet how vexed is the kinship of translation with annotation. Rosa Maria Bosinelli, an attentive reader of how Joyce is translated, has written that Joyce "invites us to overcome the frustration of obscurity and accept the universal truth that misunderstanding, equivocation, misinterpretation, and misreading are part of any attempt at communication" (407) – yet this is an invitation that annotation effectively rescinds and simultaneously accepts, as though to say, "I understand very well that I cannot fully or accurately convey this information or this sensation, but I nonetheless endeavour to do so by other means." And this preposterous, delightful bit of sophistry is also recognizable as every translator's necessary working credo and *apologia pro vita sua*.

Lavergne's *Wake* includes a total of 621 notes, which might at first blush seem a large number, but ultimately it is not how *many* there are that startles, but how *few*, and too how *sporadic* they are. In the 924-page book – which dimensions themselves underscore how translation effectively amplifies and expands a text – there is an approximate average of three notes to every two pages. In any other book, this would signify little or nothing, but the density and pluralities of the *Wake* underscore what a singularly selective procedure this is. Annotation shares the same task of translation in having to balance the imagined reader's needs against the integrity of the text. The decision to annotate such and such a passage is no more fraught and questionable than the decision not to, and the interconnected ethical, philosophical, and political assumptions, concerns, and constraints that shapes such decisions are precisely those that shape the decisions made by a translator. Joyce brews a special headache on this point when he includes in his book a verbatim – and we might call it untranslated, in the sense that it is seemingly untransmogrified by the *Wake* effect, in the way so many partially recognizable idioms are – sentence from Edgar Quinet's *Introduction à la philosophie de l'histoire de l'humanité* (1857),[4] but appends five heterogeneous and conspicuously un-French glosses to it, from different sides of the page (281.04–13). The translator – and especially the French translator – faces a real dilemma here. While declining to alter the Quinet text might seem obvious, how then should this gesture be signalled, so as to alert the reader to the quality of the original? Since Joyce italicizes the quotation, unusually differentiating the passage with an indirect form of quotation marks, that popular ploy is unavailable to the poor translator, and Lavergne leaves the French and the typeface as they are. Moreover, the proliferation of annotation here serves to block or at least seriously hamper any editorial effort either to explain the non-translation of a non-translation or to inform the reader about the source of the quotation. "Translout that gaswind into turfish," dares (gloats?) one of the footnotes.[5] Joyce's catch-22 here is not that this sentence cannot be translated – as we have acknowledged, and undoubtedly will again, every translation begins with the understanding that it cannot be done – but that the translator is denied this favourite plea, and cannot aver to the reader that it cannot be done, indeed *has not* been done.

That total number of Lavergne's footnotes not only excludes (some might say naturally, but I am hesitant about such a claim) the various notes found in the "Nightletter" chapter but also Lavergne's prefatory note to that chapter, in which he seeks to explain its unusual page layout. This note makes for as instructive a beginning as any for understanding how Lavergne annotates, and the relationship between the notes and the translation. That this note is itself announced with the kind of Latin shorthand that the *Wake* tends to parody ("N.B.") and placed above rather than below the translated text may tempt readers to suppose at first glance that it is some device of Joyce's, perhaps part of the generally strange spatial distribution of words in this chapter. This potential confusion is, if not remedied, promptly translated: "Dans ce chaiptre les 2 jumeaux, depuis les rives opposées de la Liffey échangent des propos, arbitrés par notes en bas de page, de la main de Joyce" (402). The structural understanding conveyed here is not suggestive but assertive, definite: the who, what, and where of the entire chapter seem incontrovertibly laid out for the reader. Yet the comfort of these stage directions is short-lived, for the reader may well discern their ambiguities and ambivalences. For example, one might wonder *who* is doing this "arbitrating" at the foot of the page. The explanation – or is it an assurance? – of "de la main de Joyce" is surely intended, at the most immediate level of meaning, to distinguish Joyce's text from Lavergne's annotations (a distinction also made by the use of letters rather than numerals to signal the notes), but it oddly seems to place Joyce's hand on the same plane of reality as "les 2 jumeaux" so likewise definitively identified. That Lavergne tells his reader – *avant la lettre*, as it were – who is writing the notes on the left and the right (he inserts the names "SHEM" and "SHAUN" above the respective "riverbanks" of the page) naturally shapes that reader's interpretation; but what he declines to identify or situate likewise shapes that interpretation in the same way that it reveals how the translator approaches the original text. We can observe, for example, the implication that the text in the centre of the page is the Liffey flowing along (which suggestion may or may not be helpful) and too the omission of Issy (Lavergne calls her "Isabelle" [13]), whose voice many readers hear in this chapter's footnotes.[6] Lavergne also understands and frames the structure of the chapter in an altogether more fixed way than I read it – for example, he does not observe that the right and left commentators seem to change places.

The "Nightletter" poses an interesting problem for translators not much discussed, though it is strikingly emblematic of the more general problems of the *Wake*'s extreme heteroglossia: the concurrence of a specific site in a central text and a given footnote. In some respects this problem is similar to that of approximating a particular measure, like trying to match sentence for sentence in prose, without breaking up those sentences, or multiplying them as little as possible; or keeping equivalent (or proportional) points of enjambment in verse. These are obviously no easy tasks, since different languages do not agree on how many words and of what length and rhythm it takes to make even the most banal, simple, and universal sorts of statement, and (as I have already noted) translation most often has an expansive effect, which can likewise complicate locating the precise point of reference – the jumping-off place, as it were, where a note begins. A most pertinent example is one of the footnotes to the essay themes listed at the end of the chapter, each of whose themes is also linked with a historical or mythological figure in the left annotations. "I've lost the place, where was I?" (307F4) has lost its place in Lavergne: in Joyce's original, it's attached to "Travelling in the Olden Times" (307.10–11); in the French, "J'ai perdu l'endroit, où en étais-je?" is attached to "Le Rève le plus étrange qui fut jamais démi-révé" (479). Obviously such divergences between the texts generate incommensurable differences in interpretations of the two, and this example is not, alas, an isolated incident. Lavergne completely omits several of the chapter's footnotes, such as "Making it up as we goes along" (268F2; see Lavergne 415),[7] and others get transposed, the way 285F4 is with 285F5 (Lavergne 444–5). Many of these accidents are probably the effect of trans-syntactic displacement, though of course carelessness, either that of the translator or of the publisher, or even both, may well play a role, too.

Yet the problem of where the translation ends and the annotation begins becomes more and more apparent – even inevitable – and more and more difficult to solve the further one explores how Lavergne treats these notes within the text. When "Lawdy Dawdy Simpers" (*FW* 282F2) becomes "Lawdy Dawdy Simpers (Laus Dei Semper)" (439Fb), the translation, or the non-translation if you prefer, is parenthetically extended, but what exactly would we call what is found in those brackets – annotation (explication, clarification) or translation (retranslation, maybe reversion of the original)?[8] If it is Latin, it is not quite the Latin of the Church tag (Laus *Deo* Semper; praise to God always) but a more selfish sort of translation thereof (Laus *Dei* Semper; praise from God always). To the confusion of referents is hereby added confusion between the agencies and purposes of footnotes, and of translation itself.

However drastic Lavergne's situation is, translating and annotating a book that is itself an extreme process of perverted translation intertwined with digressive annotation, it is worth recalling Derek

Attridge's remark that the "enormous difference between *Finnegans Wake* and other literary works is, perhaps, a difference in degree, not in kind" (203). This difference ultimately lies in how readers react to and interact with the book, and so as daunting (or intimidating, maddening, impossible – choose your preferred adjective) – as the task of translating and/or annotating the *Wake* seems, it too is "a difference in degree, not in kind." The *Wake*'s specific, rather sizeable degree of difference serves to affirm, and will not let the reader ignore, that translation is always tempted to annotate, and vice versa: one is the secret impulse of the other.

Let us sketch a taxonomy that might usefully distinguish different functions served by Lavergne's footnotes, and thereby discuss more specifically the uses of annotation in translation.

• *Notes that re-present the original, untranslated text.* In those places where his translation either does not convey to his satisfaction the full or possible meanings of the original, the translator apologetically shows that original text to his reader, and perhaps too some of his own interpretation of and thinking about that text. That translators generally prefer to avoid doing this – the equivalent of a magician nervously explaining why he cannot produce the six of diamonds that his audience volunteer has assiduously envisioned in her mind: this sort of thing rather tends to kill the act – shows the persistent degree of commitment to translation as an act of illusion.

Near the end of I.6, we find the short sentence "I'll beat you so lon" (167.27). Lavergne offers, "Je te crache mon adieu" (265); "I spit you my farewell." How did the threat of a beating or defeat of some kind become an act of spitting and leavetaking? Lavergne's note reverts to discussing the original: *"I'll beat you so lon.*, a écrit Joyce. Le sens superposé est: je t'ai bien eu Solon" (265n126). But whose sense does this last sentence refer to? "Superposé" would seem to suggest that Lavergne is identifying what meaning he privileges – what, to use the etymology of translation, he has decided to carry across to the reader – in his French version. This explanation is not altogether satisfactory, however, for the name of Solon is nowhere to be found in "Je te crache mon adieu" (though "adieu" echoes a discernible "bid you so long"), and the translation of this particular *Wake* passage makes for an interesting paradox, since Joyce's reference to Solon, who decreed that the words of Homer were not to be changed, is interwoven with a muddled and ironic discussion of imperial law and divine logos: "My unchanging Word is sacred" (*FW* 167.28). The reader of the *Wake* is compelled to be both its translator and annotator, even as the *Wake* issues garbled warnings against such desecrations. The translator of the *Wake* must come up with a similarly contradictory admonishment, and thereby disregard the original – *traduttore, traditore* in a nutshell.

This use of annotation sometimes effectively acts as a transpositioning of annotation and translation. That is – this quickly gets confusing! – the translated text functions as an annotation of the original text, and the annotation to the translated text functions as a translation of that annotation. The reader of Lavergne's text might well blink at the phrase "le Saturday Evening Post" (160) and wonder whether this is an English phrase found in the original and left un-Frenchified because it is a proper name (of a newspaper). Lavergne's footnote to the phrase, surely inspiring a few more blinks, squelches these hypotheses: "Orthographié par Joyce: *Scatterbrains' Aftening Posht*" (160n13; see *FW* 99.34–5). The difference, it seems, is one of spelling (*orthographie*), but what Lavergne has done in the body of his text (the alleged translation) is correct Joyce's spelling, and thereby present an editorial interpretation not as a footnote but as the text itself, while adding a footnote to translate or retranslate Lavergne's puzzling English back into Joyce's language. Here we have the problem of "Lawdy Dawdy Simpers (Laus Dei Semper)" in stereo.

• *Notes that draw attention to a specific pattern, trope, or structural feature of the original text (perhaps understated or not reproduced in the translation).* Where the first type of note is generally site-specific, offering focussed commentary on the translation difficulties that a given word or phrase poses, this type of note will have a broader frame of reference, taking in the whole work being translated. Thus the translator/annotator can highlight either or both how the original text as a whole operates or how the translation strategy as a whole operates (or, as the case may be, doesn't operate).

A newcomer to *Finnegans Wake* can find assurance of some sort of method to the muchness of madness in the recurrence of certain clusters of letters, most noticeably HCE and ALP, and simply recognizing (and often underlining, a first gesture of annotation) those patterns where they appear can be heartening. Alas, the translator not only has to recognize such patterns but try to preserve them – an utterly impossible task in languages with completely different alphabets, such as Korean and Japanese (though the *Wake* has been translated into both of these languages), but only slightly less impossible in French.

Lavergne sometimes – with no detectable pattern of his own – points out these patterns in his notes. For instance, in "*Edwin Hamilton's Christmas*" readers are instructed to remark upon "HCE, dans le désordre" (761n35). The note also serves to explain why these three words have not been translated, apart from their being italicized, which may seem to signal that they remain untranslated (unlike the Quinet case discussed above) but at the same time introduces some confusion. The matter of who performed what and where in "Edwin Hamilton's Christmas pantaloonade, *Oropos Roxy and Pantharhea* at the Gaiety" (*FW* 513.21–2) is rearranged in "d'un drôle de pante *Edwin Hamilton's Christmas*, issu tout droit d'une pantalonnade, Le Roi Europe et Pantharée à la Gaité" (761–2), leaving the reader of the first to infer that *Oropos Roxy and Pantharhea* is the title of the "pantaloonade," and the reader of the second to infer that its title is *Edwin Hamilton's Christmas*. Moreover, there is no apparent reason why Lavergne should want to draw attention to the "HCE" convention here, almost eight hundred pages into the book, when he does not do so elsewhere, at least in no consistent fashion. "*Et Cur Heli!*" (*FW* 73.19), for example, retains its original form, italics included, in Lavergne's translation, but no note lurks below to reveal "HCE, dans le désordre." A more puzzling instance occurs a couple of chapters later, in I.5's list of titles for the "mamafesta" (disappointingly masculinized by Lavergne as "son manifeste" [166]). "*Amy Licks Porter While Huffy Chops Eads*" (106.32) undergoes only a very slight transformation to become "Amy Licks Porter quand *Huffy Chops Eads*" (169), with the effect that the italics trace the constellation of HCE (Lavergne otherwise expels Joyce's italics for these collected phrases) while the ALP constellation warrants no notice.[9]

It needs to be emphasized that this second kind of note depends no less than the previous kind on the interpretation(s) that the translator-annotator chooses to privilege, despite the fact that such and such a feature of the whole original might seem obvious or important to any one reader, and precisely because it might not to another reader. Here again we can see how translation and annotation share mutual anxieties (precisely about both how these functions "use" a text and how the products they wield might be "used"), and Lavergne presents a good example in how he approaches Joyce's sentence, "In the Dee dips a dame and the dame desires a demselle but the demselle dresses dolly and the dolly does a dulcydamble" (*FW* 226.15–17). The French text reads: "Vers le Lough Dee descend une dame et la dame désire être demoiselle mais la demoiselle fait un dressoir à sa poupée dorée et la poupée dorée dort un doux sommeil" (350). The alliteration remains, though it is slightly diffused, and Lavergne succinctly notes: "Douze mots commençant par la lettre 'd'" (350n27). For reasons not given, Lavergne draws specific attention to the number of words that begin with "d." This might have something to do with his preceding footnote, which recounts, in the manner of the first kind of note discussed above, Joyce's own text (though not exactly), because in that instance Lavergne was unable to keep the "d"-alliteration: "Still we know how Day the Dyer works, in dims and deeps and dusks and darks" (*FW* 226.12–13) becomes "Cependant nous savons comment opère Day Dyer, dans le vague, profond, crépuscule, sombre" (Lavergne 350). Yet this note also functions as the second kind being considered here, for it too accentuates number as an ordering principle: "Défilé des quatre: *dim, deep, dusk, dark*" (350n26). Lavergne effectively informs his reader that these configurations of four and twelve are important, but gives no hint about how or why. In a sense, both the translation and the annotation are incomplete, and each begs questions the other does not fully answer. It is useful to compare Lavergne's text on this question with Endre Bíró's (partial) Hungarian translation, which renders the sentence beginning "In the Dee dips a dame" as "Az M mélyén egy madonna, a madonnát mardossa a manci, de manci mindig maskarázik, s a makara maga mákonymézes" (80–1), and the earlier "dims and deeps and dusks and darks" as "mély, méla, mályvaszín matricákkal" (80). Bíró appears to agree with Lavergne that the number of alliterative words ought to be retained, but esteems the number over the particular sound, taking the liberty of replacing "d" with "m." Though not altogether averse to annotation and commentary, Bíró declines to remark on this change.[10] One might just as readily imagine a translator who would retain the "d" sounds without, for whatever reason, having exactly twelve of them; or a translator who insists that the monosyllables of "dims and deeps and dusks and darks" are of equal importance to their number. And one can thereafter imagine further variations on these possible translators by imagining with what styles and extents of argumentation or apologetics they might expound on these respective foci in footnotes – or not.

These inconsistencies, idiosyncrasies, and uncertainties, while troubling, bespeak the annotator's dilemma in general: how to match the design of the text (again, as he or she perceives it) with a workable, coherent design of explication that does not needlessly interfere with or occlude the reader's own perception of that text's design (presuming, of course, that one cares about such things) – or, to put it another way, how best to reconcile the perceived design of the (original) text with the anticipated "uses" of the translated or annotated version. What is the right or best incident of "HCE" at which to inform the reader of its larger importance within the book? To thus tag "Howth Castle and Environs" (*FW* 3.03) on the first page would be to peremptorily rob the reader of the satisfaction of determining for herself that these three letters significantly travel together. (Imagine an annotated murder mystery in which a footnote identified the guilty party at the moment of his first appearance in the text.) Lavergne declines to be such a killjoy to his "Howth Castle et Environs" (though he identifies HCE as a character in his introduction – but the marvellous thing about introductions is that they can be – and often ought to be – skipped). On the other hand, he does annotate the very first word (the rather nice "erre-revie") so as to delineate nothing less than "la nature de *Finnegans Wake*" (its musicality, its memories, the way the final sentence loops around to rejoin the beginning).

• *Notes that explain allusions within or provide extratextual glosses of the original text*. Unlike the first two kinds of note, these notes do not refer to the original text as a material object with specific, intrinsic properties that can or cannot be reproduced or approximated in translation. They are more intertextual and less infratextual, though an absolute distinction on this point is untenable and the slippery "more" and "less" qualifiers are not to be elided. They also perforce serve a generally more didactic purpose by constructing (or, if you prefer, illuminating) *selective* contexts in which to read and understand the original text.

Perhaps not surprisingly – since the *Wake* continually has all of us guessing, not always safely – some of these ventures are less plausible than others. "Maggy" in the phrase "veuille penser toujours et encore à ce Galway, ne l'oublier jamais, et à cette envoyée sœur de Maggy" ("please kindly think galways again or again, never forget, of one absendee not sester Maggy" [458.08–10]) is matter-of-factly identified as "Nora, la femme de Joyce" (682n6). Lavergne was presumably remembering that Nora was from Galway, though he does not say so, and indeed gives no explanation for or evidence to support his claim – an otherwise uninformed reader presumably just has to trust his word on this. Looking elsewhere in the texts at other appearances by "Maggy," we find no similar identifications: for example, Lavergne renders "Muggy well how are you Maggy" (111.15–16) as "Muggy comment vas-tu cher Maggy" (176) without comment, and, a few pages later, "Maggy's tea" (116.24) is readily strained into "thé chez Maggy"

(184), again without any footnote. Perhaps the translation of the question "And how war yore maggies?" (142.30) to "Et que faisaient les Maggies, tes Marionettes?" (224) invokes Molly (Marion) Bloom, and so Nora by crude association; but this is hardly explicit or even definite.

The absence of a clear system or policy of annotation in Lavergne is in some respects hard to fathom. While selectivity in annotation is, as it is in translation, the unavoidable nature of the exercise, a coherent, articulated, or at least deducible organization – governing what fields of allusion are to be surveyed by what I have already observed is actually a small number of annotations for such a large and densely referential text – is of no small assistance (and assurance) to a reader. Recall the aforementioned lack of any annotation to the untranslated phrase "*Et Cur Heli!*" (*FW* 73.19) in Lavergne's *Wake*: in this instance, Lavergne not only declines to identify HCE for his reader, he does not point out the allusion to Joyce's earliest published poem, "Et tu, Healy," and its historical background. This might not seem odd if he did not make such gestures elsewhere, such as notes about *Stephen Hero* (200n1), Lucia Joyce (248n88 and 249n89), and the identification of "Maggy" as Nora Joyce. So it seems that biographical data and earlier writings by the author fall within the range and kind of allusions about which Lavergne will (curtly) notify his reader, but "Et tu, Healy" somehow flies under the radar, as do many other, similar references.

Deciding what allusions to identify and explain is only half of the job; the other half is deciding how to do it. Put another way – a way which will resonate with translators, who face the same pair of problems – one has to decide when to begin annotating, and when to stop. The majority of Lavergne's notes are, as we have seen, brief, and imply a metonymy that is seldom justified. In one of Issy's footnotes in II.2, she refers to "white mate" (270F2). Lavergne has "la chemille blanche (Wilde)" (419Fa). The *translational* connection between "mate" and "chenille" is no more obvious than the *allusive* one between a caterpillar and Oscar Wilde.[11] Both the translation and the annotation decisions seem arbitrary (though perhaps they corroborate each other, a possibility to which I'll return). But the length of the note ought not to be directly associated with depth, or the lack thereof. Lavergne can sometimes be more expansive in his notes, as he is in this one introducing the Butt and Taff exchange in II.3:

> Dans tout le dialogue qui suit, Butt et Taff jouent la scène du tableau pendu au mur du cabaret d'Earwicker: pendant la guerre de Crimée, un

cadet tire sur son général. Pour saisir toute l'implication de l'incident il faut se reporter à la confession de Stavroguine dans *Les Démons* de Dostoïevski. (519n1)

Throughout the following dialogue, Butt and Taff enact the scene depicted on a tableau [or painting] hanging on the wall of Earwicker's cabaret: during the Crimean war, a cadet shoots his general. To fully understand the meaning of this incident one must refer to Stavrogin's confession in Dostoyevsky's *Demons*.

My own translation here of Lavergne's note irons out some of the original's ambiguous wrinkles. At the very least, these two sentences seem a pile of non-sequiturs – but then, so does so much *Wake* commentary, so perhaps that should be taken in stride. Yet there is also the determinism of "saisir toute l'implication" (singular, take heed, and not plural), the direct instruction. Did Joyce read this work of Dostoyevsky's, or is this just some sort of affinity detected by the translator? What exactly should I, the hungry reader, be looking for in Stavrogin's confession? Is *all* of this dialogue's meaning ("toute l'implication") in Dostoyevsky? (And is it specifically in the *French* Dostoyevsky?)

As these examples show, Lavergne's referential contexts are biographical and literary/intertextual, though the relationships or even the distinctions between these contexts remain as occluded as the sources for such information as why Nora is called Maggy and Oscar Wilde is a caterpillar. Moreover, his notes simply point rather than explain or discuss, though this is not because (or at any rate not entirely because) he wants to resist or avoid circumscribing the field of interpretation available to a reader, for the preamble to Butt and Taff's dialogue unapologetically does just that.

Ambiguity is often thought to be the nemesis of both translation (think of idiomatic uncertainties and polyvalencies, the very stuff of *Finnegans Wake*) and annotation (driven by the need to be definite and authoritative). The dangers but also possible values and uses of ambiguity in translation and annotation themselves constitute too large and deep a subject for this essay, but it is worth remarking here how annotation can simultaneously narrow the reader's focus (and thus the meaning of the text) and be itself so ambiguous as to engender new puzzles and doubts. Often as not one has this experience in consulting Roland McHugh's *Annotations*, in which this or that expression is called "slang" but its provenance (whose slang, where?) and on what authority it is thus identified remain gaping questions. The footnote to the word "Flumen" in Lavergne's phrase "C'était un Flumen dans son genre" (313), a translation of Joyce's "She had a flewmen of her owen" (*FW* 202.05–6), reads: "Un phénomène." It is hard to dispute that, even if the reader feels none the wiser. Perhaps all glosses are eccentric, or at least more elliptical than they are commonly supposed to be.

• *Notes that explain the translator's own allusions (understood to differ in some respect or degree from those of the original text).* This function would seem the most obvious to recognize, when in practice it can be the opposite – especially, of course, for a reader unfamiliar with the original.

To the sentence "Arrête-toi et baisse-toi pour conquérir" is appended this reference: "*She stoops to conquer*, de Goldsmith" (360n54). This seems a straightforward sort of identification of a literary allusion, exactly like what is found in McHugh's *Annotations*. The inference (or assumption) that Lavergne has neatly managed to carry a reference by Joyce to Goldsmith's play is overturned by a comparison of the original passage with the translated one, which reveals both a different set of operations in the translation and a different purpose for the footnote:

> He's your change, thinkyou mehim. Go daft noon, madden, mind the step. Please stoop O to please. Stop. What saying? I have soreunder from to him now, dearmate ashore, so, so compleasely till I can get redressed, which means the end of my stays in the languish of Tintangle. (*FW* 232.17–21)

> Voici votre monnaie, merci madame. Bonsoir, jeune-fille, attention à la marche. Stoppe je t'en prie. Arrête-toi et baisse-toi pour conquérir. Je me suis rendue à lui maintenant, chère Astoreth, si complètement que je puis aller me rhabiller, ce qui signifie la fin de mes stations dans le langage de Tintagel. (360)

Demonstrated here – especially in the first three sentences – is Lavergne's custom of double-translating the text: from the original to functional English, and from that to an idiosyncratic French. And again, as we noted he does with some of Issy's notes in II.2, Lavergne omits items: the two sentences "Stop. What saying?" mysteriously fall by the wayside. Even more extraordinary than what is left out is what is added. "Dearmate ashore," which to my ear sounds like a fond salutation from one at sea to a beloved on terra firma (McHugh points very plausibly to a song, "Dermot Asthore"), has been magnified to nothing less than the queen of the heavens, "Astoreth." "Please stoop O to please," part of a telegraphic refrain that echoes at different points in the *Wake*, is even more dramatically embellished: "Stoppe je t'en prie. Arrête-toi et baisse-toi pour conquérir." In the single word "stoop," Lavergne apparently detects a nod to Goldsmith, and not only does his translation exaggerate the allusion, he adds a footnote to underline it. In effect this note highlights an allusion that is pronounced in Lavergne but far less definite in Joyce.

Similar notes on Goldsmith allusions, to follow this one patterned example, test the reader's credulity while they suggest that Goldsmith is something of a touchstone for Lavergne. No fewer than three such footnotes are dedicated to a single paragraph in I.6 (262; *FW* 166.03–19), and both their claims and the translation they refer to, though they reinforce one another, strike this reader as being at least as questionable as the "stoop" instance discussed above. Lavergne metamorphoses "THREE male ones" (166.17) into "TROIS d'espèce femelle" and explains that "The Three jolly pigeons" is the name of the ale-house in *She Stoops to Conquer* (which he repeatedly calls a *novel* [262n116]). The phrase "babyma's toddler" becomes "l'enfant de Ballymahon" and the name of this Irish town begets a footnote that informs the reader that none other than Oliver Goldsmith used to live in Ballymahon (262n115).[12] There is something uncanny about all of this.

When Lavergne does carry over and amplify these sorts of disputable allusions, his reader is left to wonder whether they are warranted precisely *because* the translator has found a clever means of approximating what otherwise might be just a faint or fanciful impression, and to what extent the annotations that accompany those translations (apt as they are to blur which allusions are in the original text, which is not represented in these instances) act as a cue for admiration. Sometimes Lavergne does seem pleased – and why begrudge the translator of *Finnegans Wake* such small pleasures – by his own paronomasia. For Joyce's sentence "We calls him the journeyall Buggaloffs since he went Jerusalemfaring in Arssia Manor" (*FW* 26.03–04), Lavergne produces: "Nous on l'appelle le Va-toujours Bœuf-à-l'eau depuis qu'il alla chercher Jérusalem en Anusie Mineure" (52). A footnote on "Bœuf-à-l'eau" smirks: "Buffalo." If there are buffalo grazing in "Buggaloffs," I don't see them, but thanks to this note I cannot miss Lavergne's pun.[13]

The function of this footnote is ostensibly to explain the translation as such (rather than explain the text being translated), but the crucial question is whether "translation" is understood in this context as a process or as a product: if the latter, as in these Goldsmith and Buffalo notes, the original is not only not acknowledged but the translated text is addressed as an object with relationships to any other text or referent *except* that original. This is the "finished" translation dressed up and out for drinks, with its spouse and wedding ring left at home.

It quickly becomes apparent, as we review the functions outlined above, that the distinctions between them are very hazy and that not only may a given annotation serve more than one function, it is sometimes no easy matter to extricate one function from the other. In fact, all of these functions are inextricable from a kind of metafunction – the justification of specific translation decisions – even though it is quite possible that this metafunction is as much an illusion (even as utopian an illusion) as the achievement of complete translation. Every translator's note is, as I said at the beginning of this chapter, a gesture of surrender and a vow to fight on, a most sincere apology and yet an act of bad faith, too.

The system or policy by which one decides to supplement a text could be called a poetics of annotation. Like a poetics of translation, whether it is outlined for the reader or left for the reader to make out for herself, any operative poetics is going to be entirely (and rightly) open to criticism, and satisfaction is likely to be in short supply.[14] And yet again *Finnegans Wake* makes for an extreme case, even if it is a "difference in degree, not in kind" (which point is not much comfort to the translator-annotator at work with Joyce's text). One of the most disarming characteristics of the *Wake* is its "sehm asnuh" (620.16) principle: it is bad enough that a recurrent phrase such as "same anew" should be perpetually metamorphosing, but to make matters worse (especially for a translator and annotator), even when a given word reappears later in the text, looking just like it did the last time we saw it, it may not "mean" the same thing it did then. Contexts are always shifting in the *Wake*, and this distressing fact should arouse even greater sympathy for Lavergne. The identification of one instance of "Maggy" as Nora without similar identifications posited for other such instances is not inconsistent if the valences of "Maggy" vary depending on context. The *Wake* makes all annotations inconsistent, in that it reveals that they always are. Any poetics of annotation is by definition as provisional, compromised, and discrepant as any poetics of translation.

Fritz Senn's remark that "everything Joyce wrote has to do with translation, is transferential" (*Joyce's Dislocutions* 39) can be extended and modified in light of the corollary that everything Joyce wrote also has to do with annotation, and so that body of work can be called *transreferential*. Lavergne's footnotes may seem irregular, capricious, futile, or by some degree all of the above, but they simply anticipate the reader's own back-and-forth reading of the self-translating, auto-annotating text of the *Wake*, not only acknowledging these same qualities in the translation, but offering (however inadvertently this may be) ways of talking back to the translation and the original text. Put another way, they give us pause, and this is a generous and useful gift. One of the shortest of the footnotes in II.2 is the question "Hasitatense?" (296F4). Lavergne's translation answers: "Avec hésitance" (462Fa). The former might be read as a question of translation, and the latter, by way of understatement, the uncertain reply of annotation. The translator, who must commit to some more or less satisfactory formulation, may look to the footnote as a space for qualification, variation, digression – a place where hesitation is possible. This may be a sustaining fantasy when one is cracking one's forehead against the desk trying to find *le mot juste* for "mirthprovoker" (466.22) or "owlglassy" (208.09), but it is an illusion nonetheless. The annotator, even the most garrulous or digressive, can likewise complain of the restrictive constraints of the note as a form, while the imperfections of the translation seem so much more liberated by comparison. And it would be unjust to exclude the translator him- or herself from the genuine, constructive pleasures to be found in hesitating at this or that move in the translation – and complaining about it.

PART TWO

Cultural Appropriations

This book tells you how to act with all descriptive particulars. (*U* 15.2393–4)

5
Make a Stump Speech Out of It

Now, if anyone wants a little more of what the vulgar people call stuffing let him or her speak. (*D* 198)

Every time I speak in public I end up sounding like James Joyce.
– George W. Bush[1]

"Go on. Make a stump speech out of it" (*U* 15.1353). This is how the disaffected Zoe brushes off Bloom's anti-smoking homily (without, oddly, catching its more overt suggestion) in "Circe." He in turn misunderstands her rebuff as an invitation – or else, in the dream logic of this chapter, receives it as a hypnotic suggestion – to let fly with all manner of oratory. Bloom promptly assumes a confidence, an eloquence, and appreciative audiences so far at odds with what readers have hitherto seen him muster that it becomes clear that this fantasy is as remote from reality as it is dear to him, especially as this particular motif goes on at some length and is only interrupted when Bloom is supplanted by another orator, Alexander J. Dowie (15.1752–60).[2] While the utopian schemes and political fancies of this scene have been much discussed, the plain fact of Bloom's sudden ability to speak so well in public deserves closer attention because it is symptomatic of a larger crisis within Joyce's work.

The dramatic tension of so much of Joyce's work lies in the act of public speaking – or, more precisely, in the anxieties that attend this act. Once one pauses to weigh this large claim, the examples quickly multiply (and I shall of course examine several in what follows), and the implications deepen. Noting that "performance expressed and accompanied all that was most important in Joyce's life" (21), Alan W. Friedman has argued that Joyce celebrates the Irish tradition of hospitality embodied by "party pieces" (recitations, songs, and the like), but the kinds of public, verbal address are conspicuously more various in Joyce's works, which suggests a wider recognition of occasions when an individual speaks to a crowd: so we find not just recitations, toasts, and "party pieces," but lectures, sermons, political speeches, business proposals, eulogies, jokes, witness testimonies and addresses to the court, and even dramatic last words from the deathbed or the gallows.[3] Moreover, this broader consideration and accounting of the phenomenon attests to something rather more than a documentary impulse, and I think that public speaking is for Joyce more than a subject for representation. It is an aesthetically productive fount of anxiety.

Rather than enumerate each instance of public speaking in Joyce's texts, or even ponder yet again the theoretical valences of speech acts with unsurprising borrowings from Searle and Austin, I propose to explore some of the common pointers and encouragements given to would-be public speakers, as they have been disseminated from the rise of the "self-help" craze in the mid-nineteenth century to the online almagest of advice that Google cheerfully retrieves.[4] Reading the acts of public speaking and their accompanying anxieties in Joyce's work against such received wisdom yields an understanding of Joyce's work – a new conception of its *use* – as a kind of inverted toastmaster's handbook, a nearly comprehensive manual on how *not* to give a speech.

It is important to appreciate the emphasis and value affixed to oratory in order to see why such an understanding has critical value of its own. Public-speaking guides and teachers inevitably posit confidence as the key to success, and, as such, an end as well as the means. This promise of success often conflates success in the task at hand (wowing the board with your report, for example) and with success on a more comprehensive scale (not just getting that promotion but a yet fiercer surge of upward mobility), the repetition of which equation might even make it seem natural, until we consider that few popular guides to other such specific tasks make such connections – it is seldom suggested that being able to drywall a basement or tie one's own fishing lures will lead to substantial material rewards and profound self-understanding. According to English Grammar School principal Samuel Whyte, writing at length about the subject in 1800, the man who is "accustomed to speak before numbers" is an extraordinary figure, to be envied and emulated as part of a definite social program. The benefits of this ability are understood to be enjoyed by both the individual and society:

> His heart will be humanized; his understanding opened; his sentiments enlarged; his morals improved; he must be a more disinterested friend; a more rational companion; a more confirmed christian; a better man; in a word, more completely qualified to discharge every civil and social duty of life in whatever station. (7)

This magnificent series of operations thus produces a dutiful citizen. Unfortunately, Whyte goes on to observe, the art of public speaking is in decline, which is not simply an embarrassment to society but a danger to it:

> That the English are the only free nation recorded in history, possessed of all the advantages of literature, who never studied the art of elocution, or formed any institutions, whereby they, who were most interested in the cultivation of that art; they, whole professions necessarily call upon them to speak in public, might be instructed to acquit themselves properly on such occasions, and be enabled to deliver their sentiments with propriety and grace, is also a point as true as it is strange. (10)

The characterization of "the only free nation" deserves notice, for despite the fact that Whyte's *An Introductory Essay on the Art of Reading, and Speaking in Public* was printed in Dublin, this remark does not seem at all an Irish jab at English complacency, but rather part of an imperial logic in defining citizenship. As Whyte's subsequent examples of language usage suggests, "English" is conceived here as a language and an empire, a "free nation" that almost incidentally includes Ireland.

The simultaneously civic, national, and imperial duty bound up in this conception of the capable public speaker is in its own way an answer to the riddle of postcolonial theory: "Can the subaltern speak?" Reports of an Irish gift for the gab are all very well, but public address might well inspire a skeptical examination of such a "gift" (maybe even to look it in the mouth). Consider Parnell's speech of thanks upon becoming a Home Rule candidate in 1874, as described by A.M. Sullivan, editor of the *Nation*:

> He faltered, he paused, he went on, got confused, and pale with intense but subdued nervous anxiety caused everyone to feel deep sympathy

> with him. The audience saw it all, and cheered him kindly and heartily; but many on the platform shook their heads, sagely prophesying that if ever he got to Westminster, no matter how long he stayed there, he would be either a silent Member or be known as 'single-speech' Parnell. (qtd. in Kee 59)

Though this prophecy obviously missed the mark, it is instructive to note how poor a public speaker the man often renowned for his rhetorical powers could sometimes be. On another occasion, in 1876, Parnell was observed to have a "bad, halting delivery" in which "he seemed constantly stuck for a word" and stood "with clenched fists which he shook nervously till the word he wanted came" (Kee 126). Perhaps these incidents (and to them we might add that Parnell was a childhood stutterer) ought not to be set aside as aberrations in an otherwise glorious career of public speaking, but considered integral to a strategy for resisting the allegedly self-improving subjection that the institution of effective public speaking offers. I will return to this question of Parnell's strategy later, but this provisional suggestion allows us to consider anew how and why Joyce repeatedly depicts faltering, hesitant, and anxious attempts at public speaking.

Tip #1: Know Your Audience

The use of the phrase "dramatic tension" invites remembrance of Stephen's definition of "dramatic," which survived the transition from *Stephen Hero* to *A Portrait* without changes to its terms:

> Lyrical art, he said, is the art whereby the artist sets forth his image in immediate relation to himself; epical art is the art whereby the artist sets forth his image in mediate relation to himself and others; and dramatic art is the art whereby the artists sets forth his image in immediate relation to others. (*SH* 77; see also *P* 179–80)

Although the terms of this intriguing definition, which links the dramatic with self-performance before others, do not change between texts, its presentation and in effect its full meaning does, for it moves from the unspoken, narrated description of Stephen's thinking to a spoken Socratic dialogue with Lynch. That is, Joyce found greater force – a dramatic tension which allows for a wider possible range of conflicts and ironies – in compelling Stephen to utter his thoughts aloud, and letting them be interpellated.[5] In the paragraph from *Stephen Hero* that I have just quoted, Stephen is not just mulling over his speech (which he is still two dozen pages away from actually giving) but trying to justify his doing such a thing at all: "his essay was not in the least the exhibition of polite accomplishments. It was on the contrary very seriously intended to define his own position for himself" (*SH* 76). How different all of this is from the showy unravelling of *Hamlet* in "Scylla and Charybdis," which performance John Gordon has argued is as significantly if not altogether improvisational, "a production very much in its pre-Broadway tryout stage" (502). His trigonometric display, as it is advertised by Buck, is very much an "exhibition of polite accomplishments" but he promptly disavows that it is "his own position."

The anxiety so palpable in the anticipation and preparation of the "explosive" lecture in *Stephen Hero* is perhaps best encapsulated by Stephen's judging the period between Christmas and the second Saturday in March "an ample space of time wherein to perform preparative abstinences" (69) – that is an extraordinary last phrase. Yet it ought not to be supposed that the *Hamlet* lecture in "Scylla and Charybdis" is – as it might seem – any less worrisome an effort. Margot Norris stresses how much is at stake in the *Hamlet* lecture for Stephen, knowing as he does that "his own success or failure as an artist" may well depend upon the acceptance of the literati present in the library for the occasion (65). Stephen knows who his audience is and what possibilities of support and patronage they represent, and his attitude on this score is noticeably different from the one the alternate Stephen adopts in his Ibsen lecture. Norris writes that the *Hamlet* lecture is a "gambit" for literary prestige, "a high priority on this day with a high risk of failure unfortunately verified by its outcome" (64).

And failures both lectures are, though of different kinds. Here is the full description of the Ibsen lecture:

> He waited until a compliment of discreet applause had subsided, and until McCann's energetic hands had given four resounding claps as a concluding solo of welcome. Then he read out his essay. He read it quietly and distinctly, involving every hardihood of thought or expression in an envelope of low innocuous melody. He read it on calmly to the end: his reading was never once interrupted with applause: and when he had read out the final sentences in a tone of metallic clearness he sat down.

> The first single thought that emerged through a swift mood of confusion was the bright conviction that he should never have written his essay. (*SH* 101)

Lucky Jim this isn't. That Stephen "read[s] out his essay" rather than speaks to his audience is a formula for tedium all too familiar to anyone who has attended even a few academic conferences. The consequent note of dismay and regret readily corresponds with Gabriel's sense of "his own foolish speech" (*D* 224) and the ridiculousness of the speech's failure anticipates the same quality of Stephen's words of seduction to Emma Clery. Stephen not only doesn't know his audience, he doesn't seem to care that he doesn't know. The Stephen of *A Portrait*, by contrast, knows too well who his audience is, and can't decide how much to care.

Tip #2: Start with a Joke

In his early film *Bananas* (1971), Woody Allen is nervous before giving a speech to a hall filled with rich swells and potential benefactors for the third-world country of which he is nominally and absurdly the leader. "Open up with a joke, a funny story" he is advised, and so he begins, "I'm reminded tonight of the farmer who had incestuous relations with both his daughters simultaneously," and, pausing before the stone faces and barely polite coughing, adds, "of course, this is the wrong crowd for that joke." While we may wonder at length where that particular set-up could possibly lead, the unexpected inversion of blame – it is the audience, not the joke, that is wrong – reveals an easily overlooked egotism sabotaging any chances at a self-assured performance at the same time that it demolishes the advice. A comparably painful case is that of Gabriel Conroy, whose joke about the assembled diners in "The Dead" being the "victims" of hospitality apparently necessitates punctuating with "a circle in the air [made] with his arm" and a pause (203), the gestural equivalent of an "LOL."

But jokes are simply not Gabriel's forte. His attempt to kid Lily flops, and he proves no better at being on the receiving end with Molly Ivors: "she had no right to call him a West Briton before people, even in joke" (191). The jokes are on him, and it is hard not to notice that his self-deprecatory (and corny) reference to his own "poor powers as a speaker" (203; many public speaking guides advise against doing this)[6] is made all the more fatuous by his acknowledgment that he has performed this very same role more than once before as well as by the fact that the bait to deny the claim is taken only by Mr Browne, the blowhard of the company. Then there is his thought-tormented joke about the "Three Graces of the Dublin musical world":

> The table burst into applause and laughter at this sally. Aunt Julia vainly asked each of her neighbours in turn to tell her what Gabriel had said.
> – He says we are the Three Graces, Aunt Julia, said Mary Jane.
> Aunt Julia did not understand but she looked up, smiling, at Gabriel, who continued in the same vein ... (*D* 205)

That silly word "sally" should perhaps give us pause to wonder where it comes from – is it born of the same narrative judgment that presents all of Gabriel's speech verbatim but not a direct word of Freddy Malins's less polished attempt to entertain his listeners? – and the close proximity of "vainly" and "vein" might suggest yet another insinuating joke in a story wearily replete with them.

According to the database known as the "Ithaca" chapter, one of the six reasons that "prevented [Bloom] from completing a topical song" he was composing was his inability to locate just the right "humourous allusions" in "*Everybody's Book of Jokes* (1000 pages and a laugh in every one)" (17.441–2). Gifford seems unsure about whether this refers to a real book or is a lampoon of a popular type, but W.R. Russell and Company, London, did indeed publish a book of that title, one of thirty-nine volumes in the "Everybody's Series," which includes such gems as *Everybody's Book of Curious Facts*, *Everybody's Book of Correct Conduct*, *Everybody's Guide to Poultry Keeping*, *Everybody's Cycling Law*, and of course *Everybody's Guide to Public Speaking* (though my own favourite title is the ninth in the series: *Do You Know It? If Not, You Should*).

Everybody's Book of Jokes is not, of course, 1,000 pages, but just under 200, and, alas, the promised ratio of laughs per page is also a fiction, not improved by this reduction. Instead, this very modestly sized volume advertises "Over 3,000 Selections, Old and New" of retorts, conundrums, bulls, puns, and so on. The book seems to be intended not just as light reading with which to pass an evening of bourgeois chortles alone or with the family as captive audience, but, as its placement within a "how to" series suggests, it helpfully provides entertaining matter for private conversation and public address alike. It is not altogether surprising, though, that Bloom fails to find much of use therein for the theme "*If Brian Boru could but come back and see old Dublin now*"

(17.419) since the specifically Irish references are to buffoonish stereotypes. Here is a relatively inoffensive but apposite example:

> An Irishman telling a story as an original, was informed by one of his auditors that he had read it in the translation of a Latin work. "Confound these ancients," said the Irishman, "they are always stealing one's good thoughts." (109)[7]

The editor's note to the reader makes no small claims about the resilience of jokes:

> In nothing is the doctrine of the survival of the fittest more aptly illustrated than in jests. It is almost impossible to lose or destroy a really good joke. It comes down through the ages, surviving civilisations and monuments. It is revamped, changed, and disguised by an hundred would-be humorists, but at heart it is the same old joke. An old joke is of necessity a good joke. In arranging this little book, no effort was made to exclude that which was old; and the editor has a lurking suspicion that in this, as in other books of its class, the best things are the oldest, and the least witty those most nearly original. (3)

These claims, however they might be judged, are worth bearing in mind when we discover this item among the numerous jokes about the Irish:

> An Irishman, who has jumped into the water to save a man from drowning, on receiving a sixpence from the rescued man, looked first at the sixpence, and then at the man, saying: "Be jabbers, I am overpaid for that job." (10)

Even if we set aside the inviting but uncertain and possibly incautious supposition that Joyce cribbed material from this book, the problem still stands that the "awfully good one that's going the rounds about Reuben J and the son" (6.264–5) is not exactly fresh. Recall that Bloom's attempt to recount it is not just "thwarted" by Martin Cunningham, who interrupts to tell the story with brutal concision, but ultimately surmounted by Simon Dedalus, whose wit Bloom has to admire: "Most amusing expressions that man finds" (6.599). That Simon Dedalus, the acknowledged raconteur and regular at the pubs, should be the one member of the company who has not heard the story may seem implausible enough to warrant some doubt about whether Simon's ignorance of this anecdote ("I didn't hear it" [6.268], he asserts) is entirely genuine, and thus whether his well-timed witticism is as spontaneous as it appears. Moreover, if this story is indeed an old joke (and thus "of necessity a good joke") dutifully preserved and disseminated in *Everybody's Book*, its "revamped, changed, and disguised" appearance in *Ulysses* confirms that the ancients are indeed always stealing one's good thoughts.

Tip #3: Show Enthusiasm

Probably the most zealous, animated, and uninterrupted speech in all of Joyce's work is Father Arnall's hellfire sermon in *A Portrait*. While this sermon has been read and characterized a number of different ways – as terrifying, ridiculous, or tedious – its effectiveness, as measured by the example of young Stephen, cannot be doubted,[8] and Joyce likes to remind his readers against underestimating the spontaneous (or spontaneous-seeming) power of rhetoric. Though Dan Dawson's overcooked speech about *"the peerless panorama of Ireland's portfolio"* is mocked as "a recently discovered fragment of Cicero" (7.270) in the newspaper offices, Bloom reflects: "All very fine to jeer at it now in cold print but it goes down like hot cakes that stuff" (7.339–40). Here Bloom's admiration for the combination of silver tongue and courage (however uneven the mixture) is tempered somewhat by a recognition that popularity and quality are not synonymous (in the same way that he matter-of-factly envies Philip Beaufoy's accomplishment but not his skill).

Enthusiasm does quickly catch on but of course this is a good reason in itself to be suspicious of it, and for all of the figurations of Bloom as an ordinary, common, or somehow representative man of the early twentieth century, he is able to hear the dangerously alluring songs of the sirens and sail away safely. Robert Emmet's speech to the court that condemned him, as favoured by the busy mouths in the Ormond Hotel as Dawson's speech is derided by those in the editorial office, is underscored and undercut by Bloom's eloquent flatulence: "done." With such ironies Joyce cautions against the grand and ultimately consuming use of those unhappy-making big words. Norris points out that Bloom's being burned at the stake is "merely Zoe's figure of speech – 'Talk away till you're black in the face'" (15.1958) but it also shows that messianic ambition "requires self-immolation" (176).

The object of considerable distrust in the Enlightenment, "enthusiasm" has seen a reversal of fortunes with the growth of the public relations industry in the early twentieth century. Bloom's ineptitude at public speaking is ironic precisely because he is a salesman and a believer in "self-help" just at the historical moment that these two discourses will be blended. Harken to this hymn to the wonderful, persuasive power of enthusiasm, taken from *The Art of Public Speaking* (1915):

> Enthusiasm sent millions crusading into the Holy Land to redeem it from the Saracens. Enthusiasm plunged Europe into a thirty years' war over religion. Enthusiasm sent three small ships plying the unknown sea to the shores of a new world. When Napoleon's army were worn out and discouraged in their ascent of the Alps, the Little Corporal stopped them and ordered the bands to play the Marseillaise. Under its soul-stirring strains there were no Alps.

Well, as Groucho Marx once observed, "the Lord Alps those that Alps themselves." It hardly needs to be pointed out that without exception these inspired feats are all aggressive imperial ventures.[9] The authors of this best-selling, exuberantly American guidebook contend that "it is impossible to lay too much stress on the necessity for the speaker's having a broad and deep tenderness for human nature," though there an open contradiction in the book's recognition that "self-preservation is the first law of life, but self-abnegation is the first law of greatness." One of these authors is Dale Carnagey (later spelled Carnegie), whose name is synonymous with the "self-help" boom in America, and who is best known for his later book, *How to Win Friends and Influence People* (1936), an unexpected contemporary of *Finnegans Wake*. Carnegie is, as a stylist, no less dependent on collage than Joyce, and his books are thick with quotations. As a teacher (or "professor of public speaking") Carnegie encourages clarity, sincerity, and perseverance via experiments, offering themes and subjects for the learner to speak about – these include "Woman's Suffrage," "A Larger Navy," "Love," "Kindness," "Child Labor," "The Most Dramatic Moment of My Life," and "What I Would Do with a Million Dollars."

The high point of the chapter on "Feeling and Enthusiasm" in *The Art of Public Speaking* is this story of one such pedagogical experiment, worth recounting in full:

> When the men of Ulster armed themselves to oppose the passage of the Home Rule Act, one of the present writers assigned to a hundred men "Home Rule" as the topic for an address to be prepared by each. Among

> this group were some brilliant speakers, several of them experienced lawyers and political campaigners. Some of their addresses showed a remarkable knowledge and grasp of the subject; others were clothed in the most attractive phrases. But a clerk, without a great deal of education and experience, arose and told how he spent his boyhood days in Ulster, how his mother while holding him on her lap had pictured to him Ulster's deeds of valor. He spoke of a picture in his uncle's home that showed the men of Ulster conquering a tyrant and marching on to victory. His voice quivered, and with a hand pointing upward he declared that if the men of Ulster went to war they would not go alone – a great God would go with them.
>
> The speech thrilled and electrified the audience. It thrills yet as we recall it. The high-sounding phrases, the historical knowledge, the philosophical treatment, of the other speakers largely failed to arouse any deep interest, while the genuine conviction and feeling of the modest clerk, speaking on a subject that lay deep in his heart, not only electrified his audience but won their personal sympathy for the cause he advocated.[10]

That substance is eclipsed by style is warmly commended, but the fullness of this eclipse is most pointedly marked by the statement, "It thrills yet as we recall it." The speech was so marvellous that it cannot be reproduced, only recalled – strange to say, this may even be *why* it is judged such a success. This is the point that Bloom is making with "All very fine to jeer at it now in cold print."

It is interesting to compare this description of the clerk's impassioned plea against Home Rule with the 1901 speech of John F. Taylor "recalled" in a somewhat different fashion in "Aeolus." The speech was a response to Justice Gerald Fitzgibbon, another opponent of Home Rule, of whom Professor MacHugh tells Myles Crawford that because he knows the man, "you can imagine the style of his discourse" (*U* 7.798–9). Taylor, by contrast, is "gone with the wind" (7.880), among the dead and now known as a legend, and MacHugh, caught up in the manly competition of My Orator is Better than Your Orator, has to outdo J.J. O'Molloy's recitation of Seymour Bushe. It is difficult to judge whether MacHugh truly believes that Taylor's speech is "the finest display of oratory I ever heard" (7.792–3), or whether he has hit upon it because of the Moses connection with the Bushe quotation. "Wait a moment," he says. "Let me just say one thing": Dale Carnegie would shake his head at such a beginning, which suggests a man unsure of exactly what he is going to say.

Unlike the clerk's speech, however, Taylor's words are presented in full – or so it seems. No known and verified copy of the full text of this speech has been found, apart from an anonymous leaflet titled *The Language of the Outlaw*, and it is also not known for certain whether Joyce himself was in attendance when the speech was made (though recent scholarship has produced compelling suggestions).[11] Thus it might be more accurately said of Taylor that "you can imagine the style of his discourse," for that is what both MacHugh and Joyce (who in 1924 chose to read this passage from the novel for an official recording) are doing. *Ulysses* and *The Art of Public Speaking* may be in unspoken agreement that the effect of a speech is the measure of its success, and the effect is in its turn measured not by how we correctly remember it as how vividly we "recall" or imagine it. MacHugh's gassy bluster notwithstanding, Joyce's admiration for Taylor's performance can be seen in how he imagines it: his embellishments to the text (when compared with the leaflet) and the fact that, even as the words come filtered to the reader through Stephen's interpellating thoughts, they are not cut up like Deasy's letter, another case of cold print versus hot cakes. And the enthusiasm catches: silent no longer, Stephen leaps into the fray: "I have a vision, too" (7.917).

It doesn't turn out to be such a hit. But I'll come back to that.

Tip #4: Be Direct and Enunciate Clearly

There are a number of problems and paradoxes in the common advice given to *Finnegans Wake* readers, but one of the best must be to read aloud for better comprehension from a book of whose every word pronunciation is far from certain. Perhaps this is a way of evening the score with bygone teachers who would on some unknown authority correct the pronunciation of students compelled to read Latin lessons aloud. At any rate, Joyce's work offers an interesting pattern of command performances, where someone is goaded into making a public pronouncement which, like the two Stephens' respective lectures, flops. Examples abound, but I'll just mention the way that baby Boardman is coerced into announcing, "A jink a jink a jawbo" (13.28) to satisfy his superior, bemused audience, because it serves as an emblematic miniature of the poor vocalizations championed by the *Wake*.

Though the problem of pronunciation is most glaring in his last book, Joyce's work as a whole is something of a continuous deliberation on it. *Ulysses* is a book about a man who worries about his wife's Italian accent (her "voglio") and entertains the idea of acquiring a young live-in tutor – a bit of a twist on *Pygmalion*, one might say. In *Dubliners* accents are – well – accentuated as the signs, if not the causes, of strife, miscommunication, and disappointment. "Counterparts" in particular is about saying the right thing the wrong way. Its agitating opening sentence connects a "furiously" ringing bell with "a piercing North of Ireland accent," slyly switching the more familiar combinations of a piercing bell and a furious voice. When Mr Alleyne bullies his employee with what is supposed to be a rhetorical question –"do you take me for a fool? Do you think me an utter fool?"– Farrington surprises himself as well as everyone else:

> The man glanced from the lady's face to the little eggshaped head and back again; and, almost before he was aware of it, his tongue had found a felicitous moment:
>
> – I don't think, sir, he said, that that's a fair question to put to me.
>
> There was a pause in the very breathing of the clerks. Everyone was astounded (the author of the witticism no less than his neighbours) and Miss Delacour, who was a stout amiable person, began to smile broadly. (*D* 87)

The crucial element to this scene is the presence of an audience: the clerks and the important Miss Delacour. Farrington's reaction to his own public triumph here is contradictory. Well does he know that his boss will make his working life "a hell to him," and he rebukes himself: "Could he not keep his tongue in his cheek?" (*D* 88). This, too, seems a rhetorical question, and I don't think that it's a fair question to put to the reader. The phrase "tongue in cheek" means rather more than simply "keep quiet." Is Farrington's problem that he is too much in earnest ("from the heart") or that he is too ironic ("tongue in cheek")?

Farrington is a mimic attentive to different intonations and rhetorical devices (he notices the alliteration of "*Bernard Bodley be*" in the course of his monotonous copying) but incapable of controlling his own. He has been caught imitating Alleyne's accent and at the end of the story begins "to mimic his son's flat accent" (94). The "London accent" of the young woman at the bar arouses a muddle of volatile feelings in him, which later explodes into violence when young Tom's "O, pa" echoes, in the wrong register, her earlier "*O, pardon!*" (91). The story of his eloquence gradually becomes itself a matter of mimicry for others: the drinking company only truly roars with laughter when it is retold, with something called "great vivacity" and an explicit imitation of Farrington ("*as cool as you please*" [90]) by a co-worker named Higgins – another unexpected *Pygmalion* turn.

At this point we can return to Zoe Higgins, with whom this chapter began:

> BLOOM
> (*fascinated*) I thought you were of good stock by your accent.
> ZOE
> And you know what thought did?
> (*She bites his ear gently with little goldstopped teeth, sending on him a cloying breath of stale garlic. The roses draw apart, disclose a sepulchre of the gold kings and their mouldering bones.*)
> BLOOM
> (*draws back, mechanically caressing her right bub with a flat awkward hand*) Are you a Dublin girl?
> ZOE
> (*catches a stray hair deftly and twists it to her coil*) No bloody fear. I'm English. Have you a swaggerroot? (*U* 15.1335–47)

This flirtatious exchange, which leads to Bloom's extraordinary "stump speech," is worthy of more comment than it usually receives. Joyce inverts (or perhaps perverts) Shaw's dynamic of the Cockney flower girl and the presumptuous Professor Henry Higgins by giving the latter's surname to a prostitute whose accent (she has just recited biblical Hebrew) is admired by a man who sometimes goes by the name of Henry (and whose mother's maiden name is also Higgins).[12] Zoe's pointed answer, "No bloody fear," is a recognizable echo of the most notorious line of Shaw's play, Eliza Doolittle's "Not bloody likely" (78). All of this plays to Bloom's fantasies of "correction" at the hands of a superior woman, and in this connection it is worth remembering that Martha Clifford might well be called Bloom's "flower girl" ("I'll advertize it in the papers that your duchess is only a flower girl that you taught," Eliza threatens Higgins at the end of *Pygmalion* [132]), and the retrospective significance of Bloom's musing on the austere silence of sculpted goddesses in "Lestrygonians": "Suppose she did Pygmalion and Galatea what would she say first? Mortal! Put you in your proper place" (*U* 8.924–5).[13] The subtlest detail in this scene, though, is Zoe's "little goldstopped teeth," for this is an unexpected recurrence of the theme of "Chrysostomos" (3.26), the golden mouth of the skilled orator. Prior to meeting Zoe, Bloom claims to be "Leopold, dental surgeon" (15.721), which credentials presumably enable him to judge the quality of her accent (though the reader never does find out whether she is a Cockney or a Yorkshire girl), while Stephen Dedalus is mocked as "Toothless Kinch" (1.708): whether the quality of the teeth determines the quality of the tongue seems as uncertain as whether goddesses have anuses.

There may be more ingredients than Shaw in the making of Zoe, whose name (from the Greek Ζωη, "life") is itself intriguing and perhaps a little unlikely for a Yorkshire girl, though it was once popular among Hellenized Jews). The female characters of *Ulysses* tend to be literary composites, for Joyce borrows salient details from his reading of women's writing (which reading deserves a longer study in itself), from popular fiction to personal and ephemeral texts. Gerty MacDowell's debt to Maria Susanna Cummins's *The Lamplighter* (1854) has become, by virtue of repeated annotation, the best-known instance, but more startling is Joyce's use of Queen Victoria's journal (first printed in 1865) in his creation of – of all people – Molly Bloom.[14] Bearing in mind that it is incautious to underestimate the range of Joyce's reading, it is tempting to wonder whether Zoe Higgins might to some extent be drawn from another sentimental nineteenth-century novel, Geraldine Jewsbury's *Zoe: The History of Two Lives*, published nine years before *The Lamplighter*. *Zoe* is a "novel of doubt," a swoon-filled narrative not only of apostasy and recovery but, more sensationally, of women's sexual desire for men of the cloth, a theme that also runs through *Ulysses* (from "Don John" Conmee to Gerty's crush on Father Conroy to Molly's hierophilia: "Id like to be embraced by one in his vestments and the smell of incense off him like the pope" [*U* 18.119–20]). One of Jewsbury's contemporaries called it "the first novel in which the hero's career is made dependent on the victory of modern scepticism over ancient belief" (Espinasse 136), and in case that description does not seem Joycean enough, there is the fact that the novel even has a Marian (though she's no Molly).

At the heart of *Zoe* is a struggle with rhetoric. The unfortunately named Everhard Burrows, the priest with whom the married Zoe Gifford falls in love, is instructed early in the novel, when he first doubts his calling, to become an excellent preacher: "Eloquence (and you have it) opens the way to every heart, to every thing to be desired in this world; it can cover a whole decalogue of sins; it is a regular enchanter's wand!" (53). Much later in the novel, Zoe and her friend Clara decide to attend a sermon by a Protestant minister to whom Clara is attracted.

> "I never heard him," said Clara, "and I am very curious to know whether he is as eloquent in the pulpit as out of it. I have heard he is a very fine orator."

> "I don't fancy that it will be oratory that will take much hold on me," said Zoe, "there will be more words than thoughts. I never yet heard any thing that came up to my idea of eloquence in public speaking." (334–5)

Joyce's Zoe, a displaced Yorkshire girl with a hinted but quite unclear sort of Jewish identity, seems as immune to the speechifying of Bloom as Jewsbury's Zoe, a half-Greek of disreputable background, is circumspect about "eloquence in public speaking."

It is possible that even if he did not read *Zoe*, Joyce might have heard of the novel by reputation; but a more definite textual source for the Bloom-Zoe exchange is Jonathan Swift's *Polite Conversation*, an ironic "how to" manual first published in 1738. "What is gravely introduced as a model of good behavior," writes Mackie L. Jarrell, who first pointed out this allusion, "turns out to be a holocaust of manners" (545). Jarrell catalogues a variety of phrases and proverbs from "Circe" appropriated from Swift's bores, including such conversational gems as "Fingers was made before forks" (15.2718), "After you is good manners" (15.2027–8) and many others (Jarrell 546–8). Swift (masked as Simon Wagstaff) guarantees that "there is not one single witty Phrase in this whole Collection, which hath not received that Stamp and Approbation of at least one hundred Years, and how much longer, it is hard to determine; he [the reader] may therefore be secure to find them all genuine, sterling, and authentic" (10). This assurance anticipates that of the editor of *Everybody's Book of Jokes*: "the best things are the oldest, and the least witty those most nearly original." Joyce thus takes the implied advice and borrows freely from these auspiciously certified sources.

One such point of advice from Swift is echoed in many more recent guides to public speaking: vocalization is crucially supported by body language. Swift recommends "the true Management of every Feature, and almost of every Limb" and adds that

> there is hardly a polite Sentence in the following Dialogues which doth not absolutely require some peculiar graceful Motion in the Eyes, or Nose, or Mouth, or Forehead, or Chin, or suitable Toss of the Head, with certain Offices assigned to each Hand; and in Ladies, the whole Exercise of the Fan, fitted to the Energy of every Word they deliver; by no means omitting the various Turns and Cadences of the Voice, the Twistings, and Movements, and different Postures of the Body, the several Kinds and Gradations of Laughter, which the Ladies must daily practise by the Looking-Glass, and consult upon them with their Waiting-Maids. (11)

In case the reader is not already practising gradations of laughter by the time he or she reaches the phrase "by no means omitting," there is the even thicker laying-on of "Circe," an episode resplendent with extraordinary twistings and movements. In fact, it is rare that a line of dialogue is not qualified (which is altogether too pale a word for it) by instructions about how it is to be enacted, and many of these venture further than even Swift would imagine. Nibbling on someone's ear or recoiling a stray hair while speaking seem simple operations compared to, say, "spout[ing] walrus smoke through her nostrils" (15.2561) or, in holding another's hand, using one's forefinger to give "his palm the passtouch of secret monitor, luring him to doom" (15.2012–13). And of course "the whole Exercise of the Fan" will bring us to Bella Cohen, perhaps the most outspoken woman in *Ulysses*.

If these performances – forced admissions, displaced accents, the vintage vacuity of "polite conversation," and a zany array of accompanying gestures[15] – are unsatisfactory, they may well signify defiance, a Joycean rejection of a stressed and stressful normative. Recall the prophecy of "one-speech" Parnell: it might not be so inaccurate after all if we think of the way the *Wake* reiterates and distorts the famous statement about setting a boundary to the march of a nation that Parnell himself repeated in different arrangements on different occasions, one version of which can be found on that uptown Dublin statue that so kindly points the way to the airport. For that matter, the gratuitous meanderings and orotundities of "Cyclops," "Oxen of the Sun," and "Eumaeus" (and perhaps too, in a different key, "Penelope") might be the textual and syntactic equivalence of the parliamentary obstructionism practised to no little effect by Parnell – and so *Ulysses* appears less a blockbuster than a filibuster.

How unlike the "resonant assurance" of Father Purdon, who "told his hearers that he was there that evening for no terrifying, extravagant purpose" (*D* 13–74) is the mad sort of jabbering that goes on in the *Wake*, such as we hear in the sermon of III.2:

> Divulge, sjuddenly jouted hardworking Jaun, kicking the console to his double and braying aloud like Brahman's ass, and, as his voixehumanar swelled to great, clenching his manlies, so highly strong was he, man, and quite gradually warming to her (*FW* 441.24–8)

Besides the thick clutch of orator's clichés here (the "hardworking" speaker whose voice swells as he warms to his subject), this sermon made to mount is illustrative of the way the public speaker is, ever and again, imagined as male, and the most susceptible audience female. Purdon is a man speaking to other men (men of the world), out to assure them of their state of grace, but "Jaun the Boast's last fireless words of postludium of his soapbox speech" (469.29–30) is such a jumble of instruction and excitation that there is little wonder that his audience, his sister in twenty-nine variations, is beside herself. The public speaker is seducer, and the act of public speaking affirms and flaunts a masculinity which may win the respect of other men or the erotic submission of women.

"Penelope" offers a counterpoint to this formula, though perhaps not an obvious one. Matthew Bevis sees "Joyce's technical innovation," the interior monologue, as "unpublic speech": but it "is often conceived in public terms, as if to highlight how the mind itself might be considered a debating chamber" (Bevis 235). This is especially important to bear in mind when reading the last chapter of *Ulysses*, though it might not immediately seem so. Though it contains no spoken dialogue and there is no apparent audience to Molly's thoughts, still the chapter is often referred to as a "soliloquy" – or, as Derrida qualifies it, "at most a soliloquy" (74) – and this in turn inculpates the reader as the audience, at least an audience, perhaps even something more.[16]

More than any other episode, "Penelope" is to be enacted, given voice. That it is the most performed and recorded scene in the book attests to this. The silent reader finds none of the customary comfort and support afforded by punctuation, and has to "sound out" the words to give them comprehensible, auditory form. "Penelope" is, of course, not a phonetic exercise, such as those assigned to Eliza Doolittle offstage, though it nonetheless represents a challenge that any would-be orator would find useful. Figuring out just how to pace Molly's words, where to place emphasis, when to breathe: these are problems that each and every performance deals with in its own way.

And there is a genuine political force to the performance of Molly's words, at least as strong as any of the grandiloquent sermons and speeches of men in Joyce's works (real or imaginary). It is an act of unsilencing, and what's more, it is a collective act among readers. How many readers of *Ulysses* – and this question may have special weight for women readers – have found themselves reading "Penelope" aloud, perhaps even aloud to others? This "Penelope Effect," which transforms silent, textually isolated readers into a community of public speakers, is comparable with the "human megaphone" strategy of Occupy Wall

Street protesters who, forbidden by police to use any sound amplification technology, relied upon concentric rings of people repeating outward, phrase by phrase, the words of the central speaker. This mode of transmission broadens the agora, democratizes public speech. What seems the most silent chapter in *Ulysses* (a sleepless woman thinking private thoughts) is in fact the most pronounced, an exhortation.

Tip #5: Know When to Stop

Stephen Daedalus professes an inability to use what he scornfully calls "phrases of the platform" (*SH* 56), yet the attraction of and anxieties about the platform are always there in Joyce. But one of the perplexing omissions of so many public speaking guides is the best way to conclude, though it has to be clear when you are done, and perhaps the two most appreciated words in any lecture hall are "to conclude." The funereal oration that is *Finnegans Wake* seems so altogether averse to saying farewell to the departed as to be an effort to forestall mortality. Yet as its refrain of "stop ... please stop ... please do stop" attests, it knows too well that it has gone on too long, but can't stop now. And this may be what distinguishes Joyce from the able speakers he studied with fascination and ambivalence: he didn't know how to stop, and so he became a writer, who by definition – perhaps most spectacularly by Joyce's own definition – is not constrained by time.

Poor Stephen tends to have to punctuate his speeches with the full-stop of a barked laugh (his own, unfortunately). This is followed by the "echoed dismay" of his students in "Nestor" (2.17) and after the parable of the plums, Myles Crawford's "Finished?"

And if you have to ask ...

6
Win a Dream Date with James Joyce

I don't care this fig for contempt of courting. (*FW* 145.16)

Would you describe yourself as lonely? Do you find it difficult to meet people? Is there no one who seems to understand you? You're in luck: there is hope for you in modern literature, for all of your dating problems are addressed in the works of that "moist moonful date man aver" (*FW* 347.07), James Joyce. With some understanding of his groundbreaking work in contemporary courtship, you too can meet that special someone.

The proposition is not so ludicrous as it first seems. Consider the following personals ad found in the Toronto newspaper *The Globe and Mail* for 27 September 1997:

MOLLY BLOOM SEARCHING...

> for Ulysses? Could be. Receptive, creative woman, slender and very alive in my 40s. Seeking earthly gentleman, 48+, with unaffected style and grace. Please call for details.

Unfortunately, my unsuitable age and fierce doubts about my earthliness prevented me from calling for those details, but the temptation is obvious; and what's more, such an advertisement represents a salient hint at the extent to which Joyce has been absorbed into a significant field of popular consciousness, by which I mean what I am going to describe as "romantic culture." Richard Ellmann's conviction (shared by many and here crudely summarized) that love is the overarching theme of *Ulysses* is as popular as it is almost unassailably general. I – perhaps a softie – am vulnerable to such arguments, but for the purposes of this discussion a greater focus is needed: after all, love is not a small concept. While much has been said and written of marriage in Joyce, comparatively little has been made of the equally polymorphous though rather less tangible problems of courtship. The theory and practice of "dating," the sometimes confusing ritual of modern love ("love's young fizz" [*FW* 462.09], we shall see, is as marketable as Pepsi: "the choice of a new generation"), are part of the dedicated overturning of romantic ideals found to occur in Joyce's works. "You love a certain person," *Ulysses* assures its reader (12.1499–1500). What are you going to do about it?

One of the most unusual – if not altogether unlikely – commodifications of Joyce is this assimilation into popular "romantic" culture, a phenomenon which itself represents an economic commodification. In outlining another probably unforeseen kind of "use" for Joyce, this chapter seeks to examine the protocols and probabilities of dating of Joyce's time, within Joyce's work, and (strangest of all) because of Joyce. Put another way, I propose to trace here the salient but previously unexplored connections between two public and commercial institutions, the reading of Joyce and the modern rites of courtship. In an entertaining essay titled "The Joycean Unconscious, or Getting Respect in the Real World," Vincent J. Cheng reflects on the currency of Joyce in popular culture and relates a personal anecdote about a time "when I was dating a young woman who happened to be named Joyce":

> My friends (and I myself) found this Joycean serendipity very amusing, but Joyce herself did not – since she had no idea who this James Joyce I kept talking about was. And yet I discovered, as I got to know her better, that her responses to some Joycean names or concepts I would sometimes bring up were neither completely clean slates nor random Rorschach tests: for example, she had heard of the name Molly Bloom and associated it vaguely with female sexuality. This made me start to wonder about the ways in which Joycean terms and concepts might enter the popular consciousness at unconscious, subliminal levels – and what those effects would be, even effects that could be used and manipulated to sell products. (181)

Cheng does not tell us how things turned out with Joyce, but the use of the past tense is suggestive, and the essay turns out to be bizarrely *un*-self-conscious as Cheng does not reflect upon his own use and manipulation of Joyce (both the author function in the broadest sense and the young woman as an example or study subject). Also, of course, he does not answer the question his anecdote clearly opens: is repeated conversation about Joyce a good way to pitch the woo?

As this intriguing blind spot in Cheng's essay indicates, one cannot wholly remove a given element or artefact from the cultural continuum in which it is or was born and thereafter thrives. My own attempts to address the subject of "dating and Joyce" which follow allow the conjunction of that phrase to serve as a two-way swinging door, allowing discursive movement from consideration of dating as a social phenomenon and its documentation by Joyce to discussion of the sometimes perverse ways in which Joyce, as both an artist and a cultural icon, has thereafter affected that phenomenon.

The Book of Dates

> If she knew to what his mind had subjected her or how his brutelike lust had torn and trampled upon her innocence! Was that boyish love? Was that chivalry? Was that poetry? (*P* 97)

In her interesting volume *Consuming the Romantic Utopia*, Eva Illouz recognizes the shift in courtship beliefs and practices in the twentieth century as inextricable from the expansions of capitalism.

> The "commodification of romance" designates the process by which evolving conceptions of intimacy and sexuality came to be defined by the new business of leisure and new technologies of leisure (e.g., the automobile, the movie theater). More precisely, romantic encounters were enclosed within temporal, spatial, and artificial boundaries defined by the technologies and forms of leisure offered by increasingly powerful industries. (54)

The notion of a "date" presents an intriguing semiotic intersection, for the various meanings of the term may coincide: thus, one may simultaneously be said to be on a date, with a date, on a given date; and even some of these phrases are ambiguous (to "be a date," for example, besides signifying one of the counterparts in an appointment, can also mean to be a "foolish or comic person" [*OED*]). In the same way, I can argue that *Ulysses* is all "about" a date: a meeting between two people at a specific time and place (both in subject and, if we recall the occasion of Nora Barnacle's first walking out with her Jim, in inspiration).

Stephen and Bloom have the most prominent date with destiny, but the book is filled with appointments real and imaginary. For example, there is a kind of contest in *Ulysses* between M'Coy and Bloom as to whose wife still makes performance dates (and "[w]ho's getting it up" [*U* 5.153]). In "Grace," however, Mrs M'Coy's singing schedule is a ploy for her husband, who is notorious for his "crusade in search of valises and portmanteaus to enable Mrs M'Coy to fulfil imaginary engagements in the country" (*D* 159). Bloom asserts that *his* wife is on "a kind of tour" (often how his own 16 June events are characterized by readers of the novel), but it is a mental tour of past dates with old beaux:

> I never thought hed write making an appointment I had it inside my petticoat bodice all day reading it up in every hole and corner ... I remember shall I wear a white rose and I wanted to put on the old stupid clock to near the time (*U* 18.764-6, 768–9)

The struggles to make and keep appointments will later drive the collapsing of time and place in *Finnegans Wake*, "till their hour with their scene be struck for ever and the book of dates he close, he clasp and she and she seegn her tour d'adieu" (580.15–17).

Making and keeping a date is the source of anxiety for not just Molly Bloom (either by setting "the old stupid clock to near the time" or by advertising in Canadian newspapers), but for many of Joyce's characters. The most striking example of a very wrong way of getting a date is found in *Stephen Hero*, whose protagonist's idea of a pick-up line is ridiculous: "Just to live one night together ... and then to say good bye in the morning and never to see each other again!" (*SH* 177). Such are the only slightly defended remnants of "Romance" (in every sense of the word) in Joyce; and I would argue that the death of young and "very delicate" Michael Furey (*D* 220) marks the death of premodern romance, and the début of a less languorous, more rapid, aggressive, and commercial style of courtship – a love-during-wartime dynamic which the *Wake* calls "agincourting" (*FW* 009.07).[1]

Flirting, teasing, "walking out" with another – these activities began to assume new importance, as divorce rates conspicuously rose, much to the anxiety of the general and especially the parental public (LeMasters 8–9). Bloom notes among other public notices in the newspaper the "divorce suits" (*U* 7.199), and the infamy of the 1890 Parnell divorce case resounds throughout *Ulysses*. New economic and professional interests divided the family, and, ultimately, war exploded. In the midst of these tumultuous events, schemes of "family life education" (LeMasters 3) began to form: a new moral code was being drafted, and new expectations and presumptions quickly gained weight.[2] Consider how easily Bloom constructs a wistful (but completely unsuitable) girlfriend for Stephen Dedalus:

> In the nature of single blessedness he would one day take unto himself a wife when Miss Right came on the scene but in the interim ladies' society was a *conditio sine qua non* though he had the gravest possible doubts, not that he wanted in the smallest to pump Stephen about Miss Ferguson (who was very possibly the particular lodestar who brought him down to Irishtown so early in the morning), as to whether he could find much satisfaction basking in the boy and girl courtship idea and the company of smirking misses without a penny to their names bi or triweekly with the orthodox preliminary canter of complimentplaying and walking out leading up to fond lovers' ways and flowers and chocs. (*U* 16.1556–65)

Having the *sine qua non* is a tricky business in Joyce, as one finds in the similar postulation of a "sweetheart" every boy has and must not have, presented in "An Encounter" (*D* 17–19). In his cheeky (at least, for 1954) *A History of Courting*, E.S. Turner notes the way in which dating applied new pressures on young people to engage with that unknown quantity, the opposite sex; but he exculpates the older and wiser generations by calling dating "a raw new tradition": "[t]his, it should be stressed, was not an imperative enforced by adults" (256). Joyce knows better. Bloom's assessment of slurred Yeats leads him to think Stephen goes with Ferguson: "A girl. Some girl. Best thing could happen him" (*U* 15.4950–1). The misguided, patronizing concern for another male's romantic welfare is strangely reminiscent of that of the "queer old josser" in "An Encounter" (*D* 18): in both cases, the concern comes from older men, given to public masturbation and the occasional bit of pornography.

Certainly, the roles of adults had changed as the courtship process changed: the collapse of ideologies which structured arranged marriages is echoed in "The Boarding House" and its epilogue within *Ulysses*. Social pathways were being reoriented, as it were, by the growth of the modern city and its demands:

> increasing urbanization meant that many young people were on their own, working in the cities ... Because rules of propriety dictated that a

> young woman could not have a gentleman in her apartment, boarding-house or dorm room, courtship activities had to take place in the public domain. Eventually the wealthy saw the less formal system of courtship in public as something to emulate, and the fun and excitement of "dating" became an upper-class phenomenon as well. (Cate and Lloyd 21)

Mrs Mooney's boarding-house is an archaism (confirmed by the unimpeachable moral judgment of the "Cyclops" narrator), as it tries to contain and regulate within its domestic structure those "courtship activities" which were moving to public spaces. The boarding-house, like the "marble halls" of which Maria sings in her "tiny quavering voice" (*D* 102), is a faded fantasy, as out of touch with modern ways as are many of the would-be lovers in *Dubliners*, including Maria, Mr Duffy (and his stuffy "distaste for underhand ways" [*D* 106]), and Gabriel Conroy's mooning aunts. However, all of these instances signal the persistence with which elders seek to dictate the mores and practice of relationships. Courtship was at this time quickly shifting "from the private to the public sphere" (Bailey 3); but the public sphere has never been managed by the young.

Who would sell the cosmetics young girls bought, and the "flowers and chocs"[3] Bloom mentions; and who would produce the cinema (home of the "flimsyfilmsies" [*FW* 279.F1]) and the automobile? Who else but those adults made exempt from responsibility for the "raw new tradition" by Turner's account (and this from someone who also penned a book called *The Shocking History of Advertising!*)? By way of contrast to Turner, the attitude of E.E. LeMasters on the issue is more indicative of the truth, but at least equally laughable for its rhetorical tone: "If we reflect for a moment, it becomes obvious that complete anarchy and chaos would prevail if young men and women were left completely to themselves during the courtship period" (69). Supervision, as usual, would pull us back from the brink.

Dating was such a perilous mystery that the build-up of an industry of explication occurred very quickly, replete with a proliferation of dating instruction manuals – "mating manners" – as numerous, various, simple, and usually as unnecessary as reading guides to Joyce (which had begun to appear, coincidentally, at about the same time).[4] As I noted in the introduction to this book, among the titles Stephen peruses on the bookcart in "Wandering Rocks" is one instructive volume on "How to win a woman's love" (*U* 10.847), a precursor to the deluge of works coming to prevent social instability, turpitude, and ruin.

(Coincidentally, one of the more popular guides produced after the Second World War was written as the confessions of a fictitious teenager named – yes – Joyce.)[5] Whereas the medical status of the hearts of so many were cared for – as one early proponent of computer dating put it – the "heart hungers" (qtd. in Mullan 67) required professional attention, too. The sociologist who probably broke the most ground in this field with his assessment of the "Rating and Dating Complex" in 1937 had the unlikely name of Willard W. Waller. Waller called dating "a sort of dalliance relationship," and recognized the upsurge in "thrill-seeking" in courtship practices going on in the early part of the century, facilitated by "[d]ancing, petting, necking, the automobile, the amusement park, and a whole range of institutions and practices" (171–2). An anthropology of dating culture was being constructed by members of an inquisitive older generation who were self-appointed to the task. As Beth Bailey sums up the situation: "The new arbiters of convention were academics – social scientists in the main – who sought to bring youth's experience in courtship and marriage under the authority of educators and experts" (119).

The easy comparison between Waller's "Rating and Dating" process and "shopping practices," which LeMasters acknowledges (95) invokes "the gentle art of advertisement" (*U* 7.607), whose practitioners have always been ready to capitalize on social interactions. As Garry Leonard puts it, "it was not only Freud who wanted to know exactly what it is a twentieth-century woman wants; retailers, advertising executives, and department store managers ask themselves the same question" (660–1). The Bloom-Boylan struggle for Molly is, in a sense, a competition between a canvasser and a billsticker for the consumer; though it is Boylan who actually has the four o'clock date.

The pro-dating campaigns could endorse almost any product, though it was understood that the promise each product held was of the same loving bliss. A 1908 issue of *Ladies Home Journal* identified romance with a man as the goal of "girlhood": "It should be the bloom and blossom, the normal unfolding of all our young years" (qtd. in Illouz 29). Mass-produced products would complement and eventually actively formulate dating practices. "Still the thrill of courtship," trilled a 1920s advertising slogan for that sweetest of totems in *Ulysses*, soap (qtd. in Illouz 40). The market was not simply becoming sentimentalized; the principles of the market were being so effectively merged with the values of young romance that the consideration of one inevitably provoked a recognition of the other. The institution of Hallmark Cards provides a good example. A somewhat daring card from 1900 portrays a dark-featured man embracing a young woman from behind as she sits on his lap; the pair are on a rock before a picturesque strand of beach. "To my Valentine" the red-lettered legend reads at the top, while the bottom corner offers more lascivious text: "no time to write hands full!"[6] It is a veritable Joycean picture of girlhood; a seaside Gerty with the "bad writing, am in a hurry" (*U* 4.413) habits of a Milly.

It was true that "the vocabulary of economic exchange defined the acts of courtship" (Bailey 5), and though this sort of connection was not new per se in social practices any more than it was in literary representation prior to the twentieth century (one thinks of the deft narrative devices of Jane Austen and Henry James), the system of economic exchange was changing as the so-called free market hegemonically marched into the western world, and so too did the corresponding definitions of "the acts of courtship." Just as money became less and less a means to an end, but rather an end in itself, so too did courting become an ongoing, teasing expenditure, not necessarily yielding a final product like marriage (thus, "the pleasure each will preen her for" rather than "the business each was bred to breed by" [*FW* 268.05–6]). *Finnegans Wake,* in which Richard Beckman says that "Joyce gives marriage an air of dreary farce" (89), pointedly recognizes the struggle: "These old diligences are quite out of date" (*FW* 167.26). "Dating was about competition," writes Beth Bailey in her study, *From Front Porch to Back Seat*: "In the 1920s, dating provided a new frontier for public competition through consumption, and in the 1930s it accepted competitive energies denied outlet elsewhere" (25–6). "One must sell it to some one" (*FW* 268.F1) *somewhere.* The marriage market became distinct from what has more recently been recognized as the "meet (or meat) market."

The market itself varies in form, and there are other sites for its manifestation besides those of technologies of entertainment. Education, for instance, as an institution, was quickly transformed into a supervised forum in which the desegregated could "go steady" and give or be given fraternity pins (an activity slyly termed "pinning"). The campus is central to Waller's study and others like it; and though by now the joke about a female student acquiring an "MRS" to complement her "BA" is a stale one, Joyce was already observing the trend in the *Wake*: "when I slip through my pettigo I'll get my decree and take seidens when I'm not ploughed first by some Rolando the Lasso, and flaunt on the flimsyfilmsies for to grig my collage juniorees" (*FW* 279.F1). Issy's is here the self-assertive voice of change, unable to take seriously what she wryly terms "[t]he law of the jungerl" (268.F3). The grandmotherly advice on courtship in the *Wake* (the "dative" case in "gramma's grammar" [268.17]) is undermined by Issy, whose wisecracks about "mens uration" (269.F3) and the "jinglish language" (275.F6) challenge the paired traditions of language education (perhaps especially its rules concerning "gender") and equally stolid moral standards for matrimony. Besides demonstrating the usual rejection of written grammar's constraints by Joyce's female characters, Issy is comparable in this regard to Lily in "The Dead," who recognizes that "palaver" (*D* 178) is often the tool of untrustworthy men. Both young women know the value of education on these matters.

In the successful date, a new ethical problem presents itself – or rather, an old one assumes a new form and importance for modern life. With all of these economic structures to interpersonal relationships, the definition of prostitution becomes disturbingly blurred, as desperately vague a state as being "about town," as John Corley is in "Two Gallants." While the collapse of ideologies which structured arranged marriages is echoed in "The Boarding House" and its epilogue within *Ulysses*, the so-called "raw new tradition" of chivalric courtship is nowhere more satirized than in "Two Gallants." Bob Doran, a naïf, pays his rent and board but wins a wife. By contrast, the "gallants" – a term Joyce always employs, like "artistes," with ribald connotations – are street-smart, and represent debased romantic knights insincerely sallying forth unto a half-baked quest. As a Sancho Panza to Corley's Don Quixote, Lenehan expresses extreme interest in Corley's pursuits, something which Corley is going to try to "pull off" with a certain woman whom he describes – with frank immodesty – as a "bit gone" on him. There is a significant separation of terms in their slang: the "ticklish job" Corley is undertaking is understood to be entirely different from the "mug's game" of "go[ing] with girls" (*D* 46–7). A "job" guarantees earnings; a "game" must have its losers. Revulsion, ultimately, is perhaps not too strong a word for what the reader experiences at the revelation of the gold coin, whose status is bitterly confirmed by Lily in "The Dead": "The men that is now is only all palaver and what they can get out of you" (*D* 178). Many young women know about this "mug's game," too (Cissy Caffrey does, if Gerty MacDowell does not).[7] Accordingly, the "Circe" brothel features as dancing music "My Girl's a Yorkshire Girl," a song of working-class romance ("Though she's a factory lass / And wears no fancy clothes" [*U* 15.4130–1]). Do prostitutes "date" – is it a job or a game? Can Corley be said to be *dating* (or having, as the prostitutes call out invitingly in *A Portrait*, "a short time" [*P* 86])? The problem recurs in modern narrative, from the machinations of Lorelei Lee in Anita Loos's *Gentlemen Prefer Blondes* (1925)[8] and the moves of the "professional dancing partners," Babs and Milly, of Evelyn Waugh's *A Handful of Dust* (1934) to present-day Hollywood saccharine (consider the hooker with the heart of gold in *Pretty Woman* [1990] or the equally scintillating dilemma concerning the retail value of fidelity in *Indecent Proposal* [1993]). Such parasitic interaction is what the *Wake* may in part mean by "the wrong type of date" (*FW* 309.17). Here in miniature we find a problem as central for the reader of Joyce as it is for the recipient of an invitation to a date: determining the distinction between meaning and intention.

The unsuccessful date, by contrast, is an image of pathetic ruin, directly comparable to a bad financial investment. While the modern urban affair between Brenda Last and John Beaver is in full swing in *A Handful of Dust* (ironically conducted under the pretenses of her studying economics: again the tie to education and "collage juniorees") while Brat's Club profits off of the "men in white ties and tail coats sitting by themselves and eating ... They are those who have been abandoned at the last minute by their women": "Chucked," in other words (67). *Ulysses* offers the direct equation of courtship with a monetary value, and in particular the case of failed courtship, in the news story, "Lovemaking in Irish £200 damages" (*U* 16.1240–1): Gifford recognizes the trial of Frank P. Burke, whose "rather circumstantial courtship" with one Maggie Delaney eventually cost him the sum Joyce mentions, and very probably some embarrassment besides (552). The stakes are sometimes high.[9]

Joyce's lovers (and would-be lovers) tend to use writing as an erotic invitation: Stephen has his "foul long letters" to Emma (*P* 97; though they are undelivered) and even Molly, so widely regarded as unlettered, remembers that her first date wrote to her, and still receives confirmation of appointments from Boylan's rather unimaginable pen. Bloom, who contemplates the "[b]est place for an ad to catch a woman's eye" (*U* 13.919), knows that some intentions have to be couched in metaphors, so the possible ad, "Wanted smart lady typist to aid gentleman in literary work" (*U* 9.326–7), conceals at least in part what sort of help is really wanted. Thus, the *Globe and Mail*'s Molly newspaper ad, however unMollyesque its author sounds ("slender," "in my 40s," and capable with punctuation), is not a phenomenon unanticipated by Joyce. For that matter, it is disarmingly easy to imagine the Blooms' marriage transplanted into the digital world of Tinder, Ashley Madison, and sexting. "[L]iterary work" is another idea that Joyce regularly imbues with a measure of prurience. Bloom occasionally fancies himself a literary man in the same way that he fancies himself a "gallant," and the fancy gives rise to Henry Flower, Bloom's *nom de plume et d'amour*, who has "the romantic Saviour's face with flowering locks, thin beard and moustache" and an "amorous tongue" (*U* 15.2483–4, 2487). It is this same man of letters who savours the rich prose and economic meditations of *Sweets of Sin*: "*All the dollarbills her husband gave her were spent in the stores on wondrous gowns and costliest frillies*" (*U* 10.608–9). Footloose Shem has his own "literary work" style of "ABORTISEMENT" (*FW* 181.33) in the *Wake*:

> Jymes wishes to hear from wearers of abandoned female costumes, gratefully received, wadmel jumper, rather full pair of culottes and onthergarmenteries, to start city life together. His jymes is out of job, would sit and write. He has lately committed one of the then commandments but she will now assist. Superior built, domestic, regular layer. (*FW* 181.27–32)

Note the conspicuous specification of "city life" here. The *Wake* enjoys parroting the mannerisms of classified ads (for another example, consider the style of question 5 of the quiz [141.08–26]) while effectively erasing their differences of purpose. Here are conflated requests for informative accounts of undergarments, a secretary, domestic help or assistant, and a female lover ("layer") or made-to-order bride. If "Molly" of the *Globe and Mail* faces a challenge in finding her "Ulysses," Jymes or Shem, whose words appear embarrassed within editorial brackets, will likely find it impossible to find someone to fit this extraordinary set of criteria (how can someone wear an abandoned costume? What kind of relationship moves between "then commandments" and "now assist"?). That this passage follows an indictment of plagiarism exacerbates the reader's anxiety about what is being advertised, and its both business-like and salacious tone and its hints of double-entendre and euphemism obscure more than they reveal. The fragmentary invitations of any "Personals" section in a newspaper or posted at any online dating service follow suit, alternating between seemingly straightforward data, rather codified expressions, and dubious descriptions (of age, physique, and of course prowess), and can make for reading as perplexing and entertaining as *Finnegans Wake*.

"Have you read Joyce?" he asked roguishly

> Let us cheer him up a little and make an appunkment for a future date.
> (*FW* 536.03–4)

The business of writing to initiate a date returns us to the burning question of how Joyce (in that multiple identity situation Foucault notes that an author status necessarily generates) can get dates. The new rituals of dating necessarily changed how courtship was written about, and, unusual though it may sound, dating has been changed by Joyce in turn. The "Molly" ad is a very minor example: there are some rather bizarre connections to (and commodifications of) Joyce in popular discourses on modern romance. This is only unusual, however, if it is forgotten that Joyce is one of those writers around whom and whose work miniature subcultures may and will form and faithfully revolve: the author's function (to carry on with Foucault) is in this instance to stand for a cause for communal interaction, intellectual or otherwise.[10] Thus, one finds Woody Allen joking in the famous movie line-up scene in *Annie Hall* about the pretentious couple behind him (just before he fantastically produces Marshall McLuhan with whose authority he quashes the blowhard):

> Probably on their first date, right? Probably met by answering an ad in *The New York Review of Books*: 'Thirtyish academic wishes to meet woman who's interested in Mozart, James Joyce, and sodomy.'

Here Joyce, like an astrological sign or an interest in water-skiing, signifies what the catechist narrator of "Ithaca" would call "common factors of similarity between their respective like and unlike reactions to experience" (*U* 17.18–19) – reasons for one's date-ability. One can actually be "rated and dated" by one's Joyce-ness; though, to be sure, it is not in this instance suggested as such a desirable quality.

The invocation of the catechist method is pertinent here, as it is in this style that Marilyn Hamel, in *Sex Etiquette: The Modern Woman's Guide to Mating Manners*, poses and answers questions like "Does a lady converse with strangers at bus stops, elevators, and the like?," "Who bankrolls the baby-sitter?" and "Do I need to be concerned about inflicting 'blue balls'?" Hamel's counsel to the Modern Woman worried about "floundering out of [her] depth with an intellectual type" recognizes the literary "common factors of similarity" as elusive (and, by implication, as desirable) as material wealth:

> Highbrow palaver is as much a flaunting of credentials as passing around photos of one's yacht. You'd feel completely at ease admitting you've never been on so grand a cabin cruiser and urging him to elaborate. Respond to his intellectual rhetoric in precisely that way. "Why, no, I haven't read Proust ... do tell me more, I'm fascinated." He'll be overjoyed to be your enlightener. (18)[11]

This may say as little for Proust as it does for the Modern Woman; but substituting "Joyce" for "Proust" strikes an unexpected resonance from within Joyce criticism. Derrida's wonderful (but little-heeded) remark about the "irresistible effect of naivety" to the claim of "having 'read' Joyce" ("Two Words" 148) pays some similar tribute to the slyness of a properly modest formulation: "Why, no, I've not read Joyce." Perversely, not having read Joyce is as universal as Joyce could have wished his writing to be; but it is the declaration that is subtly empowering in the warm exchange of eroticized intellectual "credentials."

These credentials surface in the most unlikely waters. In its 1997–8 season the NBC television network's public service announcement campaign entitled "The More You Know" sought to offer counsel on relevant issues to young adults. One of these spots offered advice to young men from sitcom actor David Schwimmer on the problem of date rape. Rather than employ criminal techniques, such as the infamous "date rape drug," Rohypnol (Flunitrazepam), Schwimmer advises instead, of all things, talking about *Finnegans Wake*. It cannot be serious advice; and yet the message is obviously serious. Chatting about the *Wake* is being offered not as a genuine cruiser's trump card, but as the craziest, furthest-flung yet still socially acceptable pretext for flirtation (could it be that the intoxicating *Wake* is a more amiable sort of drug?). Silly-sounding, perhaps – but if a television hunk suggests it, following here the advertising logic in full swing, it just might work. Just as it is in *Annie Hall*, in this ad a taste for Joyce is both absurd and sexy.

A more recent film, just as much a milestone in romantic pop culture for its audience's generation, I think, as *Annie Hall* was for its own, can claim to have a very Joycean sense of dating and romance. *Before Sunrise* (1995), directed by Richard Linklater, is a story of an impromptu date, an encounter on a train between characters played by actors Ethan Hawke and Julie Delpy, and a subsequent "walking out together" into Vienna. The narrative of the film bears a startling number of similarities to *Ulysses*, including impoverished poets, pub visits, mention of diseased cows, a cemetery scene, palmistry, a fugue of restaurant conversations, a marked preoccupation with time and its passing, and even a woman nodding off to sleep in the last shot. However, the most important trace of Joyce in this romance is the uncertainty which accompanies the meaning of the date itself; for they enjoy one another's company for a single day, 16 June, and contrary to the policy and paradigm of Hollywood happily-ever-after-ism, there is no clear indication that they will ever meet again, or that the intense bond is anything more than momentary.[12] The sense of connection is powerful, but equally ambiguous; emphatically Joycean.

There are other examples of Joyce's presence in popular romance culture, from Kate Bush's 1989 hit love song "The Sensual World"[13] to the famous cheesecake photo of Marilyn Monroe studiously looking into *Ulysses* (implicit message: glamorous sex symbols enjoy Joyce, too). A number of Joyce's letters to Nora have been reprinted across the internet as examples of "Classic Love Letters" – though not (yet) those letters which porn-screening browsers would block.[14] Joyce's cultural capital has had a suggestive tint to it since the recognition of *Ulysses* as a naughty read, and a number of subsequent writers, particularly Irish writers, have confessed to having consulted this infamous book for purposes of instruction mixed with delight. From this perspective, today's erotic fetishization of Joyce is a natural outgrowth of this persistent mystique.

Basking in the Boy and Girl Courtship Idea

Illouz concludes her analysis of the "romantic utopia" with a grand statement:

> Modernity has brought irretrievable losses in the meaning of love, most notably the connection between love and moral virtue and the dissolution of the commitment and stability of premodern love, but these losses are the price we pay for greater control over our romantic lives, greater self-knowledge, and equality between the sexes. (296)

Sufficient unto the date, it seems. The unclear use of "modernity" here is no aid to the reader's understanding, but I find the scheme of replacing one score of utopianism with another somewhat suspect. In addition, there is an unappealing acquiescence to the "meet/meat market" in the language here, which would not be out of place in a corporate financial report or bank commercial: "commitment and stability" and "these losses are the price we pay." Perhaps, though, it is only to be expected that, at least in a society in which material goods and lifestyles grow more and more interchangeable, the commodity commonly held to be least eligible for public bidding should turn out to be the most treasured items in a steady buyer's market. As the *Wake* has it, "[o]ne must sell it to some one, the sacred name of love" (*FW* 268.F1).

In Joyce there are sighs aplenty, a contrast always of dates missed, expected, and hoped for. However, a strong sense of the ridiculous resides within the resignations, as the sentimental strains of a *Wake*-phrase like "Lead us seek, lote us see, light us find, let us missnot Maidadate" (*FW* 267.01–2) illustrates. Fanciful Bloom smiles on the pairing of Stephen and the "lodestar" Miss Ferguson, but simultaneously entertains doubts as to "whether he could find much satisfaction basking in the boy and girl courtship idea," while Stephen himself, ever the romantic, acknowledges that deflowering a virgin is "the ambition of most young gentlemen" (*P* 208) but kicks himself too for the ambition: "O, give it up, old chap!" (*P* 213).

Fritz Senn once voiced to me his suspicion that devoted readers of Joyce are essentially lonely people. I would be amiss, however, were I to neglect to note in this conclusion the date of celebration, for among Joyceans (that buzzword which marks us as surely as would an astrological sign in a personals ad) there is always a mark to be made on the calendar. Bloomsday is our date with Joyce and with each other – and it is not the case that there is no romancing going on during this date with Joyce, for, to paraphrase the *Wake*, we all know we dote on him even unto date (see *FW* 395.31–2).

7
The Stephen Dedalus Diet

guide me by gastronomy (*FW* 449.11)

The word "diet" is surprisingly confounding for its various definitions: it signifies simply "food," and more specifically "one's habitual food," yet it is also a metaphenomenon, "a manner of sustenance, as regards the food eaten." But it is its own antithesis, too; for like Oscar Wilde's sly definition of modern culture as an understanding of which books one shouldn't read, "diet" also connotes the regulation or restriction of foods, the popularization of which usage accompanied the late nineteenth-century advent of diet pills and the expanding commercial discourse of weight management.[1] And while we are sampling from the *OED*'s smorgasbord, let us note that "diet" can signify "a day's journey; an excursion" as well as "a meeting formally arranged for discussion ... a conference, a congress." Joyce's beloved Skeat likewise gives "an assembly, a council" (169). It is thus entirely fitting to consider *Ulysses* as a dietary text, not only for its much-studied preoccupation with food, since Joyceans unfailingly gather on the sixteenth of June each year, serving to each other, consuming, and not infrequently regurgitating their ideas.

The famously gustatory introduction of Leopold Bloom seems to underline (or "relish") how dietetic a book *Ulysses* is, and while Mr and Mrs Bloom's respective acts of consumption and digestion are richly, sometimes lasciviously detailed, the same cannot be said for Stephen Dedalus, who appears to eat so woefully little in *Ulysses* as to beggar the materialist realism for which the novel has been both celebrated and deplored. Perhaps because abundance offers more immediate promise, critical studies have preferred to lunch with Bloom, that self-professed "stickler for solid food" (*U* 16.811), rather than scavenge with Stephen, and so discussions of the novel tend to present Bloom's digestive tracts as a schematic metaphor for the workings of the text and/or a picture of modernist health.[2] The explanation that this difference between these characters is simply a matter of thematic contrasts, in which the ascetic life of the mind is counterbalanced by the sensual life of the body, is not altogether satisfactory, since it reduces these characters to embodiments of Cartesian abstractions. Although Frank Budgen recounts Joyce's insistence on how his characters have minds and bodies because they are codependent phenomena,[3] a programmatic reading of *Ulysses* in which Bloom functions as a kind of refutation of Stephen assumes that while Joyce's characters all have both minds and bodies, some have more or less of one than the other.[4] Even more troubling, such a reading elides the fascinating paradoxes, contradictions, and inconsistencies nestled in the details of the characters and, I'd ultimately like to suggest, thereby simplifies the ethos, structure, and composition of Joyce's work to pedantic allegory and mythical totalization. I propose here a contrary reading of the novel as composed of anisometric eating habits and attitudes among characters who share only the need to eat, just as readers of *Ulysses* may all seek the nourishment of meaning but what they find has much to do with what they will and will not eat.[5] In particular I will argue that Stephen's apparent rejection of eating destabilizes interpretations that rely on either mimetic realism or allegory as frameworks.

Stephen's account to Bloom in "Eumaeus" of having last eaten "the day before yesterday" (*U* 16.1577) is something of an exaggeration, an exhibition of his (affected) disregard for such matters, but symptomatic of a larger problem for the equation of Joyce's fine culinary details with realism. A catalogue of what Stephen eats in *Ulysses* is not simply short but altogether vexing for its uncertainties. He partakes of a traditional Irish fry for breakfast in the Martello tower with Mulligan and Haines, of course, but exactly what does he consume? On offer are eggs, bread, butter, honey, milk, and tea (Haines announces that he is diluting Mulligan's strong tea with "two lumps each") but the single phrase "Stephen said as he ate" (*U* 1.374) employs the most generic, non-descriptive verb ("ate" and not, say, "munched" or "chewed" or "sipped"; more visceral terms which might suggest what kind of stuff is being eaten or perhaps even the degree of satisfaction or enjoyment taken) as a blank intransitive. A couple of pages later, Stephen "let honey trickle over a slice of loaf" (1.476–7), which detail is more savory than conclusive, since this action might smack of simply playing with one's food.

"If we could live on good food like that," Mulligan opines, "we wouldn't have the country full of rotten teeth and rotten guts" (1.411–12); a statement which implies that "we" (whomever that may include) *can't* live on good food like that, and yet this is the only solid food that Stephen is seen to eat throughout the novel. There's a liquid lunch at Mooney's, where, as Lenehan later recounts, Stephen was among those not sternly refusing to partake of strong waters, though this is one of those intriguing "offstage" moments in *Ulysses*, an event to which the reader is not invited, and there is no way for the reader to be certain what was consumed then and there. After that – if we set aside alcohol, something approximating coffee ("or whatever you like to call it" [*U* 16.1170]), and a cocoa – nothing, nil by mouth. And it might as well be added by way of clinical footnote that if Stephen that day has, like Bloom, a bowel movement, it is not represented.[6]

Yet may readers well recall our Stephen in his boyhood, merrily eating that "slim jim out of his cricketcap" (*P* 78) or munching from "a fat bag of gingernuts in his pocket" (*P* 53), and later proudly taking his family out to dinner with his essay prize money, purchasing "[g]reat parcels of groceries and delicacies and dried fruits" and "squares of Vienna chocolates" (*P* 82). Whatever happened to that healthy appetite?

Ultimately the drama of *A Portrait* pivots on what Stephen will not swallow and digest (be it muscatel grapes, sacramental wafer, or repressive ideologies). As a docile child he watches his father pour him sauce with the ambiguous promise of its curling his hair (*P* 25) and, to distract him from scandal and "bad language," "[heaps] up the food on Stephen's plate" and coaxes him to "Eat away now" (*P* 27). The best diet forms the best – and perhaps by extension, most pliable – subject. As Stephen matures in the course of *A Portrait*, the consumption of food becomes inherently associated with lust, pleasure distinct from aesthetic pleasure, bestial complacency, disgust, and shame. Recall the deflowering kiss from the prostitute:

> With a sudden movement she bowed his head and joined her lips to his and he read the meaning of her movements in her frank uplifted eyes. It was too much for him. He closed his eyes, surrendering himself to her, body and mind, conscious of nothing in the world but the dark pressure of her softly parting lips. They pressed upon his brain as upon his lips as though they were the vehicle of a vague speech; and between them he felt

an unknown and timid pressure, darker than the swoon of sin, softer than sound or odour. (*P* 85)

How strange it is that all of the five senses are evoked in this kiss but one, taste, the one that might most reasonably be expected to assume the lead in judging the experience. As the next chapter opens right after this passage, Stephen's belly speaks: "Stuff it into you" (*P* 86). His subsequent repentance begins with the recognition of his having "sunk to the state of a beast that licks his chaps after meat" (*P* 94).

Little surprise then, that Stephen's "applied Aquinas" aesthetic,[7] which eschews desire and loathing, likewise excludes consideration of taste (an exclusion implicit in the gesture of recognizing Lynch's having eaten dried cowdung as an experience removed from "normal natures" and so beneath discussion [*P* 172]). Such an aesthetic might be best satisfied by the genre of the still life, the well-laid table of uneaten food, or, to use his own example, an empty basket (and we might recall that young Stephen's first rejection of food –"[h]e sat looking at the two prints of butter on his plate but could not eat the damp bread" – occurs when he is "sick in [his] breadbasket" [*P* 10]). The community of meals leaves him alienated, glaring at the squalid remnants of tea in his family's impoverished household (137) and he imagines his love poems mocked by their subject with others "at breakfast amid the tapping of eggshells" (187). No wonder, then, that Stephen is not much of a table companion at the breakfast that begins *Ulysses*, just as Telemachus scornfully watches the suitors dine at the beginning of *The Odyssey*.[8]

With what disquiet comes the notice that this man who apparently has so little to do with eating seems to be always talking of it? Recall Stephen's quotable epigrams, aphorisms, and other displays of wit: the sow eating her farrow, the parable of the plums, the riddle of the crocodile set to eat the child. It turns out that *The Works of Master Dedalus* is ... *a cookbook!*[9]

His Hungry Will Be Done

By these lights we might reassess Joyce's remark to Budgen that Stephen "has a shape that can't be changed" (Budgen 107) to understand that Stephen can gain no weight: flying as he believes he must past those nets, Stephen has good reason to shun any extra weight, and so he eats, as they say, like a bird. In this too, Bloom is more down to earth, for one of his oft-remembered and more precise titbits of scientific knowledge is the rate of acceleration of (terrestrial) falling bodies, itself the phenomenon of weight, which he tellingly associates with eating habits when he skeptically considers faddish Fletcherism: "thirtytwo feet per second per second" (*U* 8.57–8) becomes "thirtytwo chews to the minute" (*U* 8.360). Yet for all this interest, Bloom has a shape that cannot help but change, and the multiple guises that prevent him from completing the statement "I AM A" (*U* 13.1256–65) and require more costume changes in "Circe" than anyone else in the chapter ought to be borne in mind when puzzling over his impossible dimensions and body weight as they are reported in "Ithaca."

Vike Plock has shown that Bloom's diet-consciousness reflects popular attitudes of the period ("Modernism's Feast on Science" 30–42), and Aida Yared has made the claim that Bloom's synaesthesia (most notably the gustatory variations) "elicits, in the reader, the synaesthesia of reading with autonomic sensations" (476). Stephen's rather less temperate outlook, so singularly out of step with these attitudes, may even signal a dysaesthesia that those who enjoy the novel would rather not experience. It might be argued, though, that those who queasily turn away from *Ulysses*, unable to stomach any more of it, should be credited as admirably sensitive readers.

Henry Staten has plausibly suggested that Bloom's understanding of life coming down to "everybody eating everyone else" (*U* 7.214) points to a larger thematic and epistemic principle in *Ulysses*, an appreciation of "the pure transitivity of the eater-eaten relation, a phenomenon that would manifest itself at the grammatical level as the reversibility of subject and object. In this reciprocal devouring, everyone is both eater and eaten" (383). However neatly Hegelian such a view of the world may be, it has an indisputably violent and mercenary basis: a dog-eat-dog world. Stephen's unease with this ethos can be seen in his fixation on vampirism and perhaps his refusal of food represents a tacit dissent from it. His declaration of "non serviam" works both ways: he will not serve, but neither will he be ungrudgingly served (to Bloom's urging he eat the proffered bun in the cabman's shelter, he merely answers, "Couldn't" [*U* 16.788]). In listing their "divergent" views, the "Ithaca" chapter explicitly links "the importance of dietary and civic selfhelp" (*U* 17.28–9). Stephen's conception of "selfhelp" is so determinedly un- and anti-institutional as to negate the term, itself a product of the growing empire of advertising of which Bloom is a part. Bloom likewise stipulates "regular meals as the *sine qua non* for any kind of proper work" (*U* 16.812–13), a kind of categorical imperative that seems a leftover from his utopian promises and decrees in "Circe" and thus another net that Stephen will at least try to fly past.

Again, if we see Bloom as the "heroic" model in contrast to whose practical outlook and lifestyle Stephen's own are diminished as youthful, obstinate, idealistic, and so on, we may perforce accept and even endorse "everybody eating everyone else," without appreciating how as a theme it conflicts with that of hospitality (albeit hospitality so vexingly declined). One of the crucial if perhaps underappreciated differences between Homer's epic and Joyce's is that the latter climaxes with an invited guest – an invitation declined as promptly as the offer of a bun – rather than a massacre of squatting usurpers. As Yen-Chen Chuang, writing about the ethical problem of eating the other, observes, the mouth – and in this context we might say the entire digestive system – "bespeaks a contested site of ethical discourse charged with deprivation, nutrition, hospitality and hostility."

Such terms inexorably lead into Irish history, where they find drastic connotations. Terry Eagleton has pointedly asked where the Famine is in Joyce,[10] and though some critics have discerned rather indirect and in some cases tenuous allusions to it,[11] I see two explicit references: the first, perhaps not surprisingly, is its fleeting enumeration among the index of well-nursed grudges that the Citizen casts as history in "Cyclops" (see *U* 12.1365–6), but the second is of greater interest here. Though it is not always clear just which of the hallucinations and phantasms that come and go bump in the night in "Circe" are perceived by whom (not unlike the problem of who can see and hear the king's ghost in *Hamlet*), Stephen Dedalus does see Old Gummy Granny, "the deathflower of the potato blight on her breast" (*U* 15.4579–80). He exclaims: "Aha! I know you, gammer! Hamlet, revenge! The old sow that eats her farrow!" (*U* 4582–3). Accordingly, the reader's thoughts may leap to the fox burying his grandmother (rather than eating her, which would seem both more natural and logical)[12] or to Stephen's horrific rejection of his mother as "chewer of corpses" (*U* 1.278; see also 15.4214) or to the sacred relic of Bloom's mother, that overloaded signifier, the potato.[13] And of course there are Mother Ireland, a.k.a. Mother Grogan, she who makes tea and brings milk; Hamlet and his mother; the pig that the Jew is forbidden to eat; the Freudian slip (lurking in the Old Testament language) of a son declaring to "know" his mother; and so on. The conflation of famine with motherhood is in fact a web of associations which, like most many-stranded, delicately constructed webs, only comes to our attention when we have bungled into it, and then endeavour to extricate ourselves. Old Gummy Granny might seem less a "character" in the novel than an allegorical figure, but the usual rules of allegory do not apply: there is no direct, ineluctable transubstantiation from figure to meaning, no clear course of instruction or enlightenment but rather a confusing array of possibilities, too many to digest. One can starve at the banquet table.

It is hard to imagine how Joyce, or for that matter any Irish writer, might meaningfully remedy a perceived absence of such an important subject by inserting some notice or mention of the Famine, and thereby reducing it to incidental data.[14] Catastrophe reveals how famished is the language that seeks to articulate or contain it – this is a truism, certainly, and perhaps even a paradox, but its repetition may give necessary comfort just as readily as it poses the problem for the writer. One of the most plausible and popular alternative strategies for discourse is allegory, and yet it comes down to a more or less covert substitution.[15] Such an approach runs the risk of either diluting or overintensifying the nutrition it wants to deliver, however, and – in this allegorical view of allegory – approaches force-feeding, with its inherent absurdity and cruelty. I admit that I don't see how, as one critic has suggested, "Bloom's experience with Bella is an extended metaphor for the Famine" (Roos 191): that seems to me a most "extended" sort of metaphor. Bloom's blithe if idiosyncratic repetitions of the bromide "you are what you eat" can be rejoined with Beckett's instructive warning: "The danger is in the neatness of identifications" ("Dante ... Bruno. Vico ... Joyce" 3). Our problem, then, comes to this: how to reconcile the abundance of meaning and the general affirmation ("yes") of quotidian life in *Ulysses* with this abstainer parading his abstention ("no") about its pages?

Although the hunger strike is not exactly unheard of in Ireland, and it would seem that Stephen has plenty of ideological and personal grievances to oppose in such a way, I do not propose to suggest that this is the reason that Stephen won't or can't eat – at least, not on the narrative level of the text – for precisely the variety and differences of those grievances, like the overwhelming diversity of interpretations available in Old Gummy Granny's appearance, problematize if they do not outright prohibit the exclusive selection of a coherent one for either acceptance or resistance. Rebel though he may be, Stephen hardly has the panache required to answer questions about what he is rebelling against with Brando's "what have you got?" but in any case the resistance to eating as eating, as acceptance of and participation in "everybody eating everyone else" or what Jacques Derrida calls "*carno-phallogocentrism*,"[16] transcends a historically localized situation. A hunger strike is a tactic, and Stephen has no tactics, apart maybe from the silence-cunning-and-exile triad, none of which in themselves requires or explains skipping meals.

Nor is Stephen's simply a case of Prufrockian persicophobia,[17] the *au fait* anxiety of a love-starved man given to long, lonesome walks but fatally unable to defend himself against fresh fruit. It is entirely possible that Stephen won't stay at Eccles Street for fear of having the melon about which he has hitherto only dreamt at last held against his face (*U* 3.365–8).[18] There is much to be gleaned in reading *Ulysses* this way – that is, as a kind of romance, a tale of sexual intrigue, with all of the attendant twists and turns of sexual politics – but overindulging with the sweets of sin necessitates neglecting the other food groups. On a larger scale we are faced again with the Old Gummy Granny problem, and we do not take in the whole of Stephen's "no" (quite like Bartleby's somewhat more explicit "I would prefer not to") when we are forced to select one allegorical channel of interpretation in isolation from others. Although there are elements of both the hunger striker and the sexually repressed in his make-up, neither entirely answers the question of why Stephen won't eat.[19] The question points us beyond the shape of the character to the shape of the novel itself.

Nuckling Down to Nourritures

In 1980, the year he died, Roland Barthes was teaching a class on "the preparation of the novel" at the Collège de France, a fascinating exploration of the readying and steadying of oneself for the task. Among the various elements of the novelist's procedure and environment that he considers is diet, something heretofore neglected "as if this were the ultimate inconsequential detail, so very insignificant that it would never be worth the effort of discussing it" (228). He then turns to Nietzsche on "the question of nutriment," wondering "how to nourish yourself so as to attain your maximum of strength, of virtù in the Renaissance style, of moraline-free virtue?" Barthes remarks

> on how it's possible to fantasize a style of food in accordance with the style of the work ... what we lack is not a *sociology* of Food (some do exist) but its Philosophy, or its Philosophies – not on the scale of a religion (fastings, vegetarianisms, etc.) but that of the individual: the more or less analogical connection between a food system and a fantasmatic or, more precisely,

> a symbolic system ... I must stress this: symbolic meaning, not necessarily of a specific food (the issue of "taboos" is somewhat different), but of systems, of dietary styles, the *gestalt* of menus (the way in which food is consumed). (*Preparation of the Novel* 228–9)

He then turns to his touchstone example, Proust, who, at the end of his life (trying to finish his novel), "went on a diet: nothing more than a little milky coffee" (229).

The topic will seem odd if not out of bounds to anyone who subscribes even slightly to the view of authorial and intentional fallacy expressed and embodied – one of Joyce's most layered ironies – by George Russell in the "Scylla and Charybdis" episode ("what is it to us how the poet lived?" [*U* 9.185]). The Shakespeare whose life and material circumstances Stephen so vividly imagines seems unconcerned with food: others, such as the "canvasclimbers" worked in as "local colour" "chew their sausages" (*U* 9.156–7). And yet Joyce stages Russell's exit to the offices of the *Irish Homestead* where the real Russell was to be found regularly and with evangelical fervour writing about proper diet. For example, in 1906 he damned tea as "the destroyer of the nervous system, the cup which cheers for half an hour and makes one gloomy for the next two, which does not inebriate but sends its devotees to the asylum"[20] – and of course tea is something Stephen does consume. Symbolic and nervous systems are materially equated in both Joyce's Shakespeare and Barthes's Proust, in the inspiration of sausages and coffee, or for that matter in the absence thereof, in the need for them. Their proof lies in the (not) eating.

The audience may eat but the artist diets – this is the conclusion to be drawn from synthesizing Barthes's thoughts here with those of his most famous (or infamous) essay of twelve years before, "The Death of the Author." There, you will recall, he posits that the author "dies" as the text is produced and the reader born. The author's diet, then, is a form of starving oneself.

Barthes's mention of extant sociologies of Food is in part a coy reference to his own contribution to the field, written twenty years earlier, in which he observes that "modern nutritional science" and the discourse in which "food is henceforth *thought out*, not by specialists, but by the entire public" are really about power, since the design and consciousness of a society's diet constitute far-reaching social economies ("Towards a Psychosociology" 25). The popularization (i.e., the commercial fetishization) of the "diet" represents a largely illusory form of self-empowerment, typical of a predatory economy, in which subscribers to a particular formula reify those very standards of body image, lifestyle, and various behavioural codifications that so distress them.

Vike Plock highlights Joyce's awareness of "an unacknowledged overlap between his fiction and the self-help movement of the Revivalist period," even if that awareness takes the form of embarrassment at his fiction being printed within a "disagreeable vicinity of dietary and self-improvement pieces in the *Irish Homestead*," pieces including "such inspiring titles as 'The Importation of Fraudulent Butter,' 'Frozen Milk and Health' and 'Bacteria in Milk.'"[21] Just as he casts a critical eye on the commodification of the body via feminine beauty products (in "Nausicaa"), photography modelling, and bodybuilding techniques (Eugen Sandow), all of which have been amply studied by critics, Joyce invites readers to see the bids for power in this fast-growing "selfhelp" dietary discourse, and at a deeper level than the agricultural nationalism of Russell. *Ulysses* offers the kind of Philosophy of Food that Barthes appeals to, a contemplation of not just "the way in which food is consumed" but the ways in which we think and talk about the way in which food is consumed, and even about the way in which food is *not* consumed, and the ways in which we do not think and talk about that. Such a Philosophy of Food is in effect a Philosophy of History, and the indelible problem of maximal comprehension (in Pound's phrase, "including history") can be addressed in these terms: first, that one cannot eat everything, and indeed that it is debatable whether history is better understood as what we consume or what gets left on the plate; and second, an attempt to awake from the nightmare of history, if history is understood as sensory recollection, might assume the form of autostarvation, a refusal to consume.

The same year that *Ulysses* appeared, Franz Kafka published a story of the insatiable self-demands of the hunger artist: "only he could simultaneously be the spectator completely satisfied with his hungering" (205–6). This impossible demand (that only the self can be the other) is reminiscent of Stephen's hunger for attention and his reflexive rejection of it: "Speaking about me. What did he say? What did he say? What did he say about me? Don't ask" (*U* 7.789–90). A kind of bulimic narcissism, we might nod and say, and think of Tom Stoppard's memorable characterization of Joyce as a man eager that the world should take notice of his indifference to it (23). But instead of dwelling on Stoppard's Joyce, let us consider Stephen's Kafka. (By interesting coincidence, Kafka's character is ultimately buried beneath the straw of his own cage and replaced there by a panther, a fearful prospect that Stephen would recognize.) Here are two tellers of parables that are not parables, seeming allegories without clear or demonstrable exegetical frameworks. Stephen's "parable of the plums" (especially under its other title, *A Pisgah-Sight of Palestine*) offers as plummy a mix of near-salaciousness, near-farce, and near-transcendence (but not quite) as one experiences in Kafka, but also the very image of the antitheses Flo and Anne slurping and spitting from above suggests near-eating, near-communion (but not quite). Stephen is a hunger artist, a more radical aesthetic position than the one announced by the equally haughty "Katharsis-Purgative" of "The Holy Office" ("Through me they purge a bellyful"), though perforce far less prolific.

Besides helping explain his conspicuous lack of literary production, Stephen's diet in *Ulysses* prevents Joyce's novel from fully becoming an allegory, and keeps the reader from satiety. Just as his role as the disembodied mind in counterpoint to the fleshier Blooms is impossible to take seriously both because it defies the novel's (admittedly fickle) mimetic realism and because it is so often belied by events, most spectacularly by a sock to the jaw (Carr acting as a Dr Johnson to Stephen's stone), Stephen's unchangeable shape will not be digested in a comprehensive reading of the novel, not even by *allegoresis*. He makes such a reading untenable.

Multifarious Aliments

The indeterminacy of what Stephen eats is in some respects symptomatic of the very textual indeterminacy that has variously troubled and excited readers, editors, and scholars of Joyce from the publication of the first chapters of *Ulysses* unto today, and we often feel compelled to seize upon whatever fragmentary clues we can find to try to limit this indeterminacy. Just as characters in the novel find and brush away unexpected crumbs and clinging twigs, readers try to figure out how such traces came to be there at all.

Part of this trail of crumbs is a possible clue about what Stephen eats, namely the "broken biscuits" that Stephen only semi-soberly discovers in his pockets while searching for a handout for Corley in "Eumaeus": "About biscuits he dimly remembered. Who now gave them he wondered or where was or did he buy" (*U* 16.190–1). Conjectures can be made about where those recherché biscuits come from, but no certainties seem available. For example, perhaps Stephen bought them in

Mooney's and is at this point still so drunk that he's simply forgotten, or maybe he has not emptied those pockets since the last time he wore that coat, a date prior to 16 June, whenever it may have been. Or maybe there is some likewise muddled recollection of Stephen's amid the doggerel conclusion of "Oxen of the Sun": "Item, curate, couple of cookies for this child" (*U* 14.1542). This might represent Stephen's fumbling through his pockets as he leaves the hospital, but it does not in itself clarify where he came by the cookies in the first place.

Still another tantalizing though phantasmal possibility occurs to me, for there is an empty biscuit tin to be found elsewhere in Dublin that same day. Earlier drafts of the "Cyclops" episode surprisingly include Stephen in Barney Kiernan's pub. It is very hard to fathom what he would be doing there, but it may be no worse a guess than any other to suppose he was helping himself to some biscuits. If we entertain this possibility, and accept what in film would be called a continuity error, we begin to see the novel not as a cohesive, singular, symmetrical whole but as a text with sometimes conflicting composition impulses, a *Ulysses* in which alternate and in some instances competing versions of *Ulysses* are unsettlingly present.

When in *Finnegans Wake* the hopelessly shape-changing hero is said to have "killed his own hungery self in anger as a young man" (126.22–3), Joyce may be confessing to his own starving of Stephen in *Ulysses*, admitting in a book of ever-changing forms his dilemma with a character whose shape could not be changed. In looking at the phrase again, we can see that Joyce does not say a "shape that Stephen cannot change," but employs the passive voice, making it unclear whether it is the author who somehow finds himself unable to change Stephen's shape, or whether the character has some sort of inexplicable agency (think of Molly's beseeching to "Jamesy" [*U* 18.1128]) with which to resist any changes, or whether perhaps these two possibilities ultimately come to the same thing. Stephen is a ghost in the machine and will not be exorcised.

Joyce's works inspire awe and sometimes terror for being all-consuming, and his characterization of the "peristaltic" composition of "Lestrygonians" has been adopted and extended within criticism and textual studies to understand his subsequent writing methods, most recently by Aida Yared (writing of *Ulysses*) and Dirk Van Hulle (writing of *Finnegans Wake*).[22] The American poet Robert Duncan admires how the *Wake* "has intestinal fortitude, true to an internal chemistry. Its seasons are rounds of digestion" (206). For all the obvious truth in these characterizations, there is a countercurrent in his work, which the possible deletion of the origin of Stephen's biscuits (part of the continued starving of the resistant character, the Hunger Artist), like other discernible traces of earlier drafts and excisions, may suggest. Although the invaluable *Finnegans Wake* notebooks confirm – if there were any serious doubt – how accretive and assimilative Joyce's method of composition is, they also reveal the surprising amount of raw material that was not digested into the *Wake*, and that genetic scholarship is faced with a poorly understood technique of refusal. Then too there is the blunt fact that so many readers turn away from these dense books, finding nothing there, the whole thing inedible, not unlike the *Wake*'s image of an empty stomach eating itself: "all this time of totality secretly and by suckage feeding on his own misplaced fat" (*FW* 79.12–13).

Among Joyce's collection of "epiphanies" is this scene, which culminates in a gesture that seems anything but precise:

> MRS JOYCE– (crimson, trembling, appears at the parlour door) ... Jim!
> JOYCE– (at the piano) ... Yes?
> MRS JOYCE– Do you know anything about the body? ... What ought I do? ... There's some matter coming away from the hole in Georgie's stomach ... Did you ever hear of that happening?
> JOYCE– (surprised) ... I don't know...
> MRS JOYCE– Ought I send for the doctor, do you think?
> JOYCE– I don't know ... What hole?
> MRS JOYCE– (impatient) ... The hole we all have ... here. (points)
> (Scholes and Kain 29)

The unknown hole, it turns out, is in the ulcerous text, "a hole through which its meanings hemorrhage," as Maud Ellmann has it (*The Nets of Modernism* 5). Joyce points us to that horizon where nature and ideology become most difficult to separate, the precipice to which postmodern theory will not venture. Despite our often reasonable aversions to general statements about the human condition, there is, after all, a word known to all men, and that word is *hunger*. If Joyce acknowledges that everyone must eat, he also less explicitly reminds us that not everyone does. The Great Hunger transcends mimetic representation and becomes "the hole we all have ... here": a hole in the textual fabric of *Ulysses*, a book of eating and not eating, and which may tantalize and even satisfy but never satiates.

Conclusion: Means Without End

And you'll see if I'm selfthought. (*FW* 147.08–09)

A book's "conclusion" may or may not be useful, but such conclusions are, by convention, all about usefulness. They generally seek to underscore how instrumental the book is for approaching or understanding a subject. This book has examined what it means to think of a book as "instrumental" at all, and what shapes and forms "useful" reading practices can, do, and might take. Joyce, whose complex works demand of their readers an open mind and a dedicated work ethic, has provided a focus for this book's probings of the differences, real or imagined, between "literary" and "functional" texts, between "interpretation" and "use." I hope that my "use" of Joyce has opened up some new ways of reading him, and suggests a larger point: while current literary scholarship habitually professes to value texts by the variety and depth of readings that they engender, polyvalency and ambiguity have been the traits by which these things are measured. Adaptability, broadly conceived, ought to be as weighty a criterion, and thus emphasize – as I have tried to do with the working taxonomy of theocratic, aristocratic, and democratic readings outlined in this book's introduction, and in the many different "uses" for Joyce proposed and examined in the subsequent chapters – the performative and selective nature of reading. The boggling degrees of polyvalency and ambiguity in Joyce have long been admired; let us now acknowledge how remarkably adaptable he is too – he has so many uses.

Those traditional literary and scholarly textual functions of quotation, annotation, translation, and editing excite most debate when the texts at issue widen the possible range of such functions. We are still quoting and annotating and translating and editing Joyce, never determining an absolutely satisfying method for any of these practices, always coming up with new approaches for all of them. New media and ever more complex questions of access (as Joyce studies expand globally) imbue the debates and new directions for such methods with a nervous sort of urgency, even as we grimly realize that so many fairly basic and preliminary tasks remain undone. As I have tried to present them here, these textual functions are inextricable from one another, and the future understanding of them is likewise inextricable from what "uses" we attribute to and imagine for Joyce's texts.

The last three chapters, gameful readings of Joyce in the Wittgensteinian sense of "game," by no means represent an exhaustion of such possibilities (what I have called, without judgment, "appropriations"), and I invite readers to come up with and explore other readings of Joyce as "self-help" author. "Pop psychology," the self-help subject *par excellence*, is an excellent example. In her sociologist's overview of the rise of self-help books, Eva Illouz observes that

> Psychoanalysis and psychology were gold mines for the advice industry because they were wrapped in the aura of science; because they could be highly individualized (fitting any and all individual particularities); because they could address a wide variety of problems, thereby enabling product diversification; and because they seemed to offer the dispassionate gaze of science on tabooed topics. With the expanding market of consumers, the book industry and women's magazines avidly seized a language that could accommodate both theory and story, generality and particularity, nonjudgmentality and normativity. (52–3)

How modernist is the promise of a "dispassionate gaze of science on tabooed topic," and how Joycean the notion of a language that encompasses "both theory and story, generality and particularity." As we have seen, *Finnegans Wake* is an entire "advice industry" of its own, and it repeatedly, ironically questions the premises and terms of all the advice it extends.[1] Psychoanalysis gets the occasional drubbing:

> But this is no laughing matter. Do you think we are tonedeafs in our noses to boot? Can you not distinguish the sense, prain, from the sound, bray? You have homosexual catheis of empathy between narcissism of the expert and steatopygic invertedness. Get yourself psychoanolised!

> – O, begor, I want no expert nursis symaphy from yours broons quadroons and I can psoakoonaloose myself any time I want (the fog follow you all!) without your interferences or any other pigeonstealer. (*FW* 522.34–5)

The *Wake*'s attention to psychoanalysis is in evidence from the earliest stages of its composition. The phrase "psoakoonaloose myself," which appears in an April 1926 draft (Rabaté, "The Fourfold Root of Yawn's Unreason" 389), anticipates the title of Joseph Ralph's book, *How to Psycho-Analyse Yourself* (1937). Thus Joyce not only kept abreast of trends in the dissemination of psychoanalysis – they were, to use Illouz's phrase, "gold mines" for Joyce's composition – but at the same time was, in an idiosyncratic way, something of a leader in this growing popularization. For instance, the *Wake* words "behaviourising" (110.25) and "behaviouristically" (149.25–6) show Joyce's bemused awareness of the psychological doctrine "behaviorism" that became popular in the 1930s. And the notion of "sanity," as modern a fiction as one can find, seems never to disappear from Joyce's mind. *Ulysses* is packed with expressions of mental disorder, and *Finnegans Wake*, as the above excerpt demonstrates, is obsessive about its own obsessions. Shakespeare, according to Haines in "Wandering Rocks," is "the happy huntingground of all minds that have lost their balance" (*U* 10.1061–2), and the Englishman diagnoses Stephen as a psychological type or category: "I am sure he has an *idée fixe* ... Such persons always have" (*U* 10.68–70; ellipsis added). The influence of books may alternately be thought of as nurturing (the premise of bibliotherapy) or damaging (the premise of *Don Quixote* and of censorship). Haines naturally disregards how enthralled he is by his own *idées fixes*: the pursuit of "real Irish cream" (10.1094) and his fears of panthers in the night and German Jews.[2] In fact, there is not a single character in *Ulysses* so untouched by any quirk, delusion, or mania as to be a picture of psychological normality (or normativity).

Psychological self-help is, as I've said, only one plausible lens through which we might read Joyce. Legal advice, another enduring topic for guide publishing, is also a hobbyhorse of Joyce's. The author's own litigious ways and the legal dilemmas faced by *Ulysses* (piracy, censorship) find bizarre counterparts in his works: Denis Breen (another conspicuous picture of a mind that seems to have lost its balance) scurries for counsel as to how to sue an unknown party for an obscure slander, while most of the bar banter in Barney Kiernan's amounts to "arguing about the law and history" (12.1235), with reference to the Zaretsky swindle case as well as the "slander" on Breen. For his part, Bloom tends to treat legislation as a matter of fancy and speculation, imagining laws for confirming death against premature burial and keeping (for some reason) "a sealed prophecy (never unsealed)" about "the consequences of the passing into law of William Ewart Gladstone's Home Rule bill of 1886 (never passed into law)" (17.1787–90). The court scene in "Circe" and trial motif in *Finnegans Wake* point to the drama and anxiety in judicial proceedings, part of the larger preoccupation with public speaking discussed in chapter 5.

Or there is health advice, perhaps the oldest subject of manuals. Young Stephen in *A Portrait* is an observer of symptoms: "And when Dante made that noise after dinner and then put her hand to her mouth: that was heartburn" (*P* 8). Sensitive and sickly, the boy notes the way that language becomes imprecise and euphemistic when it comes to illness: "Sick in your breadbasket" (10) and "Terrible thing to have the collywobbles!" (18). In "Oxen of the Sun," probably the most laborious episode for a reader of *Ulysses*, the loud and convoluted views on gynecological practices exchanged among drunken (male) medical students while, in the background, a woman suffers a protracted childbirth, do not seem to have any unqualified authorial endorsement. Medical guides and homely almanacs are blended in the *Wake* as "the hidebound homelies of creed crux ethics. Watsch yourself tillicately every morkning in your bracksullied twilette. The use of cold water, testificates Dr Rutty, may be warmly recommended for the sugjugation of cungunitals loosed" (*FW* 525.01–05). The *Wake is*, after all, a do-it-yourself guide to reincarnation, isn't it?

Or, a little further along on the spectrum of readerly desperation, there is money management. Before he initially agreed to publish *Dubliners* in 1905, and also after he eventually did publish it in 1914, Grant Richards was a "self-help" publisher, and the fourth volume of the "How To" series published by Richards, Henry Warren's *How to Choose Your Banker: A Manual for Customers and Investors* (1900), concludes with the strange gesture so often found in self-help guides, a confession of how self-evident is the answer to the guide's own question, how easily is the puzzle of the title solved: "the customer, of course, should give the preference to the bank ... which offers him the greatest guarantee for his deposit. There should be no difficulty in selecting the right bank" (172). This wisdom is very much on the order of Mr Deasy's counsel to Stephen, the Shakespearean quotation we have already discussed: "*Put but money in thy purse*" (*U* 2.239). If Deasy seems more sententious

Polonius than scheming Iago, he ought to say, "Neither a borrower nor a lender be," which if not quite the same sentiment as what he does say is no less dispiriting. Countless such wearying bromides affirm each other: "it takes money to make money," "a penny saved is a penny earned," and so on. Though the exchange between Stephen and Mr Deasy is well known and much discussed, it is worth reproducing part of it here:

> – *I paid my way. I never borrowed a shilling in my life*. Can you feel that? *I owe nothing*. Can you?
>
> Mulligan, nine pounds, three pairs of socks, one pair brogues, ties. Curran, ten guineas. McCann, one guinea. Fred Ryan, two shillings. Temple, two lunches. Russell, one guinea, Cousins, ten shillings, Bob Reynolds, half a guinea, Koehler, three guineas, Mrs MacKernan, five weeks' board. The lump I have is useless.
>
> – For the moment, no, Stephen answered.
>
> Mr Deasy laughed with rich delight, putting back his savingsbox.
>
> – I knew you couldn't, he said joyously. But one day you must feel it. We are a generous people but we must also be just.
>
> – I fear those big words, Stephen said, which make us so unhappy. (*U* 2.253–64)

Joyce's fascinations with debts, financial and literary, his own and those of others, themselves constitute a kind of substructure to his works, *Ulysses* perhaps most of all, and there is a significant body of commentary on what might be called his many and various cultural capital venture risks.[3] The narrative language ironically pampers Deasy with its "rich delight" and later dancing coins and like characterizations and conceits. What I want to underscore here is the strangeness of Deasy's question: "Can you feel that?" Does the declaration of being debt-free express a *feeling*? This is precisely the sort of suggestive language favoured by financial counsellors and bank advertisements.[4]

Joyce's works are of course filled with borrowers and lenders, several of whom make free with financial advice to others.[5] "The Irish borrower must be either extremely careless or remarkably ignorant of the value of money," concludes Warren (55), who also wrote *How to Deal with Your Banker* and *Banks and Their Customers*. Comparing dividends from English and Irish banks, he remarks, with slightly puzzling syntax: "It certainly looks as though the Irish borrower pays very full rates. Perhaps they are more unsophisticated and trustful than we in the Emerald Isle" (54–5). However that may be, Joyce by no means condemns debtorship, and relations between his characters are marked rather than measured by loans and borrowings.[6] Just as Deasy's claim about Ireland having no Jews ("she never let them in" [2.442]) is belied by the introduction of Bloom two chapters later, his admiration of the Englishman's proud boast *"I paid my way"* (2.251) doesn't jive with the previous chapter's picture of Haines, who fears for his country's economic future and whose only contribution to the settling of the milk bill is the smiling advice, "pay up and be pleasant" (2.449).

Evidence of Joyce's interest in popular guides on this subject includes the last of "the world's twelve worst books" listed in "Circe," *"Pennywise's Way to Wealth"* (which may echo such titles as Thomas Tryon's *The Way to Get Wealth* [1702] or Benjamin Franklin's *Way to Wealth, or Poor Richard Improved* [1795]),[7] and one of the books on Bloom's bookshelf: *"The Useful Ready Reckoner* (brown cloth)" (17.1366). "Ready Reckoner" is a fairly generic title in use in publishing since the eighteenth century – but we might connect Bloom's book with (if perhaps not identify it as) John Henry Norman's 1893 *Ready Reckoner,* which proposes itself "a stepping-stone to the science of money" (viii). Its full title is *A Ready Reckoner of the World's Foreign and Colonial Exchanges with the Aid of Less than 2000 Figures Whereby 756 Tables of Exchange, Consisting of from 13,800 to 200,000 Figures Each, Can Be Dispensed With.* Bloom's various get-rich schemes, especially those detailed in "Ithaca" (17.1657–1753), find encouragement in texts such as these, precursors of *The Wealthy Barber* and *Think and Grow Rich.*

Though it has been less studied, financial advice is also a theme in *Finnegans Wake,* which meditates in its anguished, absurd way on the "dime-cash problem" (149.14) and "the use of money" (421.16). Phrases copied into a 1929 notebook, "earn while you learn" (VI.B.4.185) and "my capital is safe" (VI.B.4.211), are illustrative of the sort of catchwords that Joyce collected for this purpose. The fables in *Finnegans Wake* that he was revising at this time offer contrasting images of the impecunious wretch (the gracehoper, the Gripes) and the fiscally responsible investor in the future, sure of his returns (the ondt, the Mookse). Joyce is playing with rather than inventing a traditional "use" of such fables: that of the ant and grasshopper is often used to promote a familiar kind of political economy. A 1930s Disney cartoon, in which the hard-working ants have a very CCCP-like banner, is one colourful example, and more recently, a 2010 *Financial Times* article adapted Aesop's fable to fashion an account of the imbalanced global economy: "Today, the ants are Germans,

Chinese and Japanese, while the grasshoppers are American, British, Greek, Irish and Spanish. Ants produce enticing goods grasshoppers want to buy." Whereas the original fable's moral was "Idleness brings want," the moral for this neoliberal story is "If you want to accumulate enduring wealth, do not lend to grasshoppers." The *Wake* is considerably more ambivalent, casting ant and grasshopper as eternal twins, defined by each other and dialectically tending towards interchangeability. If, as English vicar and university lecturer William Cunningham opined in *The Use and Abuse of Money* (1891), "[p]rimers and elementary manuals of economic science usually make a general assumption about human nature, and take for granted that man is actuated by a single motive, – the desire of wealth" (v), *Finnegans Wake* offers an economics lesson that neither affirms nor denies such assumptions, but suggests, in no clear terms, that opposites meet and that short-term rewards are illusory. Should reading Joyce seem insufficiently incoherent and unprofitable, however, there are always the writings of professional economists.

Thus sketched out in broad strokes are the cases for reading Joyce's works as psychological, legal, medical, and economic guides. Other possibilities, more briefly observed:

- Home repairs and decor: imagine and build your dream house (use the wondrous example of the detailed idyllic vision of "Bloom's Cottage," at which the recreations include "house carpentry with toolbox containing hammer, awl, nails, screws, tintacks, gimlet, tweezers, bullnose plane and turnscrew" [17.1580, 17.1601–2]).[8]
- Cat care and dog training: you too can become a cat whisperer, or teach your canine chum Gaelic.
- The art of self-defence: from the problem of bullies (Nasty Roche, Wells, the Citizen, Privates Compton and Carr) to the manly (and patriotic) sport of boxing.
- Coping with grief: break the lonely silence with the help of Gretta Conroy, Stephen Dedalus, the Blooms, and Bob Doran and Alf Bergan; or, by the same token, Joyce's writings might be read as one of the oldest forms of advice books, the guide to dying (for surely this is what *Finnegans Wake* is: at once a stay against death – as I suggested in chapter 5 – and a preparation for eternity).
- Memory improvement: study the methods of that terrible heretic Giordano Bruno and acquire the unfailing mnemonic tricks of Leopold and Molly Bloom ("if I could only remember the 1 half

of the things" opines Molly [18.579–80]). Learn *Finnegans Wake* by heart and your heart will thank you.

Should any or all of these suggested readings (or "uses") of Joyce seem preposterous, it is worth remembering that at least two kinds of guides that might be included in the above list have already been written and published: the travel brochure (Blamires's *The Bloomsday Book* and assorted walking tours, by no means confined to Dublin) and the cookbook (Alison Armstrong's *The Joyce of Cooking*). Moreover, one might claim that certain "critical" books – and because readers will no doubt think of specific examples of their own, I happily need not advance any – read Joyce as instrumental to their theses.

Joyce does not unconditionally confirm the usefulness of his writing. Though he was quick to assert his legal rights as an author and was far from modest, Joyce's notion of his own "awethorrorty" (*FW* 516.19) is (or, over the course of his life and career, becomes) significantly tempered by irony. Unlike such modernists as Ezra Pound – not inaccurately called a "village explainer" by Gertrude Stein – or even (in a different measure) Stein herself, Joyce never posed as an adviser to other writers. Nor did he seek to impose schemes of order on the world outside of his fiction, or seek to counsel or ingratiate himself with those in power. The advice or suggestions we find in his books are never endorsed without qualification, or presented without some shade of doubt or irony. Self-help publishers would shake their heads: that's not how it's done. And yet, as I have attempted to show, Joyce's characters struggle for and with help and assistance, not always sure what forms those might take, and Joyce's readers similarly struggle to find "user-friendly" means of better access to and understanding of his writings. Whether literary writing – let alone literary criticism – is itself potentially "useful" cannot be comprehensively or absolutely answered by this book because the question is entirely contingent on the historical context in which it is asked, but I have tried to demonstrate in this book that imagination is as crucial a factor as circumstances.

In a lecture entitled *How to Fail in Literature*, delivered "at the South Kensington Museum in aid of the College for Working Men and Women" and published as a book in 1890, the folklorist and poet Andrew Lang carefully lays out a program:

> he who would fail must avoid simplicity like a sunken reef, and must earnestly seek either the commonplace or the *bizarre*, the slipshod, or the

> affected, the new-fangled or the obsolete, the flippant or the sepulchral. I need not specially recommend to you to write in "Wardour-street English," the sham archaic, a lingo never spoken by mortal man, and composed of patches borrowed from authors between Piers Plowman and Gabriel Harvey. A few literal translations of Icelandic phrases may be thrown in; the result, as furniture-dealers say, is a "made-up article." (32–3)

This warning seems a vividly prophetic description of Joyce's later writings, and *Finnegans Wake* hearkens to all of this advice and applies it most assiduously. Joyce's reading and composition methods become – sometimes to the consternation of his associates – more and more intensely *practical*: how to repurpose the words of others as well as his own. The *Wake* is a factory of words, mass producing "made-up articles," the applications for which may found later, by readers. As for "lingo never spoken by mortal man," there are plenty of failed writers on that score, Shakespeare among them. As we have seen, he is always useful for quotation, and the diagnosis of Ophelia's madness sounds not unlike Lang's recipe for failure in literature:

> Her speech is nothing,
> Yet the unshapèd use of it doth move
> The hearers to collection. They aim at it,
> And botch the words up fit to their own thoughts (*Hamlet* 4.5.7–10)

Madness is methods without known application. Joyce is a writer of "unshapèd use": as hard a condemnation and as high praise as anyone might hope for.

Fulminating against his fellow Dubliners to his students at the Berlitz school, Joyce called them "the most hopeless, useless and inconsistent race of charlatans I have ever come across" (Ellmann 225–6). The degree to which these same terms might apply to himself and his works notwithstanding, it is incontestable that Joyce did eventually find a use for these people after all: as the ineluctable subjects of his writing. Retooling Homer is the least astonishing of his alchemical acts: he unlocks purposes in things that were hitherto without them. This is what Joyce reveals: the "useless" is that which awaits creative transfiguration: new functions, unanticipated appropriations. What uses we readers may discover for Joyce, be they ever so prosaic or improbable, will decide in what ways and to what degree we ourselves are – as all honest critics fear themselves to be – "useless."

Appendix

This chronology may help readers compare the growth of the "Joyce Industry" with the publishing of self-help books within the same historical period. Listed in the left column are Joyce's works and books about those works explicitly written for a general audience (rather than a specifically scholarly one: Cambridge guides, a debatable exception, are included here, though biographies and remembrances of Joyce are omitted); in the right column is a miscellany of self-help guides, including but not limited to many of those discussed in this book (full citations are to be found in the bibliography). This list is by no means comprehensive, but is instead simply intended to be suggestive of parallels and of the undiminished vitality of both enterprises. Not represented here are the numerous reprintings, subsequent editions, and translations of titles from both columns. I have, however, included the advent of Wikipedia as a signal event that should not be disregarded here.

What is especially interesting is the way the divisions between the two lists seem to deteriorate the longer one studies them together: for instance, titles like *Awaken the Giant Within* (1991) start to seem like (somewhat alarmingly) plausible extrapolations from *Finnegans Wake*, while an anxious and long-suffering reader of the *Wake* may find the promise of *How to Stop Worrying and Start Living* (1948) uncomfortably alluring. And it is surely remarkable that the title *Here Comes Everybody* is found in both lists (see 1969 and 2008).

1897		*Strength and How to Obtain It* (Sandow)
1903		*As a Man Thinketh* (Allen)
1904	work on *Stephen Hero* begins	*Stories of Self-Help: Recent and Living Examples of Men Risen from the Ranks* (Alexander)

1907	*Chamber Music*	*Self-Reliance: Practical Studies in Personal Magnetism, Will-Power and Success, through Self-Help, or Auto-Suggestion* (Coates)
1908		*A New Self-Help: A Story of Worthy Success Achieved in Many Paths of Life by Men and Women of Yesterday and Today* (Bryant)
1909		*The Philosophy of Self-Help: An Application of Practical Psychology to Daily Life* (Kirkham)
1910		*The Science of Getting Rich* (Wattles)
1911		*Conquest of Nerves: A Manual of Self-Help* (Courtney)
1912	"Gas from a Burner"	
1914	*Dubliners*	
1915		*The Art of Public Speaking* (Esenwein and Carnagey)
1916	*A Portrait of the Artist as a Young Man*	
1918	*Exiles*	
1922	*Ulysses*	*Self-Mastery through Conscious Autosuggestion* (Coué) *Physical Beauty: How to Develop and Preserve It* (Courtenay)
1927	*Pomes Penyeach* *A Key to the* Ulysses *of James Joyce* (Smith)	
1928		*Speeches and Toasts: How to Make and Propose Them* (Stemp)
1929	*Our Exagmination Round His Factification for the Incamination of "Work in Progress"* (Beckett et al.) *Tales Told of Shem and Shaun*	
1930	*Anna Livia Plurabelle* *James Joyce's* Ulysses*: A Study* (Gilbert)	
1933	*Haveth Childers Everywhere*	*Know Thyself: An Aid to Self-Examination* (Wareham)

1934	*The Mime of Mick, Nick and the Maggies* *James Joyce and the Making of 'Ulysses'* (Budgen)	
1935		*How to Spend Money* (Brindze)
1936		*How to Win Friends and Influence People* (Carnegie) *Self-Mastery through Psycho-Analysis: A Practical Guide for Laymen* (Hogarth)
1937	*Storiella as She is Syung*	*Think and Grow Rich* (Hill) *How to Psycho-Analyse Yourself* (Ralph)
1939	*Finnegans Wake*	
1940		*How to Read a Book: The Art of Getting a Liberal Education* (Adler)
1944	*Stephen Hero* *James Joyce: A Critical Introduction* (Levin) *A Skeleton Key to "Finnegans Wake"* (Campbell and Robinson)	
1948		*How to Stop Worrying and Start Living* (Carnegie)
1952		*The Power of Positive Thinking* (Peale)
1955	*James Joyce and the Common Reader* (Jones)	
1959	*Reading* Finnegans Wake (Boldereff) *A Reader's Guide to James Joyce* (Tindall)	
1960		*Psycho-Cybernetics: A New Way to Get More Living out of Life* (Maltz)
1962		*Sex and the Single Girl* (Brown)
1966	*The Bloomsday Book: A Guide Through Joyce's* Ulysses (Blamires)	
1968	*Giacomo Joyce*	
1969	*Here Comes Everybody: An Introduction to James Joyce for the Ordinary Reader* (Burgess)	*I'm OK – You're OK* (Harris)

	A Reader's Guide to Finnegans Wake (Tindall)	
1971	*James Joyce and the Plain Reader* (Duff)	
1973	*Joysprick: An Introduction to the Language of James Joyce* (Burgess)	*How to Be Your Own Best Friend* (Newman and Berkowitz)
1974	*Conversations with James Joyce* (Power)	
1975	*A Topographical Guide to James Joyce's* Ulysses (Hart)	
1980	*Annotations to* Finnegans Wake (McHugh; 1st ed.)	
1981	*The* Finnegans Wake *Experience* (McHugh)	
1984		*You Can Heal Your Life* (Hay) *Sex Etiquette: The Modern Woman's Guide to Mating Manners* (Hamel)
1986	*The Joyce of Cooking* (Armstrong)	
1987	*Studying James Joyce* (Blamires) *James Joyce's Odyssey: A Guide to the Dublin of* Ulysses (Delaney)	
1988	*The* Ulysses *Guide: Tours through Joyce's Dublin* (Nicholson)	
1989		*The Wealthy Barber: The Common Sense Guide to Successful Financial Planning* (Chilton) *Seven Habits of Highly Effective People* (Covey)
1990	*The Cambridge Companion to James Joyce* (Attridge)	*Women Who Love Too Much* (Norwood)
1991		*Awaken the Giant Within: How to Take Immediate Control of Your Mental, Emotional, Physical and Financial Destiny!* (Robbins) *DOS for Dummies* (Gookin): first of the "for Dummies" series

1992	*Joyce's Dublin: A Walking Guide to* Ulysses (McCarthy and Rose)	*Men Are From Mars, Women Are From Venus* (Gray)
1993		*Chicken Soup for the Soul* (Canfield and Hansen)
1994	*Joyce for Beginners* (Norris and Flint)	
1995	*James Joyce A-Z: An Encyclopedic Guide to His Life and Work* (Fargnoli and Gillespie)	
1996	*How to Study James Joyce* (Blades)	
2000	*Finding Joy in Joyce: A Readers Guide to Ulysses* (Anderson)	
2001	*James Joyce: A Beginner's Guide* (Startup)	Wikipedia (online January 15)
2002	*How to Read* Ulysses *and Why* (Hunter) *James Joyce's* Ulysses*: A Reference Guide* (McKenna) *James Joyce: A Short Introduction* (Seidel)	*Men Who Hate Women and the Women Who Love Them* (Forward and Torres)
2004	*An Aid to Reading* Ulysses (Butler) Ulysses *Unbound: A Reader's Companion to James Joyce's* Ulysses (Killeen) *James Joyce* (Murphy)	
2005	*A Word in Your Ear: How to Read James Joyce's* Finnegans Wake (Rosenbloom)	*A New Earth: Awakening to Your Life's Purpose* (Tolle)
2006		*The Secret* (Byrne)
2007	*How to Read Joyce* (Attridge)	
2008		*Here Comes Everybody: How Change Happens When People Come Together* (Shirky)
2009	*A Guide through* Finnegans Wake (Epstein)	

	Everyman's Joyce (Gordon)	
	Ulysses *and Us: The Art of Everyday Life in Joyce's Masterpiece* (Kiberd)	
	Joyce's Kaleidoscope: An Invitation to Finnegans Wake (Kitcher)	
	Joyce: A Guide for the Perplexed (Mahon)	
	Joyce's Ulysses: A Reader's Guide (Sheehan)	
	James Joyce: A Critical Guide (Spinks)	
2012		*Emotional Equations: Simple Formulas to Help Your Life Work Better* (Conley) *The Natural: How to Effortlessly Attract the Women You Want* (La Ruina)
2014	*The Cambridge Companion to* Ulysses (Latham)	
2015	Ulysses *Explained: How Homer, Dante, and Shakespeare Inform Joyce's Modernist Vision* (Weir)	*The End of Self-Help: Discovering Peace and Happiness Right at the Heart of Your Messy, Scary, Brilliant Life* (Brenner)

Notes

Introduction

1 Stephen is perhaps thinking of Joshua 13:14: "Only unto the tribe of Levi he gave none inheritance; the sacrifices of the Lord God of Israel *made by fire* are their inheritance, as he said unto them" (emphasis added). Fire's powers to create as well as consume fascinated Joyce (think of the mix of doctrinal hellfire, Promethean arrogance and generosity, and the "fire" of creative madness that Joyce despaired he had transmitted to his daughter) and the description of the dean as having "waxed old" may express some worry about his vulnerability to the flame. Scripture also contends that the Levites have not only a fiery inheritance but a fiery destiny: "But who may abide the day of his coming? And who shall stand when he appeareth? For he is like a refiner's fire, and like fullers' soap; And he shall sit as a refiner and purifier of silver; and he shall purify the sons of Levi, and purge them as gold and silver" (Malachi 3:2–3).

2 Other scholars to whom I have mentioned this have suggested that one might learn from the novel how to blaspheme and how to approach prostitutes, though the firelighting lesson seems the more helpfully detailed. In later chapters I explore some other possibilities.

3 "[P]ractical wisdom," writes Aristotle, "cannot be knowledge nor art; not knowledge because that which can be done is capable of being otherwise, not art because action and making are different kinds of thing" (1800; 1140b).

4 *Hamlet*, it is worth noting – though this is, in truth, less a note than a corollary argument *in utero* – is itself a narrative meditation on "use." When its conspicuously idle hero laments, "How weary, stale, flat, and unprofitable / Seem to me all the uses of this world!" (1.2.133–4), he identifies the

problem: he seeks new "uses of the world" and is perpetually dissatisfied with the uncertain purposes and significance of his schemes. The very word "use" is always potent in the play and often has a strong effect on the prince:

> POLONIUS: My lord, I will use them according to their desert.
> HAMLET: God's bodykins, man, much better! Use every man after his desert and who should scape whipping? Use them after your own honor and dignity ... (2.2.507–10)

He suggests, however unsure or ironic he may be in doing so, that "use almost can change the stamp of nature" (3.4.151.8). The play is a meditation on whether this is so.

5 Covert or concealed reading is a theme in Joyce worthy of an essay unto itself: think of the schoolboys' Westerns in "An Encounter," Molly's letter from Boylan, Bloom's letter from Martha Clifford.

6 The fire sermons of *A Portrait* are recalled at the end of *Ulysses*, when Bloom shows hospitality to Stephen by lighting a fire for him, which act triggers Stephen's memory of "similar apparitions" (17.134).

7 Wittgenstein has his own intriguing if not explicit ideas about "use" and "value": in one of the notes collected in *Culture and Value*, for example, he writes: "Talent is a spring from which fresh water is constantly flowing. But this spring loses its value [*wird wertlos*] if it is not used in the right way [*in rechter Weise benutzt*]" (10–10e).

8 See, for example, Bill Brown, ed., *Things* (Chicago: U of Chicago P, 2004) and *Other Things* (Chicago: U of Chicago P, 2016); Maurizia Boscagli's *Stuff Theory: Everyday Objects, Radical Materialism* (New York: Bloomsbury, 2014); and Raymond Malewitz's *The Practice of Misuse: Rugged Consumerism in Contemporary American Culture* (Stanford: Stanford UP, 2014).

9 There are two exceptions worth noting, both of which have to do with specialization. One is the term "used books," which primarily designates a financial value ("used" is not nearly so posh as what "antiquarian" means in the book trade) but also, as the synonym makes plainer, "secondhand" artifacts. The other is scholarly shorthand: "he is using *A Thousand Plateaus* to examine the matricidal impulses in Joyce's novel." This "use" does have a sense of labour to it, but it is highly unlikely in such instances that the book in question is being referred to *as an object* for use in this operation.

10 Slavoj Žižek compares the domains and limits of the literary with those of the economic this way:

> If we define literature in the broadest possible sense, as the entire field of explicit or implicit references to any kind of narrative, we can say that there is nothing which is not literature – literature serves as a kind of universal medium, even the most intense and violent political or military struggle is traversed and sustained by references to ideological myths. However, precisely insofar as everything is literature, literature is simultaneously nothing in itself: it is never present "as such," but always already withdrawn, deprived of its purity, traversed and distorted by social and political struggles, economic interests, eroticism, and so on and so forth. It may appear that we can make a similar claim about every domain of social life (is not the economy also universal and simultaneously pervaded by all other spheres – law, ideology, private traumas and interests– so that while there is nothing that is not economic, the "pure" economy does not exist?); however, "literature" (the symbolic sphere of narratives) is unique here since it is not a special sphere like economy or law but a medium structuring the entire field of social life. (379)

11 "Job" is a loaded term in Irish usage and in *Ulysses*. Bloom frequently comments on the unpleasant kinds of tasks and employment he runs across: "Tiresome kind of a job" (6.630); "unclean job" (6.20); "Devil of a job" (8.143). The word can be tellingly equated with fortune: Katey Dedalus wryly reckons her siblings' meal of crumbs "a good job we have that much" (10.288).

12 Marianne Moore once described *Dubliners* as "pretty near a manual ... of the fundamentals of composition" (*Selected Letters* 164).

13 Joyce's one-time publisher Harry Crosby once wrote a poem called "Telephone Directory" (*Surrealist Poetry in English* [New York: Penguin, 1978], 75).

14 I am not counting those who sell rare copies to Joyceans.

15 This also means that genre, because it is itself a kind of codification of use and an attempt to affix modes of interpretation, is not the solution to these problems, but a symptom of them. The discovery of a copy of Jeanette Winterson's *Oranges Are Not the Only Fruit* in the cooking section of a bookstore or library can either distress or instruct us, depending on how invested we are in the orthodoxies of this or that literary institution (publishing, university seminars, a book club).

16 For Rorty's distinction between interpretation and use, with which Eco agrees, see his "Nineteenth-Century Idealism and Twentieth-Century Textualism," in *Consequences of Pragmatism: Essays 1972–1980* (Minneapolis: U of Minnesota P, 1982), 139–59.

17 Bloom does not read *Ruby, Pride of the Ring*, but the title, the cover image, and his wife's appraisal of it are sufficient grist for his mind's mill. That is, his mind uses these things in the narratives that it composes and adapts over the course of the day – and perhaps it is true to say that *it cannot help but use them*.

18 Carolyn Lesjak has argued that Wilde, struck by the sheer strangeness of commodities and the culture that produces and worships them, makes the case that pleasure is constituted by a kind of work. See her essay, "Utopia, Use, and the Everyday: Oscar Wilde and a New Economy of Pleasure," *ELH* 67.1 (2000): 179–204.

19 Wilde surfaces again here, for Joyce's connection of immortality and ongoing commentary is an aesthetic statement very much in tune with Lord Henry Wotton's assertion that "there is only one thing in the world worse than being talked about, and that is not being talked about" (*Picture* 6). In *Dorian Gray*, it is the unageing Dorian who excites talk, while Basil Hallward's mutable portrait of him languishes in obscurity. In *Finnegans Wake*, the letter that might explain or justify all of the mysteries remains absent, while gossip around HCE, ALP, and other characters of the same and different names so flourishes as to become the book's whole discursive mode.

20 *Finnegans Wake*'s question "His producers are they not his consumers?" (497.01–02) is not answered but rather prompts a debate.

21 In a Monty Python sketch, a man who has inherited 122,000 miles of string cut into three-inch lengths, worried that it is "not really useful" is assured by a zealous (and ultimately unhinged) advertising man that it has "a million household uses" including "tying up very small parcels, attaching notes to pigeons' legs, destroying household pests" and so on.

22 Beth Blum has likewise argued for *Ulysses* as a kind of "self-help" text which readers can consult for instruction: see her essay "*Ulysses* as Self-Help Manual? James Joyce's Strategic Populism." An anonymous reader of this book for the press recalls that in *A Colder Eye*, Hugh Kenner described *Ulysses* as "a Berlitz classroom between covers: a book from which we are systematically taught the skills we require to read it" (198).

1. Guidance Systems

1 See, for example, George Steiner, *On Difficulty and Other Essays* (Oxford: Oxford UP, 1980) and Leonard Diepeveen, *The Difficulties of Modernism* (New York: Routledge, 2003). Also of interest is Jennifer Doyle's *Hold It Against Me: Difficulty and Emotion in Contemporary Art* (Durham, NC: Duke UP, 2013).

2 Search made 26 October 2014.

3 My thinking on the "use" of these notebooks (by Joyce and by readers) is laid out in the essay "Playing with Matches: The *Wake* Notebooks and Negative Correspondence."

4 Race and religion are trickier matters. For example, the currents of anti-semitism flowing beneath or within certain, broad sections of modernism obviously disallow Jews from either being or becoming anything but a pernicious influence. This makes it all the more interesting that *Ulysses* has its hero not simply a Jew but an irreligious man keen on self-improvement – and, in this sense, a more "modern" man than T.S. Eliot.

5 The most famously useless of such notes is Eliot's "a phenomenon which I have often noticed" (141n68), though probably the most self-consciously so is to one of Bunting's allusions: "O, come on, you know that one" (224).

6 A central and inevitable problem for annotation is ascertaining how annotations will be used. Many annotators, rightly worried about spoiling a plot or imposing a particular interpretation, have struggled to be unassuming, a servant not seen until summoned. Don Gifford writes:

> I have tried to balance on the knife-edge of factual annotation and to avoid interpretive remarks. This distinction is something of a legal fiction, since it can hardly be said that the notes do not imply interpretations or that they do not derive from interpretations; but the intention has been to keep the notes "neutral" so that they will inform rather than direct a reading of the novel. The ideal of neutrality, however, has its drawbacks and has tended to overweight the annotations. (xv)

All might be well if the reader – the user of annotations– were likewise "neutral," or even inclined to neutrality, but the fact is that readers want different things from different notes at different instances. Michael Groden's groundbreaking but failed hypertext *Ulysses* project proposed a staged series of notes, with specific parameters of information in each stage. So a user of this project could click once on a passage or word in Joyce's text to see a rudimentary level of gloss, and then click again for a more expansive and detailed discussion, and again for a third level of annotation that would assume a reader's familiarity with the entire novel. The benefits of this model of annotation point to the value of maximizing the reader's choices in how to engage with and use such notes.

7 This argument is laid out in greater detail in "*Finnegans Wake*: Some Assembly Required."

8 Also worth mentioning in this company is G.J. Holyoake, author of *Public Speaking and Debate* (1863), *A Logic of Facts; or, Everyday Reasoning* (1866), and *Self-Help by the People* (1867).

9 See *Virgin and Veteran Readings of Ulysses*. My review of the book can be found in the *James Joyce Literary Supplement* 26.2 (2012): 11–12.

2. Misquoting Joyce

1 The site has, at the time of this writing, seen some significant changes. In 2006 the site offered certain "sourced" quotations – including "Does nobody understand?" cited in full as "Last words (January 1941)"– selected bagatelles from *Dubliners*, *Finnegans Wake*, and *Stephen Hero*, as well as a few "unsourced" and "misattributed" quotations. *A Portrait* and *Ulysses* each warrants its own page at Wikiquote, and at the latter you can find this semi-familiar sentence:

> "A man of genius makes no mistakes. His errors are volitional and are the portals to [corrected, as of 28 July 2016, to "of"] discovery."

2 See *Joyces Mistakes: Problems of Intention, Irony, and Interpretation*.

3 http://en.wikipedia.org/wiki/Quotation. Accessed 30 October 2006. As of 4 July 2016, the site now simply reports: "Many quotations are routinely incorrect or attributed to the wrong authors, and quotations from obscure or unknown writers are often attributed to far more famous writers. Examples of this are Winston Churchill, to whom many political quotations of uncertain origin are attributed, and Oscar Wilde, to whom anonymous humorous quotations are sometimes attributed."

4 Dorothy Parker offers wise advice: "If with the literate I am / Impelled to try an epigram, / I never seek to take the credit; / We all assume that Oscar said it" (115).

5 It is of no great avail to know that is a 1947 Château Ausone, Mr Bond, if you are already fatally poisoned.

6 David Hayman introduces the notion of the "arranger" in Ulysses*: Mechanics of Meaning* (Rev. ed., Madison: U of Wisconsin P, 1982). See my discussion of it in *Joyces Mistakes* 51–7.

7 When Iago puts his rival Michael Cassio in a compromised position, and gives a self-evidently mild report of the engineered offences, Othello falls for the trick: "I know, Iago, / Thy honesty and love doth mince this matter" (2/3/229–30).

8 Wikipedia's list of popular misquotations (https://en.wikiquote.org/wiki/List_of_misquotations – accessed 24 October 2016) offers an interesting example of how misquotation can represent an attempt to give

a quoted statement context it might otherwise lack. This example is both germane to this discussion of *Hamlet* and indicative of the common frame of cultural reference that Wikipedia tends to adopt. Although Darth Vader actually says, "No, *I* am your father" in the climax to *The Empire Strikes Back*, the anonymous Wikipedia author observes that the line is typically misrepresented as "Luke, I am your father": the misquotation eliminates the unexplained negative (Vader is gainsaying Luke's previous statement) and the emphasis on "I" while it adds Luke's name to make it clear who is being addressed – not unlike how Bloom and Stephen add "Hamlet" to the ghost's speech.

9 http://en.wikiquote.org/wiki/Arthur_Wellesley%2C_1st_Duke_of_Wellington. Accessed 30 October 2006 and again 24 October 2016.

10 http://edge.org/3rd_culture/lanier06/lanier06_index.html. Accessed 24 October 2016.

11 This phrase comes from a recent but as-yet-unpublished essay, "The Potency of Error," which Fritz Senn kindly sent me.

12 Borges returns to his idea of Shakespeare's reader being Shakespeare a bit more fully in his lecture on "Immortality":

> When I recite Shakespeare, my father is living in me. The people who have heard me will live in my voice, which is a reflection of a voice that was, perhaps, a reflection of the voice of its elders. The same may be said of music and language. Language is a creation, it becomes a kind of immortality. I am using the Castilian language. How many dead Castilians are living within me? (490)

3. Limited Editions, Edited Limitations

1 For a sense of scale: at the price listed by Amazon UK at the time of this writing, you can buy forty-six copies of the Penguin "restored" *Wake* for this amount (not counting taxes and shipping). Or there's a copy of the 1939 first edition of *Finnegans Wake* in "near fine" condition" listed online for sale, at the time of this writing, by a dealer in Richmond, UK, for fifty euros less than the "special" Houyhnhnm *Wake*. On the other hand, the "special" Houyhnhnm *Wake* is a downright bargain compared to Rose's newest production, a hitherto (and, we are to understand, unjustly) unpublished "serio-comic collection of 'little epics'" called *Finn's Hotel* (Ithys Press, 2013), the "deluxe" edition of which is up for grabs for 2500 euros. Operators are almost certainly standing by – call today, and have your credit card ready.

2 I say "ill-fated" with sympathy – whatever the flaws of that edition, it was a misfortune that the Joyce Estate should have seen to its destruction – and to raise the question of what remarkable developments there must have been in Rose's relationship with the Estate since then. The copyright page of the Houyhnhnm *Wake* notes that the copyright was "revived 1995 © The Estate of James Joyce," but that of the Penguin *Wake* makes no mention of anyone's copyright prior to that of Rose and O'Hanlon (2010), and that of the Oxford *Wake* includes no mention at all of Joyce, the estate, or even 1939.

3 See also Danis Rose and John O'Hanlon, "Preface" (*FW–RH*) 7.

4 A modest proposal: if the thus far non-permitting circumstances have some sort of asking price – if it's a lack of financial wherewithal that is holding back this information, or even a lack of volunteers for menial data entry – perhaps Rose and O'Hanlon might try crowd-sourcing the project. It would make for a welcome, sensible, and twenty-first-century contrast to the "limited edition" method of dissemination, and in the interest of seeing it work, I'll put my own money where my footnote-in-mouth is and chip in the moment the option appears on Kickstarter.

5 Gabler might, however, be seen to sound one note of caution when he refers to amendments to the first edition as "textual paths not taken into the particular rose garden of the first edition" (15), for the metaphor leaves open the possibility – especially since the methodology is here taken on trust – that readers are being led up a garden path.

6 Whether textual errata and disruptions constitute such "barriers" is unclear though perhaps a weak implication, given the force with which corrections are advertised as the great virtue of this work. The aforementioned prospectus attests that this edition "incorporates some 9000 minor yet crucial corrections and amendments, covering punctuation marks, font choice, spacing, misspellings, misplaced phrases and ruptured syntax. Although individually minor, these changes are nonetheless crucial in that they facilitate a smooth reading of the book's allusive density and essential fabric." (Note the plaintive repetition of that "minor yet crucial" formula.) That a new edition may claim a corrective mandate is to be expected, but Rose and O'Hanlon assume an overstated, definitive position that is (somewhat paradoxically) at odds with Gabler's statement about the persistent possibility of texts being otherwise.

7 Incidentally, why is Joyce textual scholarship (still) such a boys' club? From the players and brawlers in the "Joyce Wars" about editing *Ulysses* of the 1980s to the nine names that comprise the editors and editorial board of the *Finnegans Wake Notebooks* series, one looks in vain for women's

voices in these technical, sometimes heated debates. Welcome exceptions, such as Ingeborg Landuyt, only confirm the rule (Landuyt is the only woman among the fifteen contributors to Crispi and Slote's *How Joyce Wrote* Finnegans Wake). The effects of this phenomenon may prove no less troubling than the causes.

8 As valuable as the *JJA* is, however, it is a work of reproduction rather than a primary textual source, so its use is best followed up with consultation of actual notebooks, manuscripts, etc.

9 This problem can be most immediately expressed in terms of translation: to what degree are the notions of a stabilized and consistent "source language" and "target language" merely serviceable (perhaps necessary) fictions?

10 See http://www.houyhnhnmpress.com/rationale.

11 Wim van Mierlo, who answers his own question as to whether Rose and O'Hanlon "have created a good edition" with a supportive "yes," writes: "Conjecture, however, is not an arbitrary decision; it is at worst an educated guess, at best a careful decision based on a critical examination of the available facts. Any conscientious editor would present a full explanation and argumentation in the Textual Notes to justify his choices" ("'For polemypolity's sake': Editing *Finnegans Wake* – A Consideration and Review").

12 Advances in textual and genetic studies have allowed us to better understand how Joyce wrote, but it must be remembered that significant limitations are implicit in that necessary word "better."

13 For this, one has to go to Fordham's *Lots of Fun at* Finnegans Wake*: Unravelling Universals* (7–33) – in which book occurs the first use of the phrase "an exegete's dream" (33) – though I wonder whether such a (truncated) schematic would not be at least as illuminating than the "chapter-by-chapter outline" in an introduction to the book itself (xxxv–xlv).

14 See Rabaté, "Modernism and 'The Plain Reader's Rights': Duff-Riding-Graves Rereading Joyce," 37–8.

4. Translation, Annotation, Hesitation

1 Vladimir Nabokov's demand for "copious footnotes, footnotes reaching up like skyscrapers to the top of this or that page" for his translation of Pushkin's *Onegin* is illustrative of this paradox ("Problems of Translation" 127). Resolutely abandoning (and condemning) any attempt to proximate Pushkin's prosody or rhymes, Nabokov wants it both ways: it is impossible to translate *Onegin*, and his extensive, exhaustive commentary *to his translation* affirms that any other approach than his own fails.

2 As is sadly usual in matters of Joycean texts, publisher delays tangle up this production timeline.
3 An apposite observation by Sidney Monas: "Too many learned articles on translation veer from the lurid tradition of the police memoir ('Some Bad Translations I Have Known') into the closely related and even more dismal atmosphere of the marriage manual ('How to Make Your Translation an Aesthetic Success')" (165).
4 Not quite "verbatim," actually: remember that Joyce is a *user* of quotations. See Ingeborg Landuyt and Geert Lernout, "Joyce's Sources: *Les Grands Fleuves Historiques*."
5 Lavergne's version of this is somewhat abstract, in part because it shifts an imperative into an infinitive, for reasons I don't see (or hear): "Traduire ce chafouin en turc" (438nb); that is, roughly, "to translate this sly into Turkish." Among other things, the interesting translation-as-bowel-movement motif in the original note is absent in Lavergne.
6 There is, I think, a compelling argument to be made that Lavergne is often deaf to Issy's voice (an argument I am not at leisure to make here, but at least some of the substance of which can be gleaned from the following paragraph), and she has a significantly muted presence in his translation. This does not seem to be because he is unaware of her: for example, Lavergne's translation of the phrase "I was so snug off in my apholster's creedle" (276F5) pointedly marks the speaker as female: "J'étais si envelopée de ma croyance aux apôtres" (430Fa).
7 Other omissions include 291F8 (see Lavergne 454); 292F1 (see 454); 296F3 (see 461); 305F3 (see 477); 307F5 (see 479); and 307F6 (see 480).
8 And as *Finnegans Wake* makes painfully apparent, translation is not just a matter of determining what to "carry over," but the subtler *a priori* problem of figuring out from and to what respective languages one is taking this message. There is, for example, the general conception of "French," but from there one must become more specific: the French of France; the French of Tours in the nineteenth century; the French of Balzac; the Frenches of Balzac's various characters. The skilful translator is always modulating to accommodate and approximate these shifting differences in the way that a pilot with a shifting, unwieldy, and quickly disintegrating cargo must modify his or her flight plan (changing as necessary not just speed and altitude but possible landing sites) at nearly every point along the voyage. But what, for the purposes of the translator, is the language of the *Wake*? "Wakese" is no more useful a designation than the general "French," since neither is monolithic and absolutely circumscribed, and besides they are not both "languages" in equivalent functional terms

(I can successfully order a pizza in French, but not in "Wakese"). Noam Chomsky offers a salutary reminder: "No individual speaks a well-defined language. The notion of language itself is on a very high order of abstraction" (54).

9 On page 233, Lavergne does take notice of her: in "ce bras d'eau alpin" ("this alpin armlet") (*FW* 148.22) he observes "A.L.P., symbole féminin., pour Joyce" (233n56).

10 Bíró's translation is less inhibited than Lavergne's, but it is not easy to say whether his refusal to annotate (to observe in a footnote, for example, that he has swapped Joyce's d's for m's) is part of that greater liberty, a more or less necessary effect of it, or even a cause of it.

11 Sam Slote, plumbing the *Scribbledehobble* text, offers the kind of context that Lavergne does not. "Wilde," Slote writes, "had been called a 'great white caterpillar' by Lady Colin Campbell ... A caterpillar is also a soldier, according to Francis Grose's *Classical Dictionary of the Vulgar Tongue* (Joyce owned a copy of this volume). This suggests an early conceptual link between Wilde and Wellington ... and 'Great White Caterpillar' is deployed frequently in the *Wake* as a reference to both Wilde and Wellington" ("Wilde Thing" 104).

12 In their 1985 review of Lavergne's *Wake*, Shari and Bernard Benstock belittle how "erudition in the form a footnote" fails to highlight certain allusions. Lavergne renders "the Ballmooney Bloodriddon Murther" (*FW* 219.19–20) as "de Murther Bloodriddon de Ballymooney" (340) and adds this footnote: "Master *Blottet*. Mr le démuni de Ballymoney. Le jeu de mot porte sur le norvégien" (340n3). The Benstocks ask: "Whatever became of the Ballyhooley Blueribbon Army or Der Bestrafte Brudermord, or are they of no importance or incapable of being rendered in the language of La Plume de ma Tante? How did money (a rare item in Ireland) come to replace mooney (as common in Ireland as murphies)?" (232–3). While everyone looks for their own favourite allusions, I think the Benstocks should rein back the rhetorical questions and appreciate that *Ballymoney* might be closer than *Ballymooney* to *Ballymahon* – where *Oliver Goldsmith* used to live!

13 Indeed, Lavergne seems a bit gone on the many meanings of buffalo: he notes of "bafflelost bull" (*FW* 118.07; rendered as "Baie-falot-bulle"): "Buffalo Bill, semble être une allusion à l'esprit balour américain de Pound, qui avouait ne rien comprendre à *Finnegans Wake*" (187n17).

14 It would be interesting to compare the kinds of adjectives and adverbs habitually affixed to translations by reviewers (the predictable and narrow range of which many translators and theorists of translation have wryly

taken notice of: "readable," "elegant," and "smooth" and so on) to those used to characterize annotations.

5. Make a Stump Speech Out of It

1 Quoted in *The Telegraph* 20 March 2001 (online).
2 Dowie earlier in the day similarly halted Bloom's eagerness to see his name celebrated by emerging as the subject of the leaflet that Bloom briefly supposes might be about himself: "Bloo. Me? No, blood." We can read this scene as part of the novel's sequence of interruptions of Bloom's efforts to articulate his own beliefs and identity.
3 The lack of drama in *Exiles* might be accounted for by its lack of public speeches: the whole play is about private conversations.
4 Typing "Joyce" and "public speaking" into the search engine finds the LinkedIn profile of someone named Stephen Joyce, a travel and tourism consultant keen on and experienced in public speaking: "If you're looking to juice up your summit or conference with a presentation on social media, technology, innovation, or leadership, let me know."
5 Matthew Bevis has ingeniously suggested that the opening pages of *A Portrait* constitute a kind of "*progymnasmata*, a set of fourteen exercises to prepare students of rhetoric for the creation of speeches" (228; see further 228–32).
6 Not all, however, and the use of this disingenuous device (and the suggested use of it) may inadvertently display the speaker's attitude towards the listeners. A 1928 guide to making toasts and giving speeches offers an example of a toast to be made to "the Ladies" of a company – it goes without saying that the speaker is male – which begins this way: "Let me say at once that I am too youthful, too unskilled in the study of the enchanting ways of womanhood to do justice to what is, no doubt, a great and inspiring subject" (Stemp 142).
7 And this is one of the *better* ones! It is debatable, though, whether the Irish come off worse on the whole than either African-Americans (not the book's term) or women.
8 It is rather odd that this long sermon ends with an expression of utter fear – which feeling is plainly encouraged in the audience – at the prospect of hearing God deliver a stern lecture Himself. Perhaps it acts as a kind of apologia by way of threat: if you think my speech is dreadful, be thankful that you're not listening to my superior, who is much, much worse.
9 Joyce uses the word "enthusiastic" twice in *Ulysses*, both times unflatteringly: once to describe Haines's feeling about Hyde's *Lovesongs*

of Connacht and to explain his absence from Stephen's lecture (9.93) and once to characterize the women driven to mass suicide for the love of Bloom in "Circe" (15.1745). The word's root meaning of (frenzied) spiritual possession resonates with Joyce's observation of the Irish as "the gratefully oppressed" (*D* 35).

10 J. Berg Esenwein and Dale Carnagey [later Carnegie], *The Art of Public Speaking* (Springfield, MA: The Home Correspondence School, 1915). Available online at http://www.gutenberg.org/files/16317/16317.txt.

11 See Ellmann, *The Consciousness of Joyce* 34–6. Bevis (238), claiming to cite Ellmann, says that he was in attendance, while in his 2011 biography of Joyce, Gordon Bowker ambiguously writes that Joyce "heard [Taylor] ... defend the power of 'the rude vernacular'" (82). See also Abby Bender's "The Language of the Outlaw: A Clarification" and So Onose's "'A Great Future Behind Him': John F. Taylor's Speech in 'Aeolus' Revisited."

12 To complicate matters, the Man in the Macintosh insists that Bloom's "real name is Higgins" (15.1562).

13 Zoe doesn't exactly "put Bloom in his place" – certainly not compared with Bella Cohen's treatment of him – but she does unsettle him. "And you know what thought did" might seem like innocuous banter, but this late nineteenth-century catch-phrase touches Bloom's anxieties: according to Eric Partridge, "If the other asks *What?*, one adds *Ran away with another man's wife*" (960).

14 See Ronan Crowley, "The Queen Is Not a Subject: Victoria's *Leaves from the Journal* in *Ulysses*," in *James Joyce in the Nineteenth Century*, ed. John Nash (Cambridge: Cambridge UP, 2013), 200–13.

15 The judicious use of body language is another standard subject in popular guides to public speaking, and Joyce's characters provide numerous examples of probably misjudged gesticulation. Gabriel Conroy's aforementioned "circle in the air" is quite restrained when compared with the exhibitions of D.B. Murphy, raconteur:

> – I seen him shoot two eggs off two bottles at fifty yards over his shoulder. The lefthand dead shot.
>
> Though he was slightly hampered by an occasional stammer and his gestures being also clumsy as it was still he did his best to explain.
>
> – Bottles out there, say. Fifty yards measured. Eggs on the bottles. Cocks his gun over his shoulder. Aims.
>
> He turned his body half round, shut his right eye completely. Then he screwed his features up someway sideways and glared out into the night with an unprepossessing cast of countenance.

– Pom! he then shouted once.

The entire audience waited, anticipating an additional detonation, there being still a further egg.

– Pom! he shouted twice. (*U* 16.389–401)

The contortions of prose in "Eumaeus" are matched by those of the sailor, and explanation and dramatization become hopelessly muddled: "as it was still he did his best to explain."

16 I have elsewhere discussed problems of "hearing" Molly: see "The Silence of the Looms: 'Penelope' as Translation," in *James Joyce's Silences*, ed. Serenella Zanotti and Jolanta Wawrzycka. London: Bloomsbury (forthcoming).

6. Win a Dream Date with James Joyce

1 In *A Portrait*, Stephen's repertoire of "curious" and "quaint old songs" with which to woo the object of his affections includes, besides "Greensleeves" and "a dainty song of the Elizabethans," "the victory chant of Agincourt" (*P* 184).

2 The end of the Second World War saw a renewed effort at this form of "education," which is perhaps best satirized by Nabokov's *Lolita* in 1955 (for example, the headmistress of Beardsley School for girls explains to Humbert Humbert that the school likes to "stress the four D's: Dramatics, Dance, Debating and Dating. We are confronted by certain facts. Your delightful Dolly will presently enter an age group where dates, dating, date dress, date book, date etiquette, means as much to you as, say, business, business connections, business success, mean to you" [177]).

3 Those most prone to romantic fancy make the best demographic targets. The flower-seller's wares which peevish Stephen rejects are better suited, he thinks, for "a tourist from England or a student of Trinity" (*P* 154), but the scene does bear interesting contrast with that in "Wandering Rocks" in which Blazes Boylan does business in the respectable florist's on Grafton Street (*U* 10.299–336).

4 To be fair, there were probably more pages printed on dating and youth courtship (before about, say, 1975) than on Joyce: LeMasters notes, for example, some 1,031 studies on courtship and marriage between 1945–54 (13).

5 *Joyce Jackson's Guide to Dating* (1957) was actually written by one Helen Louise Crounse.

6 Unfortunately and for reasons incomprehensible to me, the Hallmark Corporation will not permit reproduction of the card here or, their

spokespeople claim, *anywhere*, regardless of all promises of disinterested scholarship and non-commercial venues. As I came across the card on the Discovery Channel's website as part of a feature on the history of courtship (the feature is no longer online), this policy seems more arbitrary than the company admits. Textual and cultural historians be warned.

7 Gerty is not necessarily ignorant, as Jen Shelton points out: "Gerty's romantic musings seem a self-conscious attempt to remake the world according to a gentler standard" (90).

8 A book Joyce himself enjoyed and winks at in the *Wake*: "O loreley!" (201.35).

9 There is, of course, the option to "go dutch!" (*FW* 244.02): the *OED* records usage of the expression as early as 1914.

10 To observe virtual communities like the specialized debates of a *Finnegans Wake* listserve is to confirm this phenomenon, for the general form and tone of exchanges are not unlike what would find, say, on a listserve dedicated to *Star Trek*, The Grateful Dead, or JFK assassination conspiracy theories.

11 Hamel's lingo may be indicative of the writer's era, but the substance of the advice has been perfectly recycled from previous advisors on the subject. Bailey notes, for example, that the dating guides of the 1940s suggest that women refrain from attempting to compete with the intellectual heights of their male counterparts (*From Front Porch to Back Seat*, 113). I am thus compelled to wonder about the nature of the writing errors in the letters from Martha and Milly in *Ulysses*, and whether they might be seen as evidence of such an accepted rule in operation.

12 *Before Sunrise* is even more indebted to Joyce than is sketched here. In a self-reflexive moment in the film, Ethan Hawke's character Jesse (whose friends, he tells us, call him James) explains an idea he has for a 24-hour television documentary of "the poetry of day-to-day life" shot in different parts of the world, and focusing on different individuals for each episode. The film's sequel, the equally delightful *Before Sunset* (2004), could be described as a Proustian reply to the Joycean *Sunrise*, immersed as it is in the emotional complexities of remembering what could have been in tandem with what was.

13 The lyrics to "The Sensual World" are familiar to readers of *Ulysses* from their beginning:

> Then I'd taken the kiss of seedcake back from his mouth
> Going deep South, go down, mmh, yes,
> Took six big wheels and rolled our bodies
> Off to Howth Head and into the flesh, mmh, yes,

He said I was a flower of the mountain, yes,
But now I've powers o'er a woman's body – yes.

For reasons known only to the Joyce Estate, Bush was granted permission to re-record the song in 2011 with lyrics drawn directly from "Penelope."

14 A few years ago I taught a *Ulysses* class in which students revealed in our first meeting that the only Joyce texts which they had read were the most notorious letters to Nora. Awareness of Joyce's reputation as a pornographer thus may remain prior to recognition of any other sort of accomplishment.

7. The Stephen Dedalus Diet

1 Witness such nutritious titles as J. Milner Fothergill's *A Manual of Dietetics* (London, 1887) and, perhaps for the bedridden wife, Samuel Henry Purdon's *A Handy Book for Invalids: The Dietary in the Treatment of Disease* (Belfast: Charles W. Olley, 1890).
2 See the general discussions of eating in the novel in Maud Ellmann's entry on Joyce for *The Cambridge Companion to English Novelists*, ed. Adrian Poole (Cambridge: Cambridge UP, 2009), 328–41, and in Declan Kiberd's *Ulysses and Us: The Art of Everyday Life in Joyce's Masterpiece* 124–36. These examples also demonstrate how discussion of the subject has become a touchstone for critical introductions to *Ulysses*.
3 In *James Joyce and the Making of 'Ulysses,' and Other Writings*, Budgen reports Joyce's using the example of the "peristaltic movement" of "Lestrygonians" to illustrate how "if they [the characters of the novel] had no body they would have no mind" (21).
4 Feminist critique has taken up the question of the intellectual capacities of Molly and Gerty and how readers have (often unfairly) gauged them, but Stephen's body tends to inspire only bemusement and revulsion.
5 The *Finnegans Wake* term "scripchewer" (412.04) has relevance here: the ancient image of the written word as corporal sustenance.
6 There are, then, at least a few levels of comic irony to the fact that, though associating the library chapter with the brain seems warranted by Stephen's expounding on the ghostly meanings of *Hamlet*, the altogether unghostly Bloom undertakes an investigation of his own with an anatomical focus rather distant from the brain. The unresolved mystery of one of the finer points of divine form – whether a callipygous goddess has an anal orifice – surely permits us to likewise wonder whether Stephen has a sphincter, and, by extension, doth Shakespeare shit?

7 Stephen himself acknowledges in "Proteus" that his philosopher was not one to miss meals by calling him "Aquinas tunbelly" (*U* 39).

8 Lauren Rich carefully outlines how many of Joyce's marginalized Dubliners "find themselves eating in isolation in surroundings that mimic but never quite recreate the domestic glow" (72). To this we can add Stephen's inability or unwillingness to eat even in domestic spaces, which pointedly lack any "glow."

9 Readers with a mind to do so may insert *The Twilight Zone* theme here.

10 Eagleton, *Heathcliff and the Great Hunger: Studies in Irish Culture*, 13. At a talk entitled "Joyce Incorporated," delivered at the Dublin Joyce Summer School in 2011, Maud Ellmann posed the same question to an unresponsive audience.

11 See, for example, Bonnie Roos's essay, "The Joyce of Eating: Feast, Famine and the Humble Potato in *Ulysses*," and June Dwyer's "Feast and Famine: James Joyce and the Politics of Food."

12 Unless, of course, he is saving her for later.

13 Of the many objects in the novel that might be characterized as "useless," Bloom's potato has to be one of the most striking. Its function as Homeric proxy for the protective moly given by Athena to Odysseus seems pretty doubtful, though it does appear to have a kind of exchange value, perhaps symbolic in some other fashion, as it passes from Ellen Bloom (*née* Higgins) to her son to Zoe Higgins, and then back to Bloom: a strange gift that keeps on giving.

14 At least to some extent, it might be the very quotidian focus of the novel that effectively prohibits significant contemplation of the enormity of the Famine, in just the way that the broad sweep of the heroic epic has to imbue what might seem most tedious in day-to-day experience (all of that waiting that Odysseus and Penelope must do!) with extraordinary virtue.

15 A well-known and gripping approach to this problem is Art Spiegelman's *MAUS*, in which a contrived allegory (German Jews as mice, Nazis as cats, Americans as dogs, and so on) seems to be offered as a way to represent the Holocaust, but in fact it is the gradual (and quite moving) deconstruction of this allegory, the disintegration of the categorical essentialism that allegory and fascism both depend upon (the cartoonist-narrator not knowing how to draw a French Jew, for example), that sounds out the strain of the effort in such representation.

16 "I hope to demonstrate that [the concept of the subject as phallogocentric structure] ... implies carnivorous virility," says Derrida, and thereafter suggests a contrary possibility: "'One must eat well' does not mean above all taking in and grasping in itself, but *learning* and *giving* to eat, learning-to-give-the-other-to-eat" ("'Eating Well'" 280, 282). Stephen does not, of

course, "eat well" in this sense at all, since he appears far from "*learning* and *giving* to eat."

17 The (irrational) fear of peaches.

18 A number of online "dream dictionaries" suggest that dreaming of melons "denotes ill health" and "A melon in a dream also means that one will be struck with an adversity for which he will find no solution, and he will not understand its consequences for sometime to come." Although Gifford and Seidman cite scriptural dreams to account for Stephen's, they elsewhere stoop to consult J.E. Cirloit's *A Dictionary of Symbols* (e.g., see their note for 3.494–7).

19 In *The Hunger Artists: Starving, Writing, and Imprisonment*, Maud Ellmann notes how Stephen "compares the umbilical cord to a telephone wire" and how this connection leads him to envision a telecommunicative world "in which all speakers are enmeshed, parasiting one another's inmost thoughts. In this context, to refuse food would be to deny the other at the cost of the annihilation of the self" (55). If Stephen's disavowal of food is, for him, at some level a disavowal of subjectivity, it is not a terribly successful effort, for he is constantly being recognized, hailed, and chased after wherever he goes in the novel, constantly reinstated as a subject.

20 G.W. Russell, "In praise of milk," *The Irish Homestead* (6 January 1906), qtd. in Clarkson and Crawford 235.

21 Plock notes that Joyce "preferred to publish [these stories, "The Sisters" and "Eveline"] under the pseudonym 'Stephen Dædalus'" (33–4).

22 See Dirk Van Hulle, "Joyce, the Master Craftsman: Frank Budgen and the Making of the 'Wake,'" in *Joyce's Disciples Disciplined: A Re-Exagmination of the 'Exagmination' of 'Work in Progress,'* ed. Tim Conley (Dublin: University College Dublin Press, 2010), 24–32.

Conclusion

1 The *Wake* is a mishmash of the kinds of proverbs and homilies that, for better or worse, are passed from one generation to another as nuggets of wisdom. Some of these are more recognizable than others (though not necessarily more useful for that). "Share the wealth and spoil the weal" (579.16–17), for example, is a neoliberal renovation – or a critical expansion – of the equally unkind counsel, "spare the rod and spoil the child"). One could make the case that, along with José Saramago and perhaps Agatha Christie, Joyce is one of the most *proverbial* writers of the twentieth century.

2 The model for Haines, Samuel (Dermot) Chenevix Trench, shot himself in 1909. This fact lends a further grim irony to Haines's calling Stephen's mind "unbalanced."

3 See Mark Osteen's *The Economy of* Ulysses*: Making Both Ends Meet*; Michael D. Rubenstein's "'The Waters of Civic Finance': Moneyed States in Joyce's *Ulysses*;" and Matthew Hayward's "Reconsidering Joyce's 'Notes on Business and Commerce.'"

4 After the financial lessons of Mr Deasy, probably the money matter in *Ulysses* that has excited the most commentary is the budget for 16 June 1904 tabulated in "Ithaca" (17.1455–78), largely because of its glaring irregularities, omissions, and dubious arithmetic. I think that Joyce offers this budget as a kind of fictional genre of its own, no more a record of truth than a novel, or a memoir, or anyone's tax return. But a budget is expressly a "useful" fiction.

5 Joyce habitually counterbalances the appreciation of capital with doubt about its abstract premises, and this sometimes occurs in terms directly related to the *use* of measures of capital. For instance, where Mr Deasy recommends his savingsbox as "very handy" (2.230), debt-conscious Stephen is far less enchanted by the illusions of dancing coins: "The lump I have is useless" (2.259).

6 After Bloom returns Stephen the money he has carried for him, Bloom entertains the idea of further exchanges between the two of them but his enthusiasm is dampened by remembrances of "the imprevidibility of the future":

> once in the summer of 1898 he (Bloom) had marked a florin (2/–) with three notches on the milled edge and tendered it in payment of an account due to and received by J. and T. Davy, family grocers, 1 Charlemont Mall, Grand Canal, for circulation on the waters of civic finance, for possible, circuitous or direct, return. (17.980–4)

That final bizarre phrase recalls Reuben J. Dodd's alleged overpayment for the safe return of his son from near drowning and anticipates the circulatory design of *Finnegans Wake*, in which every bad penny can be counted on to turn up again and again.

7 Franklin's name is among the extraordinary list of "Irish heroes and heroines of antiquity" rolled out in "Cyclops" (12.187)

8 In "Bloom's Dream Cottage and Crusoe's Island: Man Caves," Austin Briggs sees the dream cottage as kin to the allure of *Robinson Crusoe*: a vision of a life of manly self-reliance, the ultimate DIY fantasy (63–75).

Bibliography

Adams, Robert M. *James Joyce: Common Sense and Beyond*. New York: Random House, 1966.

Adler, Mortimer J. *How to Read a Book: The Art of Getting a Liberal Education*. New York: Simon and Schuster, 1940.

Agamben, Giorgio. *The Use of Bodies*. Trans. Adam Kotsko. Stanford: Stanford UP, 2015.

Alexander, John. *Stories of Self-Help: Recent and Living Examples of Men Risen from the Ranks*. London: S.W. Partridge and Company, 1910.

Allen, James. *As a Man Thinketh*. 1903. Floyd, VA: Sublime Books, 2014.

Anderson, John P. *Finding Joy in Joyce: A Readers Guide to* Ulysses. N.p.: Universal Publishers, 2000.

– *Joyce's* Finnegans Wake*: The Curse of Kabbalah*. Vol. 1. Boca Raton: Universal Publishers, 2008.

Aragon, Louis. *Paris Peasant*. Trans. Simon Watson Taylor. Boston: Exact Change, 1994.

Aristotle. *Nicomachean Ethics*. Trans. W.D. Ross, revised by J.O. Urmson. *The Complete Works of Aristotle*. Ed. Jonathan Barnes. Vol. 2. Princeton: Princeton UP, 1984. 1729–1867.

Armstrong, Alison. *The Joyce of Cooking: Food and Drink from Joyce's Dublin*. Barrytown, NY: Station Hill P, 1986.

Attridge, Derek. *Peculiar Language: Literature as Difference from the Renaissance to James Joyce*. London: Methuen, 1988.

– ed. *The Cambridge Companion to James Joyce*. Cambridge: Cambridge UP, 1990.

Bailey, Beth L. *From Front Porch to Back Seat: Courtship in Twentieth-Century America*. Baltimore: Johns Hopkins UP, 1988.

Barthelme, Donald. "On the Level of Desire." *Not-Knowing: The Essays and Interviews*. Ed. Kim Herzinger. Berkeley: Counterpoint, 1997. 190–5.

Barthes, Roland. *The Pleasure of the Text*. Trans. Richard Miller. New York: Hill and Wang, 1975.

– *The Preparation of the Novel*. Trans. Kate Briggs. New York: Columbia UP, 2011.

– "Towards a Psychosociology of Contemporary Food Consumption." *Food and Culture: A Reader*. Eds. Carole Counihan and Penny Van Esterik. New York: Routledge, 1997. 20–7.

Bataille, Georges. "From the Stone Age to Jacques Prévert." *The Absence of Myth: Writings on Surrealism*. Ed. and trans. Michael Richardson. London: Verso, 2006. 137–54.

Beckett, Samuel. "Dante ... Bruno. Vico ... Joyce." *Our Exagmination Round His Factification for Incamination of Work in Progress*. New York: New Directions, 1972. 1–23.

Beckman, Richard. "Perils of Marriage in *Finnegans Wake*." *James Joyce Quarterly* 33.1 (1996): 83–99.

Bender, Abby. "The Language of the Outlaw: A Clarification." *James Joyce Quarterly* 44.4 (2007): 807–10.

Benjamin, Walter. "May–June 1931." Trans. Rodney Livingstone. *Selected Writings: Volume 2, 1927–1934*. Eds. Michael W. Jennings, Howard Eiland, and Gary Smith. Cambridge: Harvard UP, 1999. 469–85.

Benstock, Shari, and Bernard Benstock. Rev. of *Finnegans Wake*, trans. Philippe Lavergne. *James Joyce Quarterly* 22.2 (1985): 231–3.

Bevis, Matthew. *The Art of Eloquence: Byron, Dickens, Tennyson, Joyce*. Oxford: Oxford UP, 2007.

Bíró, Endre, trans. *Finnegan Ébredése (részletek)*. Budapest: Holnap Kiadó, 1992.

Bishop, John. *Joyce's Book of the Dark: "Finnegans Wake."* Madison: U of Wisconsin P, 1986.

Blades, John. *How to Study James Joyce*. Basingstoke: Macmillan, 1996.

Blamires, Harry. *The Bloomsday Book: A Guide through Joyce's* Ulysses. London: Methuen, 1966.

– *Studying James Joyce*. Harlow, Essex: Longman York Press, 1987.

Blum, Beth. "*Ulysses* as Self-Help Manual? James Joyce's Strategic Populism." *Modern Language Quarterly* 74.1 (2013): 67–93.

Boldereff, Frances Motz. *Reading* Finnegans Wake. Woodward, PA: Classic Nonfiction Library, 1959.

Boller, Jr, Paul F., and John George. *They Never Said It: A Book of Fake Quotes, Misquotes, and Misleading Attributions*. New York: Oxford UP, 1989.

Borges, Jorge Luis. "Immortality." Trans. Eliot Weinberger. *Selected Non-Fictions*. Ed. Eliot.

Weinberger. New York: Viking, 1999. 483–91.

– "A New Refutation of Time." Trans. Suzanne Jill Levine. *Selected Non-Fictions*. Ed. Eliot Weinberger. New York: Viking, 1999. 317–32.

Borges, Jorge Luis, and Osvaldo Ferrari. *Conversations, Volume 1*. Trans. Jason Wilson. London: Seagull Books, 2014.

Bosinelli, Rosa Maria Bollettieri. "Joyce Slipping Across the Borders of English: The Stranger in Language." *James Joyce Quarterly* 38.3/4 (2001): 395–409.

Bowker, Gordon. *James Joyce: A New Biography*. New York: Farrar, Straus and Giroux, 2011.

Brenner, Gail. *The End of Self-Help: Discovering Peace and Happiness Right at the Heart of Your Messy, Scary, Brilliant Life*. N.p.: Ananda P, 2015.

Briggs, Austin. "Bloom's Dream Cottage and Crusoe's Island: Man Caves." *a long the krommerun: Selected Papers from the Utrecht James Joyce Symposium*. Eds. Onno Kosters, Tim Conley, and Peter de Voogd. Amsterdam: Brill, 2016. 63–75.

Brindze, Ruth. *How to Spend Money*. New York: The Vanguard P, 1935.

Brown, Helen Gurley. *Sex and the Single Girl*. New York: Bernard Geis Associates, 1962.

Browne, Thomas. *Religio Medici. The Major Works*. Ed. C.A. Patrides. London: Penguin, 1977. 55–161.

Bryant, Ernest A. *A New Self-Help: A Story of Worthy Success Achieved in Many Paths of Life by Men and Women of Yesterday and Today*. London: Cassell, 1908.

Budgen, Frank. *James Joyce and the Making of 'Ulysses,' and Other Writings*. London: Oxford UP, 1972.

Bunting, Basil. *Complete Poems*. New York: New Directions, 2000.

Burchfield, R.W., ed. *The New Fowler's Modern English Usage*. 3rd ed. Oxford: Clarendon P, 1996.

Burgess, Anthony. *Here Comes Everybody: An Introduction to James Joyce for the Ordinary Reader*. London: Faber, 1969.

– *Joysprick: An Introduction to the Language of James Joyce*. London: Deutsch, 1973.

Butler, David. *An Aid to Reading* Ulysses. Dublin: James Joyce Centre, 2004.

Byrne, Rhonda. *The Secret*. New York: Atria Books, 2006.

Campbell, Joseph, and Henry Morton Robinson. *A Skeleton Key to "Finnegans Wake."* 1944. New York: Viking, 1961.

Canfield, Jack, and Mark Victor Hansen, eds. *Chicken Soup for the Soul*. Deerfield Beach, FL: Health Communications, 1993.

Carnegie, Dale. *How to Win Friends and Influence People*. 1936. New York: Simon and Schuster, 1981.

– *How to Stop Worrying and Start Living*. 1948. New York: Pocket Books, 1984.

Cate, Rodney M., and Sally A. Lloyd, *Courtship*. London: Sage, 1992.

Cheng, Vincent J. "The Joycean Unconscious, or Getting Respect in the Real World." *Joyce and Popular Culture*. Ed. R.B. Kershner. Gainesville: UP of Florida, 1996. 180–92.

Chomsky, Noam. *Language and Responsibility*. New York: Pantheon, 1979.

Chilton, David. *The Wealthy Barber: The Common Sense Guide to Successful Financial Planning*. Toronto: Stoddart, 1989.

Chuang, Yen-Chen. "Derrida avec Joyce: The Principle of Eating the Other in *Ulysses*." *Hypermedia Joyce Studies* 10 (2009, online).

Clarkson, L.A. and E. Margaret Crawford. *Feast and Famine: A History of Food and Nutrition in Ireland 1500–1920*. Oxford: Oxford UP, 2001.

Coates, James. *Self-Reliance: Practical Studies in Personal Magnetism, Will-Power and Success, through Self-Help, or Auto-Suggestion*. London: L.N. Fowler, 1907.

Conley, Chip. *Emotional Equations: Simple Formulas to Help Your Life Work Better*. New York: Simon and Schuster, 2012.

Conley, Tim. "*Finnegans Wake*: Some Assembly Required." *James Joyce: Visions and Revisions*. Ed. Sean Latham. Dublin: Irish Academic P, 2010. 132–52.

– *Joyces Mistakes: Problems of Intention, Irony, and Interpretation*. Toronto: U of Toronto P, 2003.

– "Playing with Matches: The *Wake* Notebooks and Negative Correspondence." *New Quotatoes: Joycean Exogenesis in the Digital Age*. Eds. Ronan Crowley and Dirk Van Hulle. Amsterdam, Brill, 2016. 171–80.

– "The Silence of the Looms: 'Penelope' as Translation." *James Joyce's Silences*. Ed. Serenella Zanotti and Jolanta Wawrzycka. London: Bloomsbury. Forthcoming.

Coué, Emile. *Self-Help through Conscious Autosuggestion*. New York: Malkan Publishing, 1922.

Courtney, William Joseph. *The Conquest of Nerves*. New York: Macmillan, 1911.

Covey, Stephen R. *Seven Habits of Highly Effective People*. New York: Simon and Schuster, 1989.

Creasy, Matthew, ed. *Errears and Erroriboose: Joyce and Error*. Amsterdam: Rodopi, 2011.

Crispi, Luca, and Sam Slote, eds. *How Joyce Wrote* Finnegans Wake. *A Chapter by Chapter Genetic Guide*. Madison: U of Wisconsin P, 2007.

Cunningham, W. [William]. *The Use and Abuse of Money*. London: John Murray, 1891.

Dalton, Jack P. "Advertisement for the Restoration." *Twelve and a Tilly: Essays on the Occasion of the 25th Anniversary of* Finnegans Wake. Eds. Jack P. Dalton and Clive Hart. London: Faber and Faber, 1966.

Deane, Seamus. "Note on the New Edition of *Finnegans Wake*." *Finnegans Wake*. Eds. Danis Rose and John O'Hanlon. Cornwall: Houyhnhnm Press, 2010. 5–6.

Deane, Seamus. "Note on the New Edition of *Finnegans Wake*." *The Restored Finnegans Wake*. Eds. Danis Rose and John O'Hanlon. London: Penguin, 2012. vii–viii.

Delaney, Frank. *James Joyce's Odyssey: A Guide to the Dublin of* Ulysses. London: Paladin Grafton, 1987.

De Man, Paul. "Walter Benjamin's 'The Task of the Translator.'" *The Resistance to Theory*. Minneapolis: U of Minnesota P, 1986. 73–105.

Derrida, Jacques. "'Eating Well,' or the Calculation of the Subject." Trans. Peter Connor and Avital Ronell. *Points... Interviews, 1974–1994*. Ed. Elisabeth Weber. Stanford: Stanford UP, 1995. 255–87.

– "Two Words for Joyce." Trans. Geoff Bennington. *Post-Structuralist Joyce: Essays from the French*. Eds. Derek Attridge and Daniel Ferrer. Cambridge: Cambridge UP, 1984. 145–59.

– "*Ulysses* Gramophone: Hear Say Yes in Joyce." Trans. François Raffoul. *Derrida and Joyce: Texts and Contexts*. Eds. Andrew J. Mitchell and Sam Slote. Albany: State U of New York P, 2013. 41–86.

Duff, Charles. *James Joyce and the Plain Reader*. New York: Haskell House, 1971.

Duncan, Robert. *The H.D. Book*. Eds. Michael Boughn and Victor Coleman. Berkeley: U of California P, 2011.

Dwyer, June. "Feast and Famine: James Joyce and the Politics of Food." *Proteus: A Journal of Ideas* 17.1 (2000): 41–4.

Eagleton, Terry. *The Event of Literature*. New Haven: Yale UP, 2012.

– *Heathcliff and the Great Hunger: Studies in Irish Culture*. London: Verso, 1995.

Eco, Umberto. *The Limits of Interpretation*. Bloomington: Indiana UP, 1994.

– *The Open Work*. Trans. Anna Cancogni. Cambridge: Harvard UP, 1989.

Eliot, T.S. *The Waste Land*. *Modernism: An Anthology*. Ed. Lawrence Rainey. Malden, MA: Blackwell, 2005. 124–43.

Ellmann, Maud. *The Hunger Artists: Starving, Writing, and Imprisonment*. Cambridge, MA: Harvard UP, 1993.

– *The Nets of Modernism: Henry James, Virginia Woolf, James Joyce, and Sigmund Freud*. Cambridge: Cambridge UP, 2010.

Ellmann, Richard. *The Consciousness of Joyce*. Toronto: Oxford UP, 1977.

Epstein, Edmund Lloyd. *A Guide Through* Finnegans Wake. Gainesville: UP of Florida, 2009.

Esenwein, J. Berg, and Dale Carnagey [Carnegie], *The Art of Public Speaking*. Springfield, MA: The Home Correspondence School, 1915.

Espinasse, Francis. *Literary Recollections and Sketches*. London: Hodder and Stoughton, 1893.

Everybody's Book of Jokes. London: W. Russell and Company, 1895.

Fargnoli, A. Nicholas, and Michael Patrick Gillespie. *James Joyce A–Z: An Encyclopedic Guide to His Life and Work*. London: Bloomsbury, 1995.

Felski, Rita. *Uses of Literature*. Malden, MA: Blackwell, 2008.

Ferrer, Daniel. "A Library of Indistinction." *New Quotatoes: Joycean Exogenesis in the Digital Age*. Eds. Ronan Crowley and Dirk Van Hulle. Amsterdam: Brill, 2016. 11–17.

Fitch, Noel Riley. *Sylvia Beach and the Lost Generation: A History of Literary Paris in the Twenties and Thirties*. New York: Norton, 1983.

Fordham, Finn. "Introduction." Henkes, Bindervoet, and Fordham. vii–xxxi.

– *Lots of Fun at* Finnegans Wake*: Unravelling Universals*. Oxford: Oxford UP, 2007.

Forward, Susan, and Joan Torres. *Men Who Hate Women and the Women Who Love Them: When Loving Hurts and You Don't Know Why*. New York: Bantam, 2002.

Friedman, Alan W. *Party Pieces: Oral Storytelling and Social Performance in Joyce and Beckett*. Syracuse: Syracuse UP, 2007.

Gabler, Hans Walter. "Foreword." *Finnegans Wake*. Eds. Danis Rose and John O'Hanlon. Cornwall: Houyhnhnm Press, 2010. 9–16.

– "Appendix I." *The Restored Finnegans Wake*. Eds. Danis Rose and John O'Hanlon. London: Penguin, 2012. 495–502.

Garber, Marjorie. "" ' (Quotation Marks)." *Talk Talk Talk: The Cultural Life of Everyday Conversation*. Ed. S.I. Salamensky. New York: Routledge, 2001. 121–46.

– *The Use and Abuse of Literature*. New York: Random House, 2011.

Gasché, Rodolphe. *The Stelliferous Fold: Toward a Virtual Law of Literature's Self-Formation*. New York: Fordham UP, 2011.

Gifford, Don, with Robert J. Seidman. Ulysses *Annotated: Notes for James Joyce's* Ulysses. 2nd ed. Berkeley: U of California P, 1989.

Gitelman, Lisa. *Paper Knowledge: Toward a Media History of Documents*. Durham: Duke UP, 2014.

Gogan, Robert, ed. *Ulysses*, by James Joyce. Sraheens: Music Ireland Publications, 2012.

Gookin, Dan. *DOS for Dummies*. New York: Hungry Minds, 1991.

Gordon, John. "Getting Past No in 'Scylla and Charybdis." *James Joyce Quarterly* 44.3 (2007): 501–22.

Gordon, W. Terrance. *Everyman's Joyce*. New York: Mark Batty Publisher, 2009.

Gray, John. *Men Are From Mars, Women Are From Venus*. New York: HarperCollins, 1992.

Hamel, Marilyn. *Sex Etiquette: The Modern Woman's Guide to Mating Manners*. New York: Delacorte, 1984.

Harris, Thomas A. *I'm OK – You're OK*. 1969. London: Arrow Books, 1995.

Hart, Clive. *A Topographical Guide to James Joyce's* Ulysses. Colchester: A Wake Newslitter P, 1975.

Hay, Louise L. *You Can Heal Your Life*. 1984. Carlsbad, CA: Hay House, 2004.

Hayward, Matthew. "Reconsidering Joyce's 'Notes on Business and Commerce.'" *Genetic Joyce Studies* 12 (Spring 2012), online.

Henkes, Robbert-Jan, Erik Bindervoet, and Finn Fordham, eds. *Finnegans Wake*. Oxford: Oxford UP, 2012.

Hill, Napoleon. *Think and Grow Rich*. Meriden, CT: The Ralston Society, 1937.

Hogarth, Basil. *Self-Mastery through Psycho-Analysis: A Practical Guide for Laymen*. London: Rider & Co., 1936.

Horkheimer, Max, and Theodor W. Adorno. *Dialectic of Enlightenment: Philosophical Fragments*. Trans. Edmund Jephcott. Stanford: Stanford UP, 2002.

Hunter, Jefferson. *How to Read* Ulysses *and Why*. New York: Peter Lang, 2002.

Illouz, Eva. *Consuming the Romantic Utopia: Love and the Cultural Contradictions of Capitalism*. Berkeley: U of California P, 1997.

– *Saving the Modern Soul: Therapy, Emotions, and the Culture of Self-Help*. Berkeley: U of California P, 2008.

Jarrell, Mackie L. "Joyce's Use of Swift's *Polite Conversation* in the 'Circe' Episode of *Ulysses*," *PMLA* 72.3 (1957): 545–54.

Jewsbury, Geraldine. *Zoe: The History of Two Lives*. London: Virago, 1989.

Jones, William Powell. *James Joyce and the Common Reader*. Norman: U of Oklahoma P, 1955.

Joyce, James. *Dubliners*. London: Penguin, 1992.

– *Exiles. The Portable James Joyce*. Ed. Harry Levin. New York: Penguin, 1976. 529–626.

– *Finnegans Wake*. New York: Penguin, 1976.

– *Letters of James Joyce*. Ed. Stuart Gilbert. New York: Viking, 1957.

– *Occasional, Critical, and Political Writing*. Ed. Kevin Barry. Oxford: Oxford UP, 2000.

– *A Portrait of the Artist as a Young Man*. Oxford: Oxford UP, 2000.

– *Stephen Hero*. Frogmore: Panther Books, 1977.

– *Ulysses*. Ed. Hans Walter Gabler. Hammondsworth: Penguin, 1986.

Kafka, Franz. "The Hunger Artist." *The Metamorphosis, In the Penal Colony, and Other Stories*, trans. Joachim Neugroschel. New York: Simon and Schuster, 2000. 301–16.

Kant, Immanuel. *Critique of Judgement*. Trans. James Creed Meredith. Oxford: Oxford UP, 2008.

Kee, Robert. *The Laurel and the Ivy: The Story of Charles Stewart Parnell and Irish Nationalism*. London: Penguin, 1994.

Kenner, Hugh. *A Colder Eye: The Modern Irish Writers*. New York: Penguin, 1984.

Kermode, Frank. "The Modern." *Modern Essays*. London: Fontana, 1971. 39–70.

Kiberd, Declan. Ulysses *and Us: The Art of Everyday Life in Joyce's Masterpiece*. New York: Norton, 2009.

Killeen, Terence. Ulysses *Unbound: A Reader's Companion to James Joyce's* Ulysses. Wicklow: Wordwell, 2004.

Kirkham, Stanton Davis. *The Philosophy of Self-Help: An Application of Practical Psychology to Daily Life*. New York: Knickerbocker P, 1909.

Knowlton, Eloise. *Joyce, Joyceans, and the Rhetoric of Citation*. Gainesville: UP of Florida, 1998.

Landuyt, Ingeborg, and Geert Lernout. "Joyce's Sources: *Les Grands Fleuves Historiques*." *Joyce Studies Annual* 6 (1995): 99–138.

Lang, Andrew. *How to Fail in Literature: A Lecture*. London: Field and Tuer, The Leadenhall Press, 1890.

La Ruina, Richard. *The Natural: How to Effortlessly Attract the Women You Want*. New York: HarperCollins, 2012.

Latham, Sean, ed. *The Cambridge Companion to* Ulysses. Cambridge: Cambridge UP, 2014.

Lavergne, Philippe, trans. *Finnegans Wake*. By James Joyce. Paris: Gallimard, 1982.

LeMasters, E.E. *Modern Courtship and Marriage*. New York: Macmillan, 1957.

Leonard, Garry. "Power, Pornography, and the Problem of Pleasure: The Semerotics of Desire and Commodity Culture in Joyce." *James Joyce Quarterly* 31.1 (1993): 615–65.

Levin, Harry. *James Joyce: A Critical Introduction*. London: Faber and Faber, 1944.

Levine, Caroline. *Forms: Whole, Rhythm, Hierarchy, Network*. Princeton: Princeton UP, 2015.

Loos, Anita. *Gentlemen Prefer Blondes: The Illuminating Diary of a Professional Lady*. New York: Liveright, 1998.

Mahon, Peter. *Joyce: A Guide for the Perplexed*. London: Continuum, 2009.

Maltz, Maxwell. *Psycho-Cybernetics: A New Way to Get More Living out of Life*. New York: Prentice-Hall, 1960.

Marx, Karl. *Capital. Vol 1: Critical Analysis and Capitalist Production*. Trans. Samuel Morse and Edward Aveling. Moscow: Progress Publishers, 1974.

McCarthy, Jack, with Danis Rose. *Joyce's Dublin: A Walking Guide to* Ulysses. New York: St Martin's P, 1992.

McGann, Jerome J. *The Textual Condition*. Princeton: Princeton University Press, 1991.

McHugh, Roland. *Annotations to Finnegans Wake*. 3rd ed. Baltimore: The Johns Hopkins UP, 2006.

– *Annotations to Finnegans Wake*. 4th ed. Baltimore: The Johns Hopkins UP, 2016.

– *The* Finnegans Wake *Experience*. Berkeley: U of California P, 1981.

McKenna, Bernard. *James Joyce's* Ulysses*: A Reference Guide*. Westport, CT: Greenwood P, 2002.

Monas, Sidney. "Boian and Iaroslavna: Some Lyrical Assumptions in Russian Literature." *The Craft and Context of Translation*. Eds. William Arrowsmith and Roger Shattuck. New York: Doubleday, 1964. 165–85.

Moore, Marianne. "Poetry." 1919. *Modernism: An Anthology*. Ed. Lawrence Rainey. Malden, MA: Blackwell, 2005. 649–50.

– *The Selected Letters of Marianne Moore*. New York: Knopf, 2008.

Mullan, Bob. *The Mating Trade*. London: Routledge, 1984.
Murphy, Michael. *James Joyce*. London: Greenwich Exchange, 2004.
Nabokov, Vladimir. *Lectures on Literature*. Ed. Fredson Bowers. New York: Harcourt Brace Jovanovich, 1980.
– *Lolita*. New York: Vintage, 1997.
– "Problems of Translation: *Onegin* in English." *The Translation Studies Reader*. 2nd ed. Ed. Lawrence Venuti. New York: Routledge, 2004. 115–27.
Nancy, Jean-Luc. *On the Commerce of Thinking: Of Books and Bookstores*. Trans. David Wills. New York: Fordham UP, 2009.
Newman, Mildred, and Bernard Berkowitz. *How to Be Your Own Best Friend*. New York: Random House, 1973.
Nicholson, Robert. *The* Ulysses *Guide: Tours through Joyce's Dublin*. London: Methuen, 1988.
Norman, John Henry. *A Ready Reckoner of the World's Foreign and Colonial Exchanges with the Aid of Less than 2000 Figures Whereby 756 Tables of Exchange, Consisting of from 13,800 to 200,000 Figures Each, Can Be Dispensed With*. London: Sampson Low, Marston and Company, 1893.
Norris, David, and Carl Flint. *Joyce for Beginners*. Cambridge: Icon Books, 1994.
Norris, Margot. *The Decentered Universe of "Finnegans Wake": A Structuralist Analysis*. Baltimore: Johns Hopkins UP, 1974.
– *Virgin and Veteran Readings of Ulysses*. New York: Palgrave Macmillan, 2011.
Norwood, Robin. *Women Who Love Too Much*. New York: Pocket, 1990.
Onose, So. "'A Great Future Behind Him': John F. Taylor's Speech in 'Aeolus' Revisited." *a long the krommerun: Selected Papers from the Utrecht James Joyce Symposium*. Eds. Onno Kosters, Tim Conley, and Peter de Voogd. Amsterdam: Brill, 2016. 46–62.
Osteen, Mark. *The Economy of* Ulysses*: Making Both Ends Meet*. Syracuse: Syracuse UP, 1995.
Parker, Dorothy. "A Pig's-Eye View of Literature." *Complete Poems*. New York: Penguin, 1999. 115–17.
Partridge, Eric. *A Dictionary of Historical Slang*. Abridged ed. Hammondsworth: Penguin, 1972.
Paz, Octavio. *The Other Voice: Essays on Modern Poetry*. Trans. Helen Lane. San Diego: Harcourt Brace Jovanovich, 1991.
Peale, Norman Vincent. *The Power of Positive Thinking*. New York: Simon and Schuster, 2003.
Pearson, Hesketh, ed. *Common Misquotations*. London: Hamish Hamilton, 1934.
Plock, Vike Martina. "Modernism's Feast on Science: Nutrition and Diet in Joyce's *Ulysses*," *Literature and History* 16.1 (2007): 30–42.

Poulet, Georges. "Phenomenology of Reading." *New Literary History* 1.1 (1969): 53–68.

Rabaté, Jean-Michel. "The Fourfold Root of Yawn's Unreason." Crispi and Slote 384–409.

– "Modernism and 'The Plain Reader's Rights': Duff-Riding-Graves Rereading Joyce." *Joyce's Audiences*. Ed. John Nash. Amsterdam: Rodopi, 2002. 29–40.

Rainey, Lawrence. *Institutions of Modernism: Literary Elites and Public Culture*. New Haven: Yale UP, 1998.

Ralph, Joseph. *How to Psycho-Analyse Yourself*. London: Watts & Co., 1937.

Rich, Lauren. "A Table for One: Hunger and Unhomeliness in Joyce's Public Eateries." *Joyce Studies Annual* (2010): 71–98.

Robbins, Anthony. *Awaken the Giant Within: How to Take Immediate Control of Your Mental, Emotional, Physical and Financial Destiny!* New York: Free Press, 2003.

Roos, Bonnie. "The Joyce of Eating: Feast, Famine and the Humble Potato in *Ulysses*." *Hungry Words: Images of Famine in the Irish Canon*. Eds. George Cusack and Sarah Gross. Dublin; Portland, OR: Irish Academic Press, 2006. 159–96.

Rose, Danis. "Introduction." *Ulysses: A Reader's Edition*. London: Picador, 1997. ix–lxxxiii.

Rose, Danis, and John O'Hanlon. "Preface." *Finnegans Wake*. Eds. Danis Rose and John O'Hanlon. Cornwall: Houyhnhnm Press, 2010. 7–8.

– "Preface." *The Restored Finnegans Wake*. Eds. Danis Rose and John O'Hanlon. London: Penguin, 2012. ix–x.

Rose, Danis, and John O'Hanlon, eds. *Finnegans Wake*, by James Joyce. Cornwall: Houyhnhnm Press, 2010.

Rose, Jonathan. *The Intellectual Life of the British Working Classes*. 2nd ed. New Haven: Yale UP, 2010.

Rosenbloom, Eric. *A Word in Your Ear: How and Why to Read James Joyce's* Finnegans Wake. East Hardwick, VT: BookSurge Publishing, 2005.

Rubenstein, Michael D. "'The Waters of Civic Finance': Moneyed States in Joyce's *Ulysses*." *Novel: A Forum on Fiction* 36.3 (2003): 289–306.

Scholes, Robert, and Richard M. Kain, eds. *The Workshop of Daedalus: James Joyce and the Raw Materials for "A Portrait of the Artist as a Young Man."* Evanston, IL: Northwestern UP, 1965.

Schork, R.J. *Greek and Hellenic Culture in Joyce*. Gainesville: UP of Florida, 1998.

Seidel, Michael. *James Joyce: A Short Introduction*. Malden, MA: Blackwell, 2002.

Senn, Fritz. *Inductive Scrutinies: Focus on Joyce*. Dublin: Lilliput P, 1995.

– *Joyce's Dislocutions: Essays on Reading as Translation*. Baltimore: Johns Hopkins UP, 1984.

Shakespeare, William. *Much Ado About Nothing*. *The Norton Shakespeare*. 2nd ed. Eds. Stephen Greenblatt et al. New York: Norton, 2008. 1416–70.

– *The Tragedy of Hamlet, Prince of Denmark. The Norton Shakespeare*. 2nd ed. Eds. Stephen Greenblatt et al. New York: Norton, 2008. 1696–1784.
– *The Tragedy of Othello the Moor of Venice. The Norton Shakespeare*. 2nd ed. Eds. Stephen Greenblatt et al. New York: Norton, 2008. 2117–91.
Shaw, Bernard. *Pygmalion: A Romance in Five Acts*. London: Penguin, 1957.
Sheehan, Sean. *Joyce's* Ulysses*: A Reader's Guide*. London: Continuum, 2009.
Shelley, Percy Bysshe. *A Defence of Poetry. Selected Poetry and Prose of Percy Bysshe Shelley*. Ed. Carlos Baker. New York: Modern Library, 1951. 494–522.
Shelton, Jen. "Bad Girls: Gerty, Cissy, and the Erotics of Unruly Speech." *James Joyce Quarterly* 34.2 (1997): 87–102.
Shirky, Clay. *Here Comes Everybody: How Change Happens When People Come Together*. 2008. London: Penguin, 2009.
Skeat, Walter W. *An Etymological Dictionary of the English Language*. Mineola, NY: Dover, 2005.
Slote, Sam. "An Imperfect *Wake*." Creasy 135–49.
– "Wilde Thing: Concerning the Eccentricities of a Figure of Decadence in *Finnegans Wake*." *Probes: Genetic Studies*. Eds. David Hayman and Sam Slote. Amsterdam: Rodopi, 1995. 101–22.
Smiles, Samuel. *Self-Help, with Illustrations of Character, Conduct, and Perseverance*. Oxford: Oxford UP, 2002.
Smith, Paul Jordan. *A Key to the* Ulysses *of James Joyce*. New York: Covici, 1927.
Spinks, Lee. *James Joyce: A Critical Guide*. Edinburgh: Edinburgh UP, 2009.
Spurr, David. "Stuttering Joyce." Creasy 121–33.
Startup, Frank. *James Joyce: A Beginner's Guide*. London: Hodder & Stoughton, 2001.
Staten, Henry. "The Decomposing Form of Joyce's *Ulysses*." *PMLA* 112.3 (1997): 380–92.
Stein, Gertrude. *How To Write*. Barton, VT: Something Else P, 1973.
– "How Writing Is Written." *The Gender of Modernism: A Critical Anthology*. Ed. Bonnie Kime Scott. Bloomington: Indiana UP, 1990. 488–95.
Steiner, George. *No Passion Spent: Essays 1978–1995*. New Haven: Yale UP, 1996.
Stemp, Leslie F. *Speeches and Toasts: How to Make and Propose Them*. London and Melbourne: Ward, Lock & Co., Limited, 1928.
Sterne, Laurence. *The Life and Opinions of Tristram Shandy, Gentleman*. Ed. Graham Petrie. London: Penguin, 1985.
Stewart, Susan. Nonsense: *Aspects of Intertextuality in Folklore and Literature*. Baltimore: Johns Hopkins UP, 1978.
Stoppard, Tom. *Travesties*. New York: Grove P, 1975.
Swift, Jonathan. *Polite Conversation*. Ed. George Saintsbury. London: Chiswick Press, 1892.

Tiffany, Daniel. *Toy Medium: Materialism and Lyric*. Berkeley: U of California P, 2000.

Tindall, William York. *A Reader's Guide to* Finnegans Wake. London: Thames and Hudson, 1969.

– *A Reader's Guide to James Joyce*. 1959. Syracuse: Syracuse UP, 1995.

Tolle, Eckhart. *A New Earth: Awakening to Your Life's Purpose*. 2005. New York: Penguin, 2016.

Turner, E.S. *A History of Courting*. London: Michael Joseph, 1954.

Van Mierlo, Wim. "'For polemypolity's sake': Editing *Finnegans Wake* — A Consideration and Review." *Genetic Joyce Studies* 12 (Spring 2012). Online.

Waller, Willard W. "The Rating and Dating Complex." *On the Family, Education, and War: Selected Writings*, Ed. William J. Goode, Frank F. Furstenberg, Jr, and Larry R. Mitchell. Chicago: U of Chicago P, 1970.

Wareham, James. *Know Thyself: An Aid to Self-Examination*. London: A.R. Mowbray and Company, 1933.

Warren, Henry. *How to Choose Your Banker: A Manual for Customers and Investors*. London: Grant Richards, 1900.

Wattles, Wallace D. *The Science of Getting Rich*. 1910. Chichester: Capstone Publishing, 2010.

Waugh, Evelyn. *A Handful of Dust*. London: Penguin, 1997.

Weir, David. Ulysses *Explained: How Homer, Dante, and Shakespeare Inform Joyce's Modernist Vision*. New York: Palgrave Macmillan, 2015.

Whyte, Samuel. *An Introductory Essay on the Art of Reading, and Speaking in Public, Part First and Second; in which an Investigation of the Principles of Written Language is Attempted*. Dublin: Robert Marchbank, 1800.

Wilde, Oscar. *The Critic as Artist. The Complete Works of Oscar Wilde*. London: Collins, 1991. 1009–59.

– *The Picture of Dorian Gray*. Oxford: Oxford UP, 2008.

Wittgenstein, Ludwig. *Culture and Value*. Trans. Peter Winch. Chicago: U of Chicago P, 1980.

Wolf, Martin. "The Grasshoppers and the Ants – A Modern Fable." *Financial Times* 5 May 2010. Online.

Yared, Aida. "Eating and Digesting in 'Lestrygonians': A Physiological Model of Reading." *James Joyce Quarterly* 46.3–4 (2009): 469–79.

Yeats, William Butler. "Lapis Lazuli." *Collected Poems*. London: Picador, 1990. 338–9.

– *A Vision*. London: Macmillan, 1969.

Žižek, Slavoj. *Absolute Recoil: Towards a New Foundation of Dialectical Materialism*. London: Verso, 2014.

Index